DATE DUE			

RACY

American Bureaucracy

Second Edition

By

PETER WOLL

BRANDEIS UNIVERSITY

W · W · NORTON & COMPANY

New York · London

TO

Robert and Lucinda

W. W. Norton & Company, Inc., 500 Fifth Avenue, New York, N.Y. 10110
W. W. Norton & Company Ltd., 25 New Street Square, London EC4A 3NT

Published simultaneously in
Canada by George J. McLeod Limited, Toronto,
PRINTED IN THE UNITED STATES OF AMERICA
ALL RIGHTS RESERVED

Library of Congress Cataloging in Publication Data
Woll, Peter, 1933–
American bureaucracy.
Includes bibliographical references and index.
1. United States—Politics and government.
2. United States—Executive departments. 3. Independent regulatory
commissions—United States. I. Title.
JK901.W6   1977   353.04   76–51361
ISBN 0–393–05615–5
ISBN 0–393–09141–4 pbk.

3 4 5 6 7 8 9 0

Contents

Preface

THIS BOOK examines one of the most important developments in modern American government, the growth of the national bureaucracy to a dominant position in areas that traditionally have been thought properly reserved to Congress, the President, and the Judiciary. American bureaucracy is deeply involved in the political process, a fact all too often overlooked or underplayed in the literature of political science. The political activities of administrative agencies are of overwhelming significance today and present problems in constitutional and political theory of current importance.

Virtually every aspect of our daily lives is regulated to some degree by one or the other of the numerous administrative agencies that make up the national bureaucracy. The powers of these agencies are extensive, being judicial and legislative in nature as well as executive. The Constitution states that these fundamental powers of government should be separated into three branches that have effective checks and balances in relation to each other. Otherwise, arbitrary government will prevail. The growth of a bureaucracy outside of the original constitutional scheme throws this neat and logical system out of kilter. It has become essential to understand the role of bureaucracy in our government in order to appreciate the meaning of fundamental changes that have taken place in the American system of constitutional democracy.

Since the first edition of this book, administrative departments and agencies have continued to gain political clout. Although Congress and the President periodically pledge to curb the bureaucracy, such promises have not been fulfilled. Under Presidents Nixon and Ford, the White House attempted to cut back federal programs, only to be stymied by Congress. Congress, in turn, saw political advantage in attacking the "bureaucracy," and proposed legislation from "sunshine" to "sunset" to deal with the problem. But while railing against the bureaucracy in public, Congress quietly protected the agencies in private. The bureaucracy has become the most powerful branch of government, not because of a conspiracy on the part of the agencies, but because, in the final analysis, the President, Congress, the courts, and the American people acquiesce in—and tacitly support—administrative power.

This second edition takes into account a number of major changes in the federal bureaucracy. Between editions, new departments and agencies have been created to deal with such areas as transportation, housing and urban development, environmental protection, equal employment opportunity, occupational health and safety, and hazardous consumer products. Important new developments have taken place in administrative law, spurred in part by public-interest groups pressing for greater public access to administrative proceedings. These developments are analyzed in a much-expanded treatment of rulemaking and adjudication as methods of administrative policymaking.

Other new discussions center on the evolving relationships between Congress, the Presidency, and the bureaucracy. New cases relating to the doctrine of delegation of legislative power are introduced. There is analysis of the effectiveness of congressional attempts to develop expertise in counterbalancing the bureaucracy through the Congressional Budget Office, the Office of Technology Assessment, the General Accounting Office, and the increased size of personal and committee staffs. The possibility of more effective congressional oversight in the future is assessed, particularly in terms of congressional incentives for change.

Finally, attention is given to presidential attempts to control the bureaucracy that reached a peak during the Nixon administration and to congressional efforts to limit presidential authority over the bureaucracy reflected in legislation such as the Budget and Impoundment Control Act of 1974.

This book owes its origins to those who first stirred my interest in bureaucracy: some teachers were particularly instrumental in molding my emphasis on the political role of the administrative branch. My initial excitement about this area came from Herman M. ("Red") Somers, who combined insight and personal experience to make the study of public administration come alive when he taught me at Haverford College. At Cornell University Arch Dotson guided my intellectual inquiries about this subject with great perception and understanding. And Clinton Rossiter deepened my appreciation of the American constitutional and political tradition, which is so important to a proper grasp of the present role of the bureaucracy. The first edition was read in manuscript by Richard H. Leach, who made many valuable suggestions. A number of others have made generous contributions of their time and knowledge to the present version. Rochelle Jones contributed valuable insights on the relationship of Congress to the bureaucracy, and alerted me to important new developments affecting the administrative branch. Neil Sullivan aided in the research and gave the manuscript a critical reading. William Medina has for many years contributed ideas and information to my writing on the bureaucracy. Trudi Rogers diligently typed the manuscript and, as always, put in hours beyond the call of duty.

It is customary, but hardly necessary, to add that all facts and interpretations presented here are my responsibility.

Peter Woll

Weston, Massachusetts

Second Edition

AMERICAN BUREAUCRACY

Second Edition

CHAPTER 1 The Nature of Bureaucracy and Constitutional Government

THE OFTEN quoted passage from Alexander Pope's *Essay on Man* states:

> For forms of government let fools contest;
> What'er is best administer'd is best.

Following this eighteenth century expression of opinion, the nineteenth century classical economists, in their zeal for a governmental system based upon the principle of *laissez faire*, might well have said:

> For forms of government let fools contest;
> What'er is *least* administer'd is best.

Today, many, if not most, Americans would agree with the latter rather than the former couplet. Disenchantment with the traditional institutions of government extends beyond the Presidency, tarnished by the Watergate episode, and Congress, widely criticized for inaction, to the bureaucracy.[1] Although attitudes toward the bureaucracy are generally not sampled in public-opinion polls, opposition to "big government" has become an effective political rallying-point. As Democratic candidate Jimmy Carter discovered in 1976, both liberals and conservatives tend to equate big government with the growth of bureaucracy. A major element of Carter's successful drive toward his nomination was his promise to reorganize and increase presidential control over the bureaucracy.

In the minds of most people the bureaucracy represents the federal government in Washington. Often, attacks upon the

---

1. The term "bureaucracy" will be used throughout this book to designate "governmental bureaucracy," unless otherwise specified.

bureaucracy are rooted in the belief that government should be kept as close to the people as possible. Cutting back on the federal government and restoring state and local initiative therefore mean reducing the power of the bureaucracy. While the mid-1970s saw conservatives and liberals in agreement on the need to do something about the bureaucracy, they were not united on exactly what course of action should be taken.

As the 94th Congress was reaching its end, Senator Edmund Muskie (D., Maine) pushed for "sunset" legislation that would automatically cause the sun to set on government programs after five years unless the departments and agencies involved could justify their continuation.[2]

Senator Muskie's bill was co-sponsored by close to fifty Senators, and similar legislation in the House was well on its way to gaining close to a hundred co-sponsors.[3] Senators and Representatives clearly wanted to be on record in support of legislation to control the bureaucracy.

Senator Muskie also introduced the Congressional Right to Information Act in the 94th Congress, stating that it would "give the Congress the means to halt the steady erosion of its power by officials who arbitrarily withhold information needed to legislate and to oversee the workings of programs Congress has authorized."[4] The Act was designed to curb the ability of the President and administrative agencies to invoke executive privilege to withhold information from Congress. Arising out of the Watergate affair, the Act made it mandatory that there be a continual flow of information between agencies and relevant congressional committees. Under no circumstances could an agency deny a direct congressional request for information. The Act was but one indication of congressional displeasure with administrative secrecy. Senator James B. Pearson (R., Kansas) and others in Congress introduced legislation establishing a new Hoover Commission to investigate the bureaucracy and make

2. S.2925, 94th Cong. 2nd Sess., 1976, would terminate automatically statutory *authorizations* for government expenditures for most programs, but would not affect statutory or administrative law.

3. Those who co-sponsor legislation are often taking a public stand that they may oppose privately. Co-sponsors do not always support the legislation in private or vote for it on the floor.

4. Congressional Record, 94th Cong. 1st Sess., 1975, Vol. 121, p. S13491.

recommendations for reform. A committee of distinguished citizens sponsored by the National Academy of Public Administration unanimously backed the proposal.

Senator Edward Kennedy, noting that "over the past few years many have come to see that one of the greatest dangers of government is bureaucracy," launched a drive to overhaul federal regulatory agencies, particularly the Civil Aeronautics Board, to reduce their power, and to eliminate red tape. He also suggested that in the welfare area, serious consideration should be given to substituting direct cash payments to the poor in order to cut down on the welfare bureaucracy.[5] Gaylord Nelson (D., Wisconsin), a leading Senate liberal, seemed to give up on the entire issue of the bureaucracy, noting that "the federal bureaucracy is just an impossible monstrosity. You can't change it, there's no way to do it."[6] At the state level, Democratic Governors Michael Dukakis of Massachusetts and Jerry Brown of California made their marks by cutting back their state governments as much as possible.

Proposals for reform have not originated solely within the governmental system. Beginning in the 1960s, Ralph Nader formed various groups to monitor the activities of administrative agencies, and especially to use the courts to make agencies responsive to their statutory mandates. Nader also attempted to get Congress to amend legislation so that the standards governing administrative action would be stricter. Nader's approach reflected a highly conservative view of government. Essentially, he wanted to return to the original separation-of-powers scheme by reducing to a minimum the discretionary role of the bureaucracy. Although he is not averse to pleading a cause before the agencies themselves, Nader prefers to use the traditional congressional and judicial branches to control administrative activity.

Recent efforts to curb the discretionary powers of the bureaucracy have also been made by the executive branch. One of the major thrusts of the Nixon administration was to centralize power in the White House. The bureaucracy was to be a tool of the political ambitions and programs of the President. In line

5. See Norman C. Miller, "The Uneasy Liberals," *The Wall Street Journal*, August 6, 1975, p. 8.

6. *Ibid.*

with this goal, President Nixon vastly expanded the Executive Office of the President, which is the staff arm of the White House, and reorganized the Bureau of the Budget into the Office of Management and Budget (OMB) to obtain stronger direction of spending programs. President Nixon took various other steps to centralize control over the bureaucracy. Many of them failed, including his attempt to create a "super-Cabinet" composed of selected members of the Cabinet who were to filter all requests from the Departments of government before they reached the President. President Nixon epitomized the managerial approach to the Presidency, and strongly pushed for presidential supremacy over the bureaucracy. Never was there a doubt in his mind that the vast administrative branch should be responsive to presidential wishes. Ironically, this had been the approach of all Democratic Presidents since Franklin D. Roosevelt; it reflected an activist view of the Presidency, a belief in the "imperial Presidency."[7] The President was to act positively in the public interest as he and his party conceived it.

President Nixon attempted to be the first active conservative President, using the full force of the White House to put into effect conservative programs. In attempting to establish White House control over the bureaucracy, President Nixon was operating entirely in line with both constitutional and political precedent. However, he stepped far beyond the boundaries of this precedent when he sought to use agencies, particularly the CIA and the FBI, as well as the Internal Revenue Service, to advance his own political ambitions and to undermine the rights of citizens. The excesses of the Nixon Presidency called into question the desirability of total White House domination of the administrative arm of the government. Misuse of the bureaucracy was the basis of one of the three Articles of Impeachment against Nixon voted by the House Judiciary Committee.

Control of the bureaucracy seemed more important than ever in the 1970s as the American people were learning for the first time of the extraordinary scope of questionable, illegal, and, in some extreme cases, immoral policy-making decisions of ad-

7. For a discussion of the concept of the imperial Presidency and its historical origins, see Arthur M. Schlesinger, Jr., *The Imperial Presidency* (Boston: Houghton Mifflin, 1973).

ministrative agencies. These included FBI burglaries of foreign embassies; CIA assassination plots and widespread political interference in the internal affairs of other countries; experiments with the drug LSD conducted by the CIA, the Army, and HEW; not to mention an experiment conducted by the Public Health Service on blacks in the 1930s in which a group of black men with syphilis was allowed to go untreated so that the agency could determine the results of the disease. In more than one case, unsuspecting American citizens died because of administrative abuse of discretionary power.

While the events and investigations before, during, and after the Nixon administration pointed to presidential and administrative abuses of power, in the background challenges have been developing to the more traditional roles of administrative agencies. For example, disenchantment with the regulatory agencies is widespread. Politicians, economists, and many others have begun to attack the entire idea of regulation, proclaiming that the free market should be restored to bring forces of demand and supply into balance in the various regulatory areas. Although proposals for reform of the regulatory process dated back at least to the President's Committee on Administrative Management in 1937, never before has such a serious challenge been made to the underlying premises of administrative regulation.

Although agencies under attack have, in some instances, responded positively to criticism by changing their policies and procedures, the bureaucracy remains the same, as powerful (if not more powerful) than in the past. Authorizations and appropriations for administrative agencies have not decreased, and while the Watergate episode has raised serious questions about the desirability of an expansion of presidential staff, a view reflected in many strong speeches on the floor of the House and the Senate, no serious efforts have been made by the Congress to reduce the President's staff. Nor has there been any diminution of the vast powers of such departments as Health, Education, and Welfare, Agriculture, and Defense. The essential reasons for bureaucratic power—independent political support, expertise, the necessity of delegation of authority because of the widespread scope of government activities, and the preoccupation of elected politicians with matters independent of administrative operations—remain the same. The bureaucracy continues to run the government and often formulates its major policies, while the President and Congress play out the power game between them, and the courts stay in the background.

The power of the bureaucracy in our government is not unique. In modern industrialized societies, regardless of the particular forms of government in operation, the bureaucracy or the administrative arm of the governments seems to be assuming more power at the expense of the legislative and judicial branches and has reduced in many instances the influence of the main executive bodies of these governments. Bureaucracy can never be dismissed as simply part of the "executive branch" of the government controlled by the President or the Cabinet.

In the United States the growth of a vast administrative branch has introduced an important new political force into the governmental system, a force which might well become dominant if it is not controlled. The remainder of this chapter will consider the political nature of administrative functions with reference to American bureaucracy and then the relationship between the functions of the administrative branch and the American constitutional system.

Administrative Functions: The Political Nature of Bureaucracy

Congress and the President are usually referred to as the "political" arms of the government because they are the only branches elected by the people. "Political" control over the bureaucracy is exerted by both Congress and the President, and constitutionally the administrative branch is an agent of both the legislature and the executive. Strictly speaking, the bureaucracy is not supposed to have a mind of its own or be capable of making independent policy-decisions. The Constitution clearly places this authority in the hands of the Congress and the Presidency. In reality, however, the bureaucracy has become one of the most political branches of our government.

From the earliest days of the Republic, administrators have been deeply involved in politics—in the attempt to solidify and expand their power within other branches of the government and over the general public. Politics concerns itself with the nature, sources, use, and distribution of power. Power has been aptly defined as "participation in the making of decisions."[8] Decisions, in turn, involve the effective implementation as well as determination of policy. Policy implementation is always in the hands of administrative agencies, and it is through implementation that policy is really shaped.

The political nature of bureaucracy is initially revealed in the behavior of administrative agencies acting as interest groups. Administrative agencies operate in a highly charged political environment. They are constantly brought into contact with external groups, both governmental and non-governmental. To retain their power, or to expand, all agencies must maintain a balance of political support over opposition.[9] Congress controls finances and has ultimate power over reorganization; thus the agencies always seek political support that can be exerted on Congress. They are responsive to the President, or his coordinating staff agencies such as the Office of Management and Budget, only insofar as they are essential to the maintenance of political support. Agencies that have strong interest group support outside the bureaucracy do not generally have to rely on the President or his staff agencies. On the other hand, some agencies without adequate outside group support must substitute presidential support in order to survive. The effectiveness of presidential control, of course, will vary with the power of the private groups concerned and their ability to influence Congress or the courts.

American bureaucracy is filled with examples of agencies that have garnered the support of outside pressure groups. The bonds that tie the Department of Defense to a huge armaments industry —what President Eisenhower once labeled the military-industrial complex—appear to be unbreakable. The armaments industry buttresses the Defense Department before the powerful Congressional Appropriations Subcommittees on defense as well as before the Armed Services Committees. The Secretary of Defense, who is supposed to follow the President, is more often than not

8. Harold D. Laswell and Abraham Kaplan, *Power and Society* (New Haven: Yale University Press, 1950).

9. For an excellent case study illustrating this point see Samuel P. Huntington, "The Marasmus of the ICC," 61 *Yale Law Journal* 467–509 (1952).

co-opted by his Department and becomes a tool of its interests. Occasionally, strong expressions of presidential will in combination with powerful and independent Secretaries of Defense, as was the case with President Kennedy's Secretary of Defense Robert McNamara, may bring the Defense Department under the wing of the White House—at least temporarily. But this is a rare occurrence. The power of the Department, of course, is not based solely on the support of powerful political allies; the complexity of military technology and planning gives specialists within the Department the edge over most Congressmen and Presidents when it comes to the intricacies of defense policy. The elected politicians, for the most part, stand as generalists in the face of highly skilled bureaucratic experts.

The list of Departments and agencies with powerful political support could be extended almost indefinitely. Clientele Departments such as Agriculture, Labor, and Commerce all have a nationwide network of interest groups supporting them. The mammoth Department of Health, Education, and Welfare, almost incomprehensible to anyone attempting to analyze or control it, has the support of varied interest groups that are connected to its many different bureaus and divisions. HEW, the second largest Department in the federal government after Defense, is in some ways less amenable to congressional and presidential supervision than any other part of the bureaucracy. Again, this is because of its size, specialization and expertise, and the general scope of its activities. If HEW stands pat, no President can effectively move it. President Nixon went after the Department with a vengeance, attempting to cut back many of its programs, only to find himself stymied not only by bureaucratic opposition but also by powerful private groups that benefit from HEW largesse. These private groups unhesitatingly and successfully challenged the President in the courts on his attempts to impound HEW funds that had been appropriated for programs he disliked.

One of the most important segments of the bureaucracy that relies on powerful political support to survive is the independent regulatory agencies. These agencies have been under attack in one form or another since the New Deal. They have been accused of being too independent, overly solicitous of the interests of the industries they regulate, inefficient, unfair, and not heedful of their mandates to advance the public interest. Although some changes have been made in the ways these agencies operate, essentially they remain intact and largely immune from outside pressures to reform them. Why? The answer lies in the powerful support they have obtained from industry groups they regulate as well as from labor unions. The Civil Aeronautics Board (CAB), for example, is considered to be nothing more than an adjunct of the airlines. Pressures from Ralph Nader have made it more sensitive to consumer interests, as have pressures from President Ford, Senator Edward Kennedy, and others seeking some degree of deregulation of transportation. But even the most intense pressures for deregulation seem unlikely to be effective in causing Congress to alter the basic structure and mandate of the CAB. The same holds true for other independent regulatory commissions. The Interstate Commerce Commission, like the CAB, has been repeatedly attacked in attempts made to reorganize or to abolish it. But the ICC, with strong railroad and trucking support, stands firm. The only successful major attempt at reform of regulatory organization came in 1974 with the passage of the Energy Reorganization Act that abolished the Atomic Energy Commission and split its regulatory and developmental responsibilities into two separate agencies, the Nuclear Regulatory Commission and the Energy Research and Development Administration. Congress finally was able to act on long-standing criticisms of the AEC, charging that its developmental arm was reducing the effectiveness of its regulatory arm by overriding considerations of public health and safety and environmental protection.

The constant marshaling of political support is but one aspect of the political nature of the bureaucracy. The activity of individuals within organizations is also highly political. Though administrators are assigned formal roles, such roles are frequently and easily short-circuited by those attempting to maintain, solidify, and expand their positions.[10]

Another aspect of the political nature of bureaucracy lies in the fact that the functions these agencies perform involve a di-

10. For further discussion of this aspect of the bureaucracy see Victor A. Thompson, *Modern Organization* (New York: Alfred A. Knopf, 1961), chap. 7–8.

rect exercise of legislative, judicial, and executive power, all of which have profound consequences to the community as a whole. The bureaucracy is not merely carrying out law; rather it is deeply involved in the determination, interpretation, and execution of law.

THE LEGISLATIVE FUNCTIONS OF ADMINISTRATIVE AGENCIES

When the Department of Agriculture issues regulations concerning eligibility for food stamps, it is making law. When the Civil Aeronautics Board determines that there shall or shall not be youth fares, it is involved in law-making. When the Environmental Protection Agency sets standards for auto emissions or permissible levels of air and water pollution, it, too, is making law or legislating. The legislative function involves the formulation of general rules applicable to the community as a whole. Administrative agencies are as much involved in legislating as is Congress, primarily because Congress has delegated to the agencies a significant portion of its law-making responsibilities. Administrative legislation, like congressional laws, affects the community on a compulsory basis, for the state is a compulsory association.

The Constitution, in Article I, gives the law-making power initially to Congress; however, Congress was never supposed to have a monopoly of it. The President, through the veto and because of his responsibility to recommend legislation to Congress, was given highly significant law-making power in Article II. Further, the framers of the Constitution recognized the implications of judicial interpretation of congressional acts, which formally became part of the constitutional system in 1803 through Marshall's broad definition of the nature and scope of judicial review in *Marbury v. Madison*.[11] The major point of the constitutional separation of powers was that while Congress would have the primary responsibility toward legislation, both the President and the Supreme Court had a measure of control in the law-making process. Congress therefore could not become an arbitrary legislative body.

11. 1 Cranch 137 (1803).

Although Congress possesses the primary legislative power, it can delegate its power to the executive or administrative branch. Any such delegation of power must be made within certain limits, and must provide standards of conduct so specific that the agency concerned, and if necessary the courts upon judicial review, can ascertain the intent and scope of the congressional grant of authority. In this way, theoretically, Congress still retains the primary legislative power, and is merely appointing an agent to act for it; in fact, however, virtually complete legislative discretion is given to the designated agency or to the President.

Almost any agency exercising regulatory functions can be used to illustrate how legislative power resides in administrative hands. When obvious need for regulation arises, and when pressure from a variety of groups is exerted on Congress to act, it establishes an administrative agency charged with the responsibility of regulation in the area in question.

The Interstate Commerce Commission (ICC), for example, was established in 1887 to regulate the railroads because of pressure from agricultural interests that were being subjected to various types of economic coercion by the railroads. Congress was aware of the charges made against the railroads, but could not take the time to investigate them and develop minute regulations to control economic abuses; the subject was too vast, complex, and fraught with political danger. Congress decided to yield to pressures for regulation by creating an independent regulatory agency; at the same time this device prevented Congress from having to make difficult decisions involving regulation which would undoubtedly cause dissatisfaction in many of the groups being regulated. In the statutes creating the ICC and more recent agencies, such as the Securities and Exchange Commission, the National Labor Relations Board, and the Federal Communications Commission, Congress specified that the respective activities should be regulated in a "just" and "reasonable" manner, and in the "public interest." Thus, in allocating radio and television channels the Federal Communications Commission must heed the "public interest, convenience, and necessity." The ICC must establish rail, trucking, and shipping rates that are "just" and "reasonable." The Civil Aeronautics Board must also uphold the "public interest" in the establishment of "just" and "reasonable" air fares.

The Consumer Product Safety Commission is mandated by Congress to promulgate safety standards for consumer products and ban those products determined by the Commission to present an "unreasonable hazard." The Nuclear Regulatory Commission and its companion, the Energy Research and Development Administration, are to regulate and develop atomic energy respectively so as to promote the "common defense and security," the "general welfare," "world peace," and to "increase the standards of living and strengthen free competition." The Nuclear Regulatory Commission, for its part, cannot issue licenses if such issuance "would be inimicable to the common defense and security or to the health and safety of the public." The administrator of the Environmental Protection Agency is to formulate standards for air pollution that allow "an adequate margin of safety, . . . requisite to protect the public health."

The result of this vague phraseology, which is considered sufficient in the writing of such statutes, is that administrative agencies are permitted wide latitude in promulgating regulations and establishing policies that are given concrete application in individual cases and controversies before the agencies. This places the burden of reconciling group conflict upon the bureaucracy rather than Congress.[12] Who is to say what constitutes the "public interest," or what is "just" and "reasonable"? Congress may on occasion investigate such policy-formulation by administrative agencies; however, it is usually done sporadically, if at all. Moreover, the courts are very reluctant to interfere in what they consider to be the "policy-making" area of administrative decision making. It is hard to estimate in an exact way the significance of administrative legislation through rule making; however, the volume of such administrative legislation during any given period almost certainly equals the volume of congressional law making. The significance of such administrative legislation also may often exceed that of Congress.

The legislative function is also exercised through direct administrative involvement in initiating and drafting laws in Congress. The President's Committee on Administrative Management estimated in 1937 that at least two-thirds of all public bills passed

12. See E. Pendleton Herring, *Public Administration and the Public Interest* (New York: McGraw-Hill, 1936), pp. 6–9.

by Congress emanated directly from the administrative branch.[13] There is a major difference in Congress between bills passed and bills that are simply introduced. Thousands of bills are introduced in each session for various reasons having to do with congressional attempts to gain constituent support and with power and status considerations internal to Congress itself. Usually Congressmen rely on their own legislative counsel in the drafting of legislation. But the major policy-expertise lies outside of Congress. It behooves Congressmen who seriously want to see legislation passed to consult the administrative agencies concerned with a particular policy area, for strong opposition from an agency can readily kill proposed legislation. Legislation must find allies, not only within but without the legislative body.

The political clout of the agencies is based both on the support of the interest groups within their constituencies and on their own expertise. It is both politically and technically desirable for Congressmen to turn to the particular administrative agency or agencies that will have jurisdiction over implementation of their legislative proposals—to seek the backing of the Defense Department for changes in defense policies; or of the Department of Agriculture for proposals concerning modifications or elimination of price supports in particular areas; or of the Securities and Exchange Commission for plans to modify existing securities laws. Since there is often a similarity between the interests of private groups and those of administrative agencies in particular areas, the Congressman who gains the support of the administrative agency concerned with an area of legislation thereby frequently is assured of private support. For example, Labor Department support of wage and price legislation usually reflects the support of the AFL-CIO.

The combination of direct administrative participation in the congressional process, and the willingness of Congress to delegate substantial legislative power to administrative agencies, results in the firm and significant position of governmental bureaucracy in the legislative process.

THE JUDICIAL ROLE OF GOVERNMENTAL BUREAUCRACY

The existence, nature, and location of judicial power within a governmental system has always been an important consideration of political theory. The exercise of judicial functions, whether by relatively independent bodies such as courts or by administrative agencies that are more directly involved in the exercise of policy and prosecuting functions, is always "political" and a vital part of any political system. The performance of the judicial function involves the use of significant governmental power.

Generally speaking, the judicial function pertains to the disposition of a *specific* case on the basis of *general* rules; thus, when the internal revenue agent settles a tax case with an individual he is specifically applying the Internal Revenue Code, a general body of rules and regulations. His act is adjudicative in nature; the Code is legislation. When the Federal Communications Commission grants a broadcast license it is exercising a judicial function, for it is deciding a relatively specific case involving a limited number of named parties on the basis of its own regulations plus such requirements as Congress may have written into the law. In a real sense a controversy is involved in the exercise of the judicial function, requiring legal disposition; without a controversy there would be no case, and hence no need for adjudication. Such a controversy does not have to be *adversary,* in the sense of placing the parties concerned into formal opposition with each other. It can be reflected in an asserted claim of an individual against the government, for example, for veterans' benefits, or disability benefits under the Social Security laws. In such a non-adversary type of case the governmental agency concerned still has to decide whether or not benefits are to be given, and if so, in what amount. On the other hand, one private party may be in controversy with another, or a government agency may feel that there is some question concerning compliance with the law on the part of an individual or group. In this case the agency will bring action against the party in question, and adjudicate the dispute between itself and the party on the basis of public policy considerations and evidence given or available to the agency.

What agencies exercise judicial functions, and what is the legal source of this form of administrative power? In general terms, judicial power is exercised on the basis of a congressional grant of authority. This is also true, as was previously noted, with regard to administrative exercise of legislative functions. Examples of important administrative exercise of judicial functions may be seen in such agencies as the Federal Trade Commission, the Interstate Commerce Commission, the Securities and Exchange Commission, the National Labor Relations Board, the Federal Communications Commission, and others usually classified as "independent regulatory commissions." In addition to these independent regulatory commissions judicial functions are exercised by numerous other agencies both independent and within the executive branch, such as the Veterans Administration, an agency which decides several million cases a year involving benefit questions. Some of these questions are routine, but in many instances administrative discretion determines the nature, amount, and recipient of particular benefits. Within the executive branch, departments such as Agriculture, Defense, and Health-Education-Welfare possess important adjudicative powers.

Through such specific application of general rules the impact of national regulation is brought home to many individuals. When significant economic interests are involved in regulation final policy is frequently implemented only through adjudication, for the stakes are high and private parties are unwilling to let governmental policy or economic competitors stand unchallenged. In terms of the day-to-day activities of the citizenry administrative adjudication is probably more ubiquitous than that carried out by courts of law, with the exception of criminal actions. Thus the prices of many services (telephone, electric, and gas utility), some food prices (milk), transportation facilities and rates, communications facilities (radio, television), banking and insurance rates and protection, are determined initially through adjudication, based on more general policy considerations. Just as Congress is unable to define standards of administrative action so precisely that administrative discretion is eliminated, the agencies themselves are unable in their regulations to be precise enough to prevent the delegation of significant discretion to adjudicative officers; thus, the process of adjudication may (and possibly should) shape policy as it is applied in individual cases. Because agencies engaged in adjudication are primarily policy-oriented, it is inevitable that an intimate relationship has grown between these two functions in the administrative process.

THE EXECUTIVE FUNCTION AND
GOVERNMENTAL BUREAUCRACY

Executive functions pertain to administrative activities aimed at increasing the efficiency of government in budgeting and disbursement, planning, personnel, and so on. Many agencies are solely "executive" in this sense; however, all agencies engaged in legislation and adjudication also perform executive functions, pertaining mainly to management. These functions have a profound, though often indirect, effect upon the community. Clearly nothing is more important to government than the type of personnel employed; individuals formulate legislative proposals and perform judicial functions. Planning, which is executive in character, may lead directly to administrative legislation. The budgeting process always becomes deeply involved in program planning, which in turn directly affects the legislative and judicial activities of agencies. The line may frequently be very fine between an executive and a legislative function; however, distinctions can and should be made.

Important examples of the exercise of executive functions may be found in such agencies as the State Department, all the major executive departments under the President, the Civil Service Commission, the Office of Management and Budget and the other components of the Executive Office of the President, and in such independent government corporations as the Tennessee Valley Authority (TVA). These agencies formulate over-all executive budgets, engage in long-range planning, and in general manage huge governmental enterprises. Agencies such as the Civil Service Commission generally implement congressional policy concerning personnel, and some discretion may be employed in establishing personnel regulations. Such policy may be classified as management policy, and although it affects the community as a whole in the sense of determining who may join the federal civil service and under what conditions, it is not generally discussed under the heading of administrative legislation. Similarly, TVA, an independent government corporation, implements its own plans and in this sense it "legislates"; however, once again, this form of legislation may be distinguished from more general regulatory legislation and classified as management policy. In some areas, of course, TVA engages in limited regulatory legislation, for example, when it establishes electricity rates for the region under its jurisdiction. Although in areas such as these functional distinctions become blurred, it is possible to distinguish between the "policy" formulated by administrative agencies which governs various aspects of internal management and procedure, or which is related to providing profitable operation of a government enterprise (such as TVA), and administrative legislation, which regulates on a national scale the various industries of the country and affects the citizenry as a whole.

In addition to managerial functions, executive power includes the power of enforcement of public policy, both foreign and domestic. President Nixon secretly—and on his own initiative—ordered the bombing and invasion of Cambodia in 1973, causing such severe congressional reaction that the War Powers Act of 1973 was passed to limit presidential prerogatives in the international arena by requiring presidential consultation with Congress before military action can be taken. President Ford, ignoring the War Powers Act, ordered direct military action on his own initiative in 1975 to recapture the container ship *Mayaguez* and its crew that had been seized by the Cambodians directly off their coast. Such dramatic uses of the enforcement power of the executive are rare in the domestic arena. President Kennedy did, in the fall of 1962, order troops to be sent to Oxford, Mississippi, and federalized the National Guard there in order to enforce a federal court order, directed at University authorities and state officials, to proceed with integration at the University of Mississippi.

Court orders require executive enforcement. But it is not just the President who has the enforcement power, since this is lodged in varying degrees throughout the bureaucracy. Regulatory agencies, for example, do not just legislate and adjudicate; they also enforce the laws under their jurisdiction by taking direct action against violators. The Internal Revenue Service, in addition to promulgating the internal-revenue code and adjudicating individual cases both informally and formally, also enforces the law by penalizing tax delinquents, garnisheeing bank accounts, and forcing the payment of bills for tax deficiencies. Both the President and the executive branch, then, in seeing that the Constitution, the laws of Congress, court orders, and presidential policies and administrative legislation are "faithfully executed," must engage in extensive enforcement activities.

Constitutional Limitation and Bureaucratic Power

Before considering the development, structure, and operation of the administrative process at greater length, it is important to point out profound initial implications of the wide scope of administrative power on the concept of the separation of powers.

Although technical constitutional norms prevail, the constitutional system to limit governmental power through the separation of powers no longer functions in the manner or to the degree thought necessary by the framers of the Constitution. The validity of this conclusion is of central concern, for if the constitutional system functions effectively then limitation of governmental power is automatic; if, on the other hand, the original system has been altered through the expansion of bureaucratic functions, then, new devices of control of administrative power must be recognized or developed in order to maintain the constitutional ideal of limited government.

GENERAL LEGAL IMPLICATIONS

In *The Federalist* (1787, 1788) Madison, Hamilton, and Jay were particularly concerned with the concept of the separation of powers, which they hoped would be established through the ratification of the Constitution. The separation of powers was to be the principal method of limiting the role of the national government in the republic. Madison noted in *Federalist 47* that "the accumulation of all powers, legislative, executive, and judiciary, in the same hands, whether of one, a few, or many, and whether hereditary, self-appointed, or elective, may justly be pronounced the very definition of tyranny." The Constitution, on the other hand, does not completely separate the powers of the three branches of government, but rather blends them so that each branch will be able to check the other branches by interfering with their functions. For example, the President can exercise the legislative veto; but at the same time Congress has various weapons it can use to interfere with presidential power including the right to approve of various appointments and control treaties. The judiciary's power to review both congressional and executive actions is checked by the President's power to appoint justices to the Court, the power of Congress to approve of such appointments, and finally congressional control over the structure and jurisdiction of the judiciary, including the determination of the number of justices on the Supreme Court and its appellate jurisdiction.

There is no constitutional objection to legislative power residing outside of Congress, nor is there to judicial functions being employed by extra-judicial departments. As Madison pointed out in *Federalist 47*, only "where the *whole* power of one department is exercised by the same hands which possess the *whole* power of another department, [are] the fundamental principles of a free constitution . . . subverted." The very fact that administrative agencies today are permitted to perform all the functions of government indicates that the courts have seen no constitutional objection to such a combination of legislative, judicial, and executive power in the hands of one branch, provided basic controls exist through congressional and judicial surveillance.

BUREAUCRACY AND THE CONSTITUTIONAL SYSTEM

The implications of present-day bureaucratic power to traditional constitutional government must be viewed not only in terms of its effect upon the separation of powers mechanism, but also in relation to the theoretical basis and the broad purposes of the constitutional system. It is interesting to observe the type of situation the framers of the Constitution thought would lead inevitably to the exercise of arbitrary power. In *Federalist 47*, Madison, in supporting the idea that powers should be blended among the various branches, uses the argument that Montesquieu, who originated the separation of powers doctrine, based his system upon the British constitution of his day, which permitted a certain sharing of functions. Madison notes that the principles of a free constitution would have been subverted in the British constitution "if the king, who is the sole executive magistrate, had possessed also the complete legislative power, or the supreme administration of justice." This was not the case, however, because "the magistrate, in whom the whole executive power resides, cannot of himself make a law, though he can put a negative on every law; nor administer justice in person, though he has the appointment of those who do administer it." He adds that he agrees with Montesquieu's statement that: "Were the power of judging joined with the legislative, the life and liberty of the subject would be exposed to arbitrary control, for *the judge* would then be *the legislator*. Were it joined to the executive power, *the judge* might behave with all the violence of *an oppressor*." (Italics are Madison's.) The framers of the Constitution were willing to permit one branch to exercise a portion of the powers of a coordinate branch, provided that one of two conditions prevailed: the exercise of power constitutes a necessary check upon the coordinate branch; the power is properly incidental to the main function of the branch—for example, the judicial power of subpoena may be exercised by the legislature if it is necessary for effective law-making.

Today, instead of this rather delicate balance between the major governmental branches, there has been a major delegation of legislative and judicial power to the administrative branch by Congress for political and regulatory reasons that do not fit the traditional constitutional pattern. The power is not employed solely for the purposes of checking coordinate congressional and judicial branches, nor is it exercised merely because it is "incidental" to the "executive" function. In other words, present administrative powers do not conform to either the theory or mechanism of the separation of powers in the Constitution. The extent of this variation from the constitutional norm will be fully explored in succeeding chapters dealing with the relationships between the administrative branch on the one hand, and Congress, the judiciary, and the President on the other.

Does the statement that the constitutional system has been

altered in substance and theory as a result of bureaucratic functions clash with the fact that administrative power has expanded and found no constitutional impediment? Many changes have taken place in our political system that have altered substantially traditional constitutional theory and practice. The development of political parties and interest groups and their present role in government was clearly not foreseen and is beyond the expectations and intentions of the framers of the Constitution. Also, various changes in the electoral system providing, for example, for the popular election of the President and members of the Senate are out of line with the original system. Although some of these changes, such as the direct election of senators, have resulted from constitutional amendment, most have occurred as a result of custom and usage.

There is nothing "unconstitutional" about the present characteristics of bureaucracy; but the constitutional changes which have occurred must be recognized and dealt with in terms of the broad purposes of constitutional government. The primary purpose of a constitutional system is to limit the powers of government; thus, if the original system does not function in limiting bureaucratic power, it is important to determine what, if anything, has replaced it.

THE PREMISE OF LEGISLATIVE SUPREMACY

Two remaining aspects of the relationship between the original constitutional system and present day bureaucratic power remain to be discussed. First, it is important to note that the Constitution was framed in an atmosphere of distrust of legislative bodies and the powers they possessed. The framers of the Constitution, of course, had to work within the boundaries of political tradition; hence, the powers they assigned to Congress were necessarily based upon the powers traditionally given to legislative bodies, particularly in the colonies. Needless to say, one of the principal reasons the Constitution was ratified was the fact that it varied only slightly from many of the colonial constitutions, and incorporated a separation of powers doctrine accepted by the colonies in their own constitutions. The problem of curbing the legislature could not be approached from the standpoint of what powers should be withdrawn from it, but rather from the approach of checking inherent legislative power. The framers knew they had to give Congress certain powers and were worried about the nature and extent of these powers.

The feelings of the framers concerning the legislature are illustrated by Madison in *Federalist 48:*

> . . . In a democracy, where a multitude of people exercise in person the legislative function, and are continually exposed, by their incapacity for regular deliberation and concerted measures, to the ambitious intrigues of their executive magistrates, tyranny may well be apprehended on some favorable emergency, to start up in the same quarter. But in a representative republic, where the executive magistracy is carefully limited, both in the extent and the duration of its power; and where the legislative power is exercised by an assembly, which is inspired by a supposed influence over the people, with an intrepid confidence in its own strength; which is sufficiently numerous to feel all the passions which actuate a multitude; yet not so numerous as to be incapable of pursuing the objects of its passions, by means which reason prescribes; it is against the enterprising ambition of this department, that the people ought to indulge all their jealousy and exhaust all their precautions.
>
> The legislative department derives a superiority in our governments from other circumstances. Its constitutional powers being at once more extensive, and less susceptible of precise limits, it can, with the greater facility, mask, under complicated and indirect measures, the encroachments which it makes on the co-ordinate departments. It is not infrequently a question of real nicety in legislative bodies, whether the operation of a particular measure will, or will not extend beyond the legislative sphere. On the other side, the executive power being restrained within a narrower compass, and being more simple in its nature; and the judiciary being described by landmarks, still less uncertain, projects of usurpation by either of these departments would immediately betray and defeat themselves. Nor is this all: as the legislative department alone has access to the pockets of the people, and has in some constitutions full discretion, and in all a prevailing influence over the pecuniary rewards of those who fill the other departments; a dependence is thus created in the latter, which gives still greater facility to encroachments of the former.

Several ideas in Madison's paper should be emphasized. First, Madison distinguishes between a democracy and a representative republic (constitutional democracy) and notes that in the former the absence of checks and balances in the system opens a path for executive domination of the legislature; hence, power seized by the executive during a time of emergency may replace the democratic process. In a constitutional democracy, on the other hand, the powers of the executive are carefully defined and limited by the constitution; thus executive usurpation is not likely to occur. The legislative branch, however, is disproportionately powerful because its democratic base provides it potentially with strong political support, which, in all probability, it will seek to use on various occasions, and its constitutional powers are necessarily vague and not capable of precise definition.

With this concept and fear of legislative power in mind the framers set about constructing a system which gave primary attention to requirements of congressional limitation. The powers of Congress were defined as carefully as possible, and although these enumerated powers later were relied upon for a vast expansion of national power their original purpose was to set the boundaries of congressional action. Moreover, Congress was established as a bicameral body, in which the interests of the House of Representatives were pitted against those of the Senate. Different powers were given to each house of the legislature, and in a sense a checks and balances system internal to Congress itself was created. Specific prohibitions were placed on congressional action, and when the Bill of Rights was added to the Constitution the first amendment set the tone:

Congress shall make no law respecting the establishment of religion, or prohibiting the free exercise thereof; or abridging the freedom of speech, or of the press; or the right of the people peaceably to assemble, and to petition the government for a redress of grievances. (Italics added.)

In contrast to this rather exalted view of the legislature, Alexander Hamilton noted in *Federalist* 72 that although

"the administration of government, in its largest sense, comprehends all the operations of the body politic, whether legislative, executive, or judiciary, [administration] in its most usual, and perhaps in its most precise signification, . . . is limited to executive details, and falls peculiarly within the province of the executive department. The actual conduct of foreign negotiations, the preparatory plans of finance, the application and disbursement of the public monies, in conformity to the general appropriations of the legislature, the arrangement of the army and navy, the direction of the operations of war; these, and other matters of a like nature, constitute what seems to be most properly understood by the administration of government."

Keeping in mind this limited view of executive power, and concentration upon the importance of the legislature, the *premises* of the constitutional system are no longer valid today. This is a further reason to support the view that present bureaucratic power does not fit neatly into the pattern of limited government established by the Constitution of 1789.

THE ROLE OF MOTIVATION IN THE CONSTITUTIONAL SYSTEM

The framers of the Constitution realized that it would not be enough simply to enable each branch of government to check coordinate branches in order to maintain the separation of powers; the branches must be motivated to remain independent and oppose any move on the part of other branches directed at limiting their sphere of power. It was assumed that institutions, as well as individuals, act in accordance with what they conceive to be their own self-interest; therefore, the framers attempted to shape what would be the political self-interest of each branch in such a way that it would jealously guard its prerogatives against encroachment. As Madison noted in *Federalist 51* the aim of the separation of powers system is "to divide and arrange the several offices in such a manner, as that each may be a check on the other; that the *private* interest of every individual, may be a sentinel over the *public* rights." (Italics added.) *Federalist 51* expands this concept in the following way:

But the great security against a gradual concentration of the several powers in the same department, consists in giving those who administer each department, the necessary constitutional means, and personal motives, to resist encroachments of the others. The provision for defence must in this, as in all other cases, be made commensurate to the danger of attack. Ambition must be made to counteract ambition. The interest of the man must be connected with the constitutional rights of the place. It may be a reflection on human nature, that such devices should be necessary to control the abuses of government. But what is government itself, but the greatest of all reflections on human nature? If men were angels, no government would be necessary. If angels were to govern men, neither external nor internal controls on government would be necessary. In framing a government, which is to be administered by men over men, the great difficulty lies in this: You must first enable the government to control the governed; and in the next place, oblige it to control itself.

Conflicting interests, based upon different electoral constituencies, powers, and terms of office, were theoretically to motivate branches to maintain independent status.

How does this constitutional system of motivation compare with the operation of the governmental branches today? It is true that there is a great deal of conflict between the President and Congress as a direct result of the constitutional separation of powers; however, this system of motivated conflicts tends to break down in the interaction of the bureaucracy and Congress. Many agencies are creatures of Congress and relatively independent of both presidential and judicial control; in these cases Congress and its particular committees involved feel no compelling need to oppose bureaucratic interests, but rather there is a definite tendency to establish a mutually satisfactory *modus vivendi*. The fact that Congress has delegated a substantial amount of its power to the bureaucracy by itself reflects both the necessities of modern democracy and the lack of fear of bureaucracy in Congress. Admittedly, there exists a common and generally unchallenged assumption that the typical congressman is highly suspicious of the "bureaucrat"; in practice however, most congressmen recognize the necessity of working with the administrative branch, and some attempt to extend their own political power, both within Congress and with constituents, through the bureaucracy. Congressmen are often identified on Capitol Hill by reference to the agencies within the jurisdiction of committees they chair. Jamie Whitten (D., Mississippi), Chairman of the powerful House Appropriations Subcommittee on Agriculture, is considered on the Hill as a permanent Under Secretary of Agriculture. Paul Rogers (D., Florida), Chairman of the House Health Subcommittee, is referred to as "Mr. Health." Both Congressmen have built up significant reputations as the result of their close relationships with the Departments of Agriculture and HEW respectively. Many such examples are found on the Hill, with Representatives and Senators gaining status and power through close working relationships with powerful parts of the bureaucracy. Naturally, this causes committee chairmen frequently to defend agencies within their jurisdiction that are under attack from sources outside of the committee. An unwritten rule of Congress, which admittedly is violated on occasion, is that committees having jurisdiction over agencies have the exclusive power both to defend and to attack those agencies. The 94th Congress (1975–1976) witnessed Senator Edward Kennedy's Subcommittee on Administrative Practice and Procedure question many of the regulatory procedures of the Civil Aeronautics Board, while Congressman Brock Adams (D., Washington), an important member of the Interstate and Foreign Commerce Committee and its Subcommittee on Transportation and Commerce, defended the ICC and the CAB against proposals to decrease their regulatory authority. Just as good relations with administrative agencies can enhance the position of Congressmen on Capitol Hill, co-operation with the bureaucracy also can gain constituent votes. Insofar as government action may be taken in any policy field, and with respect to any private interest or in any area of the country, it must finally stem from the administrative branch; thus, it is natural for congressmen and others to attempt to influence administrative agencies, as a means of securing implementation of policy in their interests.

For these reasons the picture of present relationships between Congress and the administrative branch is often one not of conflict based upon different personal political interests, but one of co-operation for the purposes of securing mutual political objectives. This is not to suggest that there is anything "wrong" or even "unconstitutional" about such legislative-bureaucratic cooperation. Moreover, the goals that both congressional and administrative politicians seek are not always "personal," or oriented directly to securing group advantages, but frequently are what these individuals feel is in the "national interest." Often national and group interests coincide in the minds of politicians. These considerations do not change the fact that the original system of motivation to maintain the separation of powers does not function today in the area of legislative-bureaucratic relationships.

Finally, although it is not explicitly stated in the Constitution, some of the framers felt that judicial review should play an important role in the limitation of government. Judicial review extends to certain decisions of the executive and administrative arms of the government, as well as to congressional acts. It can take place only where there is a "case and controversy." Theoretically, the courts are to judge the constitutionality and legality of challenged administrative decisions that can reasonably be presumed to fall within judicial competence; thus, they are supposed to review *legal* rather than *policy* issues. But the judiciary has found it necessary to delve into both areas, since they are frequently indistinguishable even to the most subtle minds. The courts can always find legal justification for reviewing almost any administrative decision, whether of an executive, legislative, or judicial nature; however, with the development of administrative law the possibility of judicial review and remedy of administrative action has been fundamentally altered. The courts themselves refuse to review most administrative decisions, simply because they do not have the time to consider the vast volume of cases that arise in the normal course of regulatory administration.

The expansion of administrative discretion in cases involving judicial matters has resulted from the agencies' specialization, and their ability to maintain some continuity of public policy. Despite their theoretical control, the courts are unable to limit the power of administrative agencies through the device of judicial review to the extent that many consider desirable in our constitutional system.

The Administrative State and Constitutional Democracy

Constitutional government in the United States subsumes the democratic process; however, constitutional limitation of power concerns far more than limitation of democracy. Originally, a clear distinction was made in constitutional theory between the "democratic" component of government, which was to be the House of Representatives, and other units, which were to represent other elements of government. The states were represented by the Senate and took part in the selection of the President through the electoral college; and the judiciary was not to have a representative function at all, but in fact was to be a definite independent force to check the whims of the coordinate branches of government. Thus the Constitution was actually concerned with limiting *governments* (both national and state) as well as with limiting the direct power of the *people*.

The framers of the Constitution were aware that representatives would in many instances act independently of their immediate constituencies. Government was not conceived to be passive, even when the interests of the people were expressed directly through the elective process. But members of the House were supposed to give due consideration to their constituents in those matters where local interests were properly involved. In areas where the framers did not feel local interests relevant, or where such interests were considered detrimental to policy formulation in the national interest—as in the field of foreign affairs—they removed primary jurisdiction from the House. In matters of national significance, requiring calm deliberation, adequate information, and detachment from the influence of the people, the Senate was to fill the obvious deficiencies of the House. (See *Federalist 63.*) With respect to the legislative branch, then, democracy was to function directly only in shaping policy where the direct and immediate interests of constituents were involved. In matters of national concern requiring information in depth, and where some continuity of policy was necessary, the Senate was to exercise the leading role; it, presumably, could pay greater heed to such national concerns because of its relative isolation from the passions of the people, and because its greater tenure gave it more time to acquire necessary information and follow up initial policy decisions. By limiting the House of Representatives in this manner the ability of the *people* to participate directly in government was curbed. This limitation of democracy was intentional.

Although the direct influence of the people was to be curbed by the Senate, it should not be forgotten that Madison noted in *Federalist 51* that "a dependence on the people is, no doubt, the primary control on the government; but experience has taught mankind the necessity of auxiliary precautions." He indicates that the electoral sanction was considered to be of central importance in the control of government. In this respect the development of a bureaucracy that is not elected and that exercises broad political functions has apparently resulted in the breakdown of a primary constitutional check on arbitrary governmental power.

THE PROBLEM OF FACTION

James Madison, in *Federalist 10,* relates the problem of constitutional democracy, that is, limited democracy, to the role of faction in society and government. He defined faction as "a number of citizens, whether amounting to a majority or minority of the whole, who are united and actuated by some common impulse of passion, or of interest, adverse to the rights of other citizens, or to the permanent and aggregate interests of the community." Faction, so defined, exists at both community and governmental levels. It becomes a serious problem, according to Madison, only when one faction becomes or threatens to become a majority:

if a faction consists of less than a majority, relief is supplied by the republican principle, which enables the majority to defeat its sinister views by regular vote. It may clog the administration, it may convulse the society; but it will be unable to execute and mask its violence under the forms of the Constitution. When a majority is included in a faction, the form of popular government, on the other hand, enables it to sacrifice to its ruling passion or interest both the public good and the rights of other citizens.

It is necessary to construct the government in such a way that a majority, once formed, will be unable to gain control of the instruments of government. For this reason a "republic" is to be favored over a "democracy."

In *Federalist 10* Madison defines a pure democracy as "a society consisting of a small number of citizens, who assemble and administer the government in person." In such a governmental system the majority, if united, can rule without limitation; hence the evils of faction will be completely uncontrolled. On the other hand a "republic," defined as "a government in which the scheme of representation takes place," may provide a cure for faction when combined with such constitutional limitations as the separation of powers and federalism. Republican government purposely checks the rule of the majority *of the people* at the same time that it prevents a combination of arbitrary governmental power. Madison notes, however, that one of the best methods of preventing arbitrary governmental power is to *limit and refine the voice of the people*. The problem of controlling faction becomes essentially one of limiting the democratic will of the community.

Madison states the crux of this matter in the following way, in *Federalist 10:*

> The two great points of difference between a democracy and a republic are: first, the delegation of the government, in the latter, to a small number of citizens elected by the rest; secondly, the greater number of citizens, and greater sphere of country, over which the latter may be extended.
>
> The effect of the first difference is, on the one hand, to refine and enlarge the public views, by passing them through the medium of a chosen body of citizens, whose wisdom may best discern the true interest of their country, and whose patriotism and love of justice will be least likely to sacrifice it to temporary or partial considerations. Under such a regulation, it may well happen that the public voice, pronounced by the representatives of the people, will be more consonant to the public good than if pronounced by the people themselves, convened for the purpose. On the other hand, the effect may be inverted. Men of factious tempers, of local prejudices, or of sinister designs, may, by intrigue, by corruption, or by other means, first obtain the suffrages, and then betray the interests, of the people.

Madison goes on to point out that in a large republic factions will be increased, but also dispersed, which will make it more difficult for any one to gain a majority in its favor. The latter consideration, concerning the problem of how to handle the *leaders,* he dismisses in *Federalist 10* with the statement that in a large republic, because it has a greater number of "fit characters," more representatives will be "fit" than "unfit." Also leaders were to be controlled through the separation of powers system.

Perhaps the most important implication of bureaucratic power and organization today is that in relation to constitutional theory and methods pertaining to the control of faction. Because of Madison's negative definition of faction, which included both political parties and interest groups, it was assumed that faction would operate to the detriment of the community as a whole. To an extent there was a feeling that any group looking after its own interests would automatically be operating against the "public interest." Federalism was to control faction through dispersion of interests geographically; and the separation of powers was to prevent any unified group from gaining control of the national governmental apparatus.

One of the central problems of dealing with this concept today is that present definitions of "faction" differ, at least in terms of emphasis, from that contained in *Federalist 10;* and, more significantly, present attitudes regarding the desirability of "faction" are totally different from Madison's original viewpoint. Generally, **a political interest group today is defined as any group with shared attitudes advocating particular political goals, and methods for** achieving political ends.[14] It should be realized that there are both governmental and private interest groups, and that any discussion of the problems of reconciling political interest groups must deal, for example, as much with the Department of Defense (or its subdivisions) as with General Dynamics Corporation; as much with the Department of Agriculture and its subdivisions as with the Farm Bureau Federation; as much with the Federal Communications Commission as with the American Telephone and Telegraph Company, the National Broadcasting Company, and the numerous other private groups within the jurisdiction of the FCC. Of course there are various differences between the governmental and private sectors; however, both conform to the generally accepted definition of political interest groups given above. One of the most complex and important implications of the rise of the administrative branch is the proliferation of such governmental interest groups.

THE BUREAUCRACY AND CONSTITUTIONAL DEMOCRACY

The initial constitutional problem that has been raised concerning bureaucratic power is its tendency to tip the balance between coordinate branches of *government.* It was noted that the administrative branch adds a fourth dimension to the constitutional system of separation of powers, a dimension which is not controlled within its framework. Because separation of powers was

14. David B. Truman, *The Governmental Process* (New York: Alfred A. Knopf, 1951), p. 33.

intended as a curb on democratic majorities, the question of democratic control is deeply involved in the enlargement of the administrative arm of government. For example, if it could be shown that the democratic "will of the people" controls administrative decision making, the scope of the democratic process would be far greater in the present system, and the limits far less, than those established in the Constitution.

Before considering the relationship between the bureaucracy and the democratic process it is important to point out that one of the major features of constitutional development has been the expansion of the democratic base of the major institutions of government at both the national and state levels. This expansion has fundamentally altered original constitutional intent; thus, when considering the office of the President today perhaps the most significant implication of presidential power is the fact that it stems from the broadest base of democratic support in the world. If one were to analyze presidential power in relation to constitutional norms it would be necessary to point out that the original system of limitation of democracy was based upon the premise that the House of Representatives alone would be subject to direct democratic influence; hence, the House was carefully controlled by the Constitution. But once democratic influence shifts from the House to coordinate branches, the President and the Senate, the nature of constitutional limitation changes. A system designed to limit democratic majorities in the House may no longer be effective in limiting democratic power expressed through the President. It is necessary to define in outline the present position of the bureaucracy in relation to constitutional democracy in a similar manner, in order to complete a framework for the more detailed analysis that will follow.

First, the original plan of the framers of the Constitution, which limited direct democratic influence to matters of local concern, is no longer accepted. The democratic election of the Senate and the President attests to this, as does the development of political parties. It is generally agreed that "the people" should participate indirectly in public policy formulation through the selection of political leaders. In this respect constitutional democracy today emphasizes the more positive aspects of popular participation rather than requirements of limitation of the people's will. This fact, however, only appears to make it more difficult to reconcile the position of the bureaucracy with the needs of constitutional democracy, for the administrative arm of government is deeply involved in the formulation of public policy and is not in many instances controlled in any meaningful way by the elected organs of government. To the extent that these two conditions prevail it is necessary either to determine alternative methods of democratic participation, or to bring bureaucracy more under the control of the elected branches of government, if a system of constitutional democracy is to remain in existence. Before reaching this stage of value judgment, however, it will be necessary to indicate in detail the role of bureaucracy in policy formulation and the relative powers to control the bureaucracy residing in the executive and legislative branches, the only ones elected by the people. These discussions of "what is" must preface any consideration of "what ought to be." The needs of bureaucracy must be balanced with the requirements of democracy.

Insofar as the control of faction is concerned, it is widely recognized that public and private interest groups *work together* in many policy fields to achieve common goals. Because of requirements of specialization the interest groups concerned with particular policy fields are frequently unconcerned with policy formulation in neighboring areas. It is quite possible, for example, that policy formulated by the Interstate Commerce Commission pertaining to railroads, trucking, or shipping will not interest those concerned with communications policy under the jurisdiction of the Federal Communications Commission; thus, the interests which determine ICC policy will be relatively free to do as they choose. This, obviously, is not always the case; however, it occurs with sufficient frequency that it may be stated as a meaningful generalization. The development of bureaucracy, then, has greatly increased "faction," or interest groups, and at the same time it has strengthened the power of such groups in their particular policy areas.

What does the Constitution have to say about this situation? Its provisions pertaining to the control of faction do not regulate this type of administrative action. In fact, paradoxically, the Constitution encourages interest group activity beyond the sphere of its own influence. The constitutional system discourages the development of any unified source of political power in the form of disciplined political parties, or "majorities" as the framers

would have said, with the ability to control the *entire governmental system*. This enables portions of that system to be governed by "factions" or political interest groups. Federalism and
the separation of powers have prevented the creation of disciplined *national* parties by giving primary strength to state political organizations, and by preventing any kind of effective
cohesion at the national level. The latter situation is the direct
result of such constitutional provisions as different electoral constituencies for the House, Senate, and the President; staggered
terms of office; and the assignment of different powers to the
various branches of government. These same provisions, however, do nothing to prevent political interest groups, private and
public, from operating with relative freedom at the national
level. What the framers clearly failed to predict was the demise
of local interest groups and the development of groups with a
national orientation. The advantage of a republic because of
the geographical dispersion of interests is no longer valid in the
limitation of "faction."

Finally, the separation of powers system, by placing Congress
in the position of an adversary of the President, motivates the
legislature to place a significant portion of the administrative
branch outside of the legal sphere of presidential control. In this
manner, the separation of powers idea, instead of limiting governmental power, results in the relative independence of the administrative branch by displacing the most natural focal point
of control. Because of the attachment between private clientele
groups and public bureaucratic interest groups, the constitutional
separation of powers often leads directly to an increase of "faction" in government. This situation is a further reflection of the
fragmentation of power in the constitutional system, and its inability to identify a central source of political power.

CHAPTER 2 The Development and Organization of Bureaucracy

The Rise of the Administrative Process

ALTHOUGH BUREAUCRACY has always been present in America, only since the latter part of the nineteenth century has it assumed characteristics recognized today as typical. There have always been a number of executive departments exercising important responsibilities in various areas. The War (Army), Navy, State, and Treasury departments were created by Congress in the eighteenth century, along with the office of Attorney General (the Department of Justice was not established until 1870). The first national administration under Washington included Thomas Jefferson as Secretary of State, Alexander Hamilton as Secretary of the Treasury, Henry Knox as Secretary of War, and Edmund Randolph as Attorney General. The activities of the departments headed by these men generally conformed to the definition that Hamilton gave of "administration" in *Federalist* 72, a passive concept that regarded the executive branch as an agent of Congress, capable only of carrying out "executive details." Hamilton himself was a vigorous and intelligent Secretary of the Treasury who seized legislative leadership in many instances from Congress; however, such executive initiative was due to the personality of one man and several key followers, not to any political power inherent in the Department of the Treasury *per se*. There is little doubt that Hamilton believed in strong executive leadership; while Secretary of the Treasury he was accused by Madison of attempting to establish in the Presidency royal prerogatives equivalent to those of the King of England. Hamilton's relationship with Congress was scored by Jefferson who, at one point, remarked that "the whole action of the Legislature was now under the direction of the Treasury." [1]

What in the early years of the republic depended upon the political skill of individuals in more recent times has become the responsibility of department and agency heads and their staffs automatically as a result of factors external to individual political astuteness. Thus the departments and agencies have become powerful in their own right, and although skillful political leadership may increase this power the lack of such leadership does not significantly alter their position of dominance in many areas over Congress, the President and the courts.

After the creation of the initial core of executive departments it was not until the middle of the nineteenth century that more were added. The only new department established before the Civil War was Interior, created in 1849.[2] Only at the close of the nineteenth century did a dramatic spurt begin to take place in

1. For the attitudes of Madison and Jefferson on Hamilton see Edward S. Corwin, *The President: Office and Powers* (4th ed., New York: New York University Press, 1957), pp. 15–18 and p. 318, n. 37.

2. The other departments were established in the following order: Justice (1870); Post Office (1872); Agriculture (1889, originally established in 1862 under the direction of a Commissioner of Agriculture); Commerce (1913); Labor (1913); Defense (1947); Health, Education, and Welfare (1953); Housing and Urban Development (1965); Transportation (1966). The major independent regulatory agencies date from even later in the nineteenth century, and were established in the following order: Interstate Commerce Commission (1887); Federal Reserve Board (1913); Federal Trade Commission (1914); Federal Power Commission (initially established in 1920, and made an independent agency in 1930); Federal Communications Commission (1934); Securities and Exchange Commission (1934); National Labor Relations Board (1935); Civil Aeronautics Board (1940, when it assumed part of the functions of the Civil Aeronautics Authority, created in 1938); Environment Protection Agency (1970); Consumer Product Safety Commission (1972); Federal Maritime Commission (1936, reorganized 1950, 1961); Nuclear Regulatory Commission (first established in 1946 as the Atomic Energy Commission, the regulatory and developmental functions of which were divided into the Nuclear Regulatory Commission and the Energy Research and Development Administration respectively in 1974); Commodity Futures Trading Commission (1975). Created in 1958, the Federal Aviation Agency was an important independent regulatory body that became part of the Department of Transportation in 1966. The Postal Rate Commission, established in 1970, is a quasi-independent regulatory commission in that it does not have the final power to implement its decisions, but can act only in an advisory capacity to the Postal Service. The United States Tariff Commission, created in 1916, is also quasi-independent; its decisions are essentially advisory to the President. There is a total of eighty agencies, counting both independent agencies and those within executive departments, that exercise regulatory functions.

the American bureaucratic system. Many of the most important agencies today were not created until the New Deal, and a few not until after the Second World War. A spurt in new agencies occurred in the 1960s and 1970s, but it in no way equaled that of the New Deal. The Department of Housing and Urban Development (HUD) and the Department of Transportation (DOT), established respectively in 1965 and 1966, were umbrella departments encompassing agencies that already were in existence. The central core of the Department of Transportation was the formerly independent Federal Aviation Agency, created in 1958. HUD contained a collection of agencies dealing with housing that had previously been scattered about the bureaucracy. In 1970, the environmental movement secured bureaucratic representation through the creation of the Environmental Protection Agency (EPA), established by an executive order of President Nixon. The EPA was given responsibility to co-ordinate government action in environmental policy-making and administration, including the regulation of air and water pollution and toxic substances.

The consumer movement was reflected in the creation in 1972, of a Consumer Product Safety Commission that establishes safety standards for consumer goods and bans hazardous products. The 1970s also witnessed a strong drive for the establishment of a Consumer Protection Agency that would be an advocate for consumers before other administrative agencies. It would, in a sense, act as a consumer's lawyer in the federal government.

The civil rights movement secured representation in the bureaucracy with the creation of the Equal Employment Opportunity Commission under the terms of the Civil Rights Act of 1964, which bans discrimination in employment based on race, color, religion, sex, or national origin. The Commission works with employers to achieve voluntary compliance, and may bring suit in a federal district court to achieve compliance if it fails to reach a voluntary settlement. In addition to banning discrimination in employment, the Civil Rights Act of 1964 prohibits discrimination in programs and activities that receive federal financial assistance. Under this (Title VI) part of the Act, various agencies that are in the business of giving grants to private groups have established civil rights offices and designated administrators to see that the law is upheld. For example, HEW has a Civil

Rights Office that, among other policies, has required all institutions of higher education receiving federal funds (which includes virtually all colleges and universities in the country) to file with it "affirmative action" plans indicating how the institution is going to ensure non-discrimination in employment in the future. A final example of an important and relatively new administrative agency reflecting the entrance of the government into a new area is the Federal Energy Administration (FEA), which regulates in various ways the allocation of energy resources and analyzes policies relating to the development and conservation of energy.

The deep involvement of the administrative branch in legislative and judicial functions did not take place to any significant degree until the early part of the twentieth century. Administrators, particularly department heads with political talent, exercised sporadic influence on Congress; but there was no intentional and continuous administrative activity in legislation and adjudication. In attempting to ascertain the reasons for the rise of the administrative process it is necessary to focus, first, upon the broad historical, economic, and political factors that have made necessary a vast expansion of bureaucracy.

ECONOMIC DEVELOPMENT

There is a direct relationship between the nature of economic development in the United States and the rise of the administrative branch. During the first half of the nineteenth century it was possible, in general, for individual entrepreneurs to pursue goals which they considered to be in their own best interest without seriously affecting the nation as a whole. The ideal of *laissez faire* was never completely accepted, but early nineteenth century America provides one of the best historical examples of an era in which this ideal was approximated. Of course numerous private economic groups and individuals appealed directly to the government from time to time for intervention in aid of their interests, and the intermittent controversies that flared over protectionism versus free trade illustrate that even in this relatively uncomplicated economic atmosphere government was not overlooked as a potential benefactor and regulator.

After 1850 inventions and technological advances provided a catalyst for revolutionary changes, which resulted in an important alteration in the relationship between government and the economy. New industries, affecting the entire nation, in some cases required government aid and protection to become established and to prosper. The nation needed a transportation system that would span the continent. Similarly, it needed accelerated development of natural resources and manufacturing. The government was a direct beneficiary of private prosperity insofar as that prosperity reflected genuine national economic development and political stability; however, it soon became evident that the prosperity of some groups came at the expense of others. Having fostered industries with subsidies of various kinds, both the national and state governments had to contend with political and social problems, such as economic instability, deceptive business practices, and the growth of monopolies, that were directly attributable to the activities of the groups they originally supported. Moreover, economic change in areas that did not involve initial government subsidy created similar problems on such a broad scale that only the national government could deal with them effectively. The development of national monopolies in such industries as oil, steel, public utilities, and transportation created inevitable difficulties for small business, labor, agriculture, and the general consumer. This led to group conflict, which was transferred to governmental bodies at all levels. On the one hand governments were faced with a demand for new controls over the private economic sphere, and on the other they were pressured by very powerful and wealthy groups to maintain *laissez faire*. The net result was the establishment of limited government control of the economy during the latter part of the nineteenth century, and the way was paved for the far more extensive regulation that was to come later.

Development of the Railroads · An excellent illustration of the way in which nineteenth century American government became involved both in the promotion and regulation of the economy is provided by the development of the railroads.[3] This industry

3. For information concerning the activities of the railroads in the nineteenth century see Samuel Eliot Morison and Henry Steele Commager, *The Growth of the American Republic* (5th ed., New York: Oxford University Press, 1962), II, chap. vii.

presented the most serious problems to government control in the century. The railroads received probably the greatest single subsidy ever given by the government to private enterprise, with the possible exception of present-day defense expenditure. The basis of the subsidy was typical: a national transportation system was needed, and there was not enough capital from private sources to develop railroads within the time felt to be necessary. The government embarked upon a program which eventually cost it one hundred and fifty-eight million acres of land. Some railroads received truly extraordinary grants: the Northern Pacific obtained forty-four million acres, while the Santa Fe, the Union Pacific, and the Central and Southern Pacific received over seventeen million acres each. In addition, other government help was given at both the national and state levels, including loans, tax relief, protection from competitors, and outright grants of money. The entire industry, which came to dominate large sections of the country, was developed as a result of such incentives. Once established, it retained intimate contacts with government, particularly Congress and state legislatures, to ensure continued prosperity. As is generally the case with government subsidies, there were beneficial side-effects from the building of the railroads. Employment was provided for tens of thousands of workers, including many new immigrants. The development of a national transportation system pushed back the frontier and led directly to a national communications network.

Although the railroads made an enormous contribution to the country, they also began to abuse their dominant economic power in the decades following the Civil War. In some instances their freight rates were so high that the farmers, who could ship by no other means, burned their crops rather than submit to the roads. Generally there was little the roads did not do to take advantage of their semi-monopolistic position: discriminatory rates; rebates to powerful shippers; payoffs to state legislators; free passes to all who had influence; high rates in areas where there was no competition coupled with low rates in competitive locations, and so on. Inevitably demands were made, especially by the agrarian West, to curb these abuses. An analysis of the development of regulation of the railroads provides a basis for understanding the causes and problems of national regulation in general, for the regulatory mechanism, devised first for the railroads, set the pattern of future regulation in many other industries.

The Failure of State Regulation of the Railroads · Both before and after the Civil War the states attempted in various ways to curb the increasing abuses of the railroads, but their failure to do so reflected their general inability to exercise sufficient power to control industries which were national in scope. Why were the states unable to meet the challenge of effective economic regulation? First, there was the inherent defect in state regulation of powerful national industries: the problems and approaches of individual states differed, and such regulatory patterns as emerged necessarily lacked uniformity. Second, it was particularly easy for the railroads, as it was later for other powerful groups, to dominate state legislatures, executives, and the special regulatory commissions that were set up throughout the country. These commissions in some instances had initial rate-making and adjudicative power, as in the case of the powerful Illinois Board of Railroad and Warehouse Commissioners, created in 1871. In Illinois, there was strong agrarian support from the Granger movement for strict control of railroads and subsidiary operations. So strong was the feeling against the railroads there that elaborate provisions for control were written into the state constitution, adopted in 1870. Third, apart from isolated examples of strong state regulation, the vast majority of states failed to implement the necessary government control.

An additional obstacle to effective regulation faced by the states, and later by the national government, was the attitude of the courts. At the end of the nineteenth century and during much of the twentieth, the judiciary was generally unsympathetic to the goals of economic regulation. The problem of legislative removal of the jurisdiction of the courts from regulatory fields occurred later, particularly at the national level. Initially the so-called "Granger laws," establishing the right of the government to regulate private property in the public interest, were upheld in the historic case, *Munn v. Illinois* (1877), which specifically involved Illinois constitutional and statutory provisions regulating railroads. In the course of his opinion, Chief Justice Waite justified public regulation on the basis that private property affected with a public interest ceases to be private. Further, he stated that "property does become clothed with a public interest when used in a manner to make it of public consequence, and affect the community at large. When, therefore, one devotes his property to a use in which the public has an interest, he, in effect, grants to the public an interest in that use, and must submit to be controlled by the public for the common good, to the extent of the interest he has thus created." [4] It seemed that there was not going to be any serious constitutional obstacle in the path of state regulation.

Although the Supreme Court at the time of the *Munn* case supported the general idea of government control of industries affected with a public interest, a serious constitutional doubt was soon raised as to the validity of state regulation over those portions of an industry engaged in *interstate* commerce. An indication of future developments came in 1877, the same year as the *Munn* case, when the Court decided *Peik v. Chicago and Northwestern Railway Co.*[5] The issue in this case was whether or not the state of Wisconsin could regulate an interstate carrier. The Court held that "until Congress acts in reference to the relations of this company to interstate commerce, it is certainly within the power of Wisconsin to regulate its fares, etc., so far as they are of domestic concern. With the people of Wisconsin this company has domestic relations. Incidentally, these may reach beyond the State. But certainly, until Congress undertakes to legislate for those who are without the State, Wisconsin may provide for those within, even though it may indirectly affect those without." [6] In this case the issue was joined, and the proponents of state regulation won; however, the *Peik* decision, like many before it left no doubt that where Congress chose to act in areas involving interstate commerce it preempted the field.[7]

The Supreme Court became more conservative in the decade of the eighties. In 1886 its decision in *Wabash, St. Louis & Pacific Ry. Co. v. Illinois* [8] essentially overruled its previous opinions in

4. 94 U.S. 113, 126 (1877).
5. 94 U.S. 164 (1887).
6. *Ibid.*, at 178.
7. For an early decision along these lines see *Gibbons v. Ogden,* 9 Wheaton 1 (1824).
8. 118 U.S. 557 (1886).

the *Peik* and *Munn* cases by holding that any firm engaged in interstate commerce could not be regulated by the states through which it passed. This, the Court held, was prohibited by the commerce clause, which gave Congress the exclusive right to regulate interstate commerce. This prohibition against state regulation did not apply to transportation solely within the boundaries of a state, provided it was not connected in any way with interstate commerce. But there was little that needed regulation that fell within the intrastate category; thus the *Wabash* decision nullified all of the efforts that the states had made to regulate the railroads. Further, the scope of this decision led to a preclusion of state regulation in other needed areas, such as antitrust control, for it was almost a foregone conclusion that the most imperative government regulation would involve interstate firms. The economy of the United States was developing on a national scale, and state regulation was not only precluded on a constitutional basis by the Supreme Court, but also because of the evident failure of those state controls that had been established.

The obvious failure of the states led directly to the establishment of the Interstate Commerce Commission (ICC) in 1887. In many other areas it was not until the New Deal period that a recognition of a similar inadequacy of state regulation, coupled with a pressing need for national standards, led to the establishment of many new agencies patterned on the model of the ICC.

THE FIRST REGULATORY AGENCY—THE INTERSTATE COMMERCE COMMISSION (1887)

The establishment of the ICC represented a historic step in the development of American bureaucracy.[9] It is important to note, first of all, that Congress decided to place regulatory power in the hands of a *commission,* i.e., an administrative agency, in order to cope with the problems of regulation of a national industry. Further, this Commission, although under the partial direction of the Secretary of the Interior until 1889, was *independent* in various ways of the President, Congress, and, later on, the

9. For a comprehensive study of the independent regulatory commissions see Robert E. Cushman, *The Independent Regulatory Commissions* (New York: Oxford University Press, 1941).

courts. At the time of the creation of the ICC there had been a long history of state commissions; therefore the ICC was not entirely a revolutionary approach to economic regulation. Initially the most important change was the transference of the concept of commission regulation from the state to the national level.

In spite of the established tradition of state regulatory commissions, there was a sharp division of opinion in Congress, particularly between the Senate and the House, concerning whether or not a commission could handle the regulatory job that needed to be done. The term *administrative* was not applied to the ICC initially, and, as we shall see, it was not until the first decade of the twentieth century that this agency was recognized as something unique in government.

Why did Congress finally decide to adopt a commission form of regulation in 1887? There can be no definite answer to this question. To some extent it was simply that the Senate proponents of the plan were able, through various types of political maneuvering, to get the bill passed. The House as a whole never thoroughly approved of the scheme, and in fact the whole idea was finally adopted only at the final conference stage, when representatives of both the House and the Senate met to iron out their differing points of view. Once the conference committee had agreed, the House was compelled to go along with the plan because of pressure for regulation from various groups and the public generally. No further delay would be tolerated.

Although the establishment of the ICC was at least in part accidental, many cogent arguments were advanced by those favoring the plan.[10] These ideas reflected much of what was later to become generally accepted as the theoretical basis of and justification for administrative regulation. First, the ICC was accepted as a more feasible regulatory body than Congress. From the very beginning it was recognized that the ability of a commission to specialize would give it more expert knowledge than could be possessed by all but a small handful of Congressmen. Further, a permanent commission could provide more continuity of public policy than an elected body. For this reason the ICC Commissioners were initially appointed by and with the advice and consent of the Senate for a term of six years, which was later

10. These arguments may be found in *ibid.*, pp. 19–65.

increased to seven. It was expected that many Commissioners would be reappointed, and in many instances this has happened, with the result that continuity of service has been far greater than might appear from the minimum legal tenure. The staff of the agency, endowed with significant power, also was seen as a permanent force. At the time the ICC was created it was not generally expected to become an independent force in the exercise of legislative or judicial functions. In both these areas it was to act more in the capacity of an advisory body to Congress on the one hand and the judiciary on the other. The ICC was to inform Congress of needed legislation, but it was to be within the exclusive domain of Congress to determine what policies would be enacted. With respect to specific implementation the Commission depended for enforcement upon the courts. It soon became evident that *without the ability to exercise legislative and judicial power on an independent basis the ICC would never become an effective regulatory body.* This point is particularly emphasized because it is fundamental to an understanding of the evolution of the regulatory process. The history of the ICC illustrates this evolution, for beginning in the first decade of the twentieth century, it was strengthened by a number of congressional acts to provide it with independent legislative and judicial power.

Another reason for the adoption of the commission form of regulation resulted from the need for a *partisan* body to represent non-railroad interests. Today there is a very strong feeling that regulatory bodies should be *impartial,* particularly in their exercise of the judicial function (see Chapter 3). But the ICC and many similar bodies in other fields were purposely created to take punitive actions against the regulated industry. Partisanship, however, was not to be based upon political parties. In fact the need to avoid political favoritism was one of the most important justifications of a commission independent of presidential control, for the President is the leader of his party. Many Congressmen objected to establishing such a commission because they felt that it would not be partisan enough. This group favored a strict statute in which comprehensive regulatory standards would be defined in minute detail, with the courts designated as the primary bodies through which enforcement would be achieved. The actual Interstate Commerce Act of 1887 defined criteria for the Commission far more carefully than later regulatory statutes;

nevertheless a large amount of discretion was still to remain with the ICC because the enabling Act contained such imprecise phrases as "just and reasonable." Moreover, the ICC did not have to enforce the law. Weak enforcement could mean nullification, the proponents of strong regulation argued, and in this they were correct.

Another important reason for vesting regulatory power in a commission was the highly *experimental* nature of the area of regulation. Despite the varied tradition of state regulation of the railroads there was not enough precedent to enable Congress to formulate anything but the roughest outlines of policy. Because of the experimental nature of the field the Commission was to advise Congress on needed legislation, and the presumption was that the experience of the ICC would weigh heavily in favor of congressional acceptance of its proposals.

The area of railroad regulation was not only experimental, it was highly volatile. Policy requirements would change from one period to the next; thus it would be impossible for Congress to keep up with the requirements for regulation even if it so desired. An administrative agency would be constantly in touch, and would be able to adjust regulatory policy in line with current problems and needs. Although these changes in policy were at first to be accomplished by Congress at the insistence of the ICC, the Commission was soon to become largely independent as a policy body.

Proponents of the ICC also pointed out that it would provide machinery for the reconciliation of disputes within the railroad industry, and the industry itself, suffering from cutthroat competition, supported this plea. In other industries it became quite common for the firms directly affected to support regulatory commissions, because they saw the commissions as a device to bring order into their relationships with competitors. Needless to say reputable businesses that operated with integrity in relation to their customers particularly favored regulation that would put an end to unfair competition. Moreover, as the economy became more interdependent it was not difficult to find strong political support for these new agencies, because business practices in one industry had repercussions throughout the country.

Although there were great hopes for the ICC in 1887, the Commission was unable to provide effective regulation as it lacked final legislative and adjudicative power. The enforcement power still resided in the judiciary. The courts insisted on reviewing Commission orders to such an extent that they were in effect substituting their judgment for that of the agency. The railroads soon saw that they could easily obstruct the ICC by appealing continuously to the courts. They even withheld evidence from the Commission on the accurate assumption that when they brought new evidence to the attention of the judiciary, on review the courts would insist on a *de novo* trial. The conservative leanings of the judiciary during the last decade of the nineteenth century essentially resulted in nullification of the powers of the ICC. The abuses of the railroads, however, continued virtually unchecked, and strong political pressure was brought to bear at the turn of the century to remedy the situation by strengthening the Commission and freeing it from the judicial hobble. Action was finally taken with the passage of the Hepburn Act of 1906, which gave the Commission final rate-making power subject to judicial review upon complaint of the carriers; thus rates established by the ICC were to become effective immediately without the need for prior judicial approval. This had the result of shifting the burden of proof upon the carriers if they wished to challenge an agency ruling. The powers of the Commission were extended at various times after the passage of the Hepburn Act, and by 1920 it was beginning to assume comprehensive regulatory authority.

Because of the debacle of the railroads in World War I, when the government took them over to avoid a complete breakdown in rail transportation, and their increasing problems resulting from the depression, it was recognized that the previous picture of a dominant and healthy industry was fading. The functions of the ICC began to shift from those which related to control in the public interest, that is, punitive actions, to those designed to foster a healthy industry, namely, promotional functions. This meant essentially that regulation in the public interest, as redefined, became equated to regulation in the interests of the railroads. This shift also reflected changing patterns of political support, which led to Commission reliance upon the very interests it was supposed to control for the necessary political support to maintain itself as an independent agency in the bureaucratic structure.

Starting in the second decade of the twentieth century regulatory commissions, analogous to the ICC, were established to control and promote various industries. The same pattern of development prevailed, and the reasons for the creation of these agencies in additional fields corresponded to those which led to the development of a strong and independent ICC. Although the railroad industry was the first to become national in character and impact, powerful national industries soon developed in other areas that required some form of regulation at the national rather than the state level. The same failure of the states to provide effective regulation that was apparent with regard to the railroad industry was evident in other fields. In some cases, of course, state regulatory agencies developed concurrently with their national counterparts; however, their powers necessarily were limited to intrastate matters.

At the national level the ICC provided a precedent for the establishment of similar commissions in new fields. The necessary increase in the powers of the ICC at the beginning of the twentieth century because of judicial nullification of legislative purpose convinced many that the best organizational structure for effective regulation was the independent agency combining significant legislative and judicial functions. The more powerful these agencies were to be, the more important a certain degree of independence seemed. Their independence of the President and to a degree also of Congress did not prevent the agencies from implementing the law in terms of the political interests involved. These interests, however, were not generally associated with the parties, but involved both private and public interest groups which exerted pressure for the implementation of policies to their particular advantage. The agencies, then, were in many cases perfectly free at first to be partisan, in the sense of favoring one group of interests over another, as long as such partisanship did not relate directly to the major political parties.

At the time of the establishment of the ICC the most clearly articulated interests, those of the agrarian mid-West and West, called for administration of the Act of 1887 in their favor. The railroads, caught off guard at first, soon remedied that situation by using the courts as destructive instruments during the first decade of the administration of the Act. By the time later agencies, such as the Federal Trade Commission were established, industry interests supported the idea of commission regulation as long as the agencies became no more than arbiters of industry disputes. No matter what an agency did it would necessarily be supporting one set of interests over another.

Apart from the breakdown of state regulation, and the precedent of the ICC, new regulatory agencies were created because of needs of specialization, knowledge, continuity of public policy, and so forth, all of which had been raised in the past by proponents of the independent commission form of organization. Further, in virtually every case these additional regulatory agencies were established as a result of political pressure for some form of national control, arising directly from economic problems associated with the industries concerned. The ICC was created because of agrarian pressure; similarly, group demands led to the creation of such agencies as the Federal Reserve Board in 1913, the Federal Trade Commission in 1914, the Federal Power Commission in 1920, and numerous New Deal agencies. The political support for these agencies was not always as well organized as that behind the ICC; however, no agency was created in an atmosphere detached from the political process. In the 1970s, the establishment of the Environmental Protection Agency and the Consumer Product Safety Commission reflected political pressures from environmental and consumer groups respectively.

The establishment of virtually every regulatory agency was considered a revolutionary step by those directly affected; therefore, extraordinary political pressure was frequently directed at Congress to prevent the passage of regulatory statutes. The statutes were finally passed because proponents of the plans were able to muster sufficient political strength to overcome the opposition of powerful groups in the industry. Not all members of the proposed areas of regulation were opposed to government controls, and some sought such regulation to provide protection against detrimental competitive practices.

It can not be too strongly emphasized, then, that the process leading to the establishment of administrative agencies is *highly political,* and administrative functions and organization are essentially determined by political factors. No administrative agency in the American system, which supports pluralism and democratic participation (however limited), has been created on a permanent basis by governmental fiat. Agencies must have strong political support from the community itself, whether from groups, political parties, or individuals, in order to become established and to survive.

Finally, it should be noted that in the twentieth century, a great expansion in the scope and responsibilities of government at all levels occurred. This culminated in the New Deal, which solidified the idea that the national government should be responsible for the welfare of the nation in numerous fields. This idea was not new, of course, but the New Deal led directly to an acceptance of the responsibility of government for economic regulation by both political parties. Until the Ford administration, no serious attempt was made to curtail the authority of regulatory agencies. And even President Ford did not recommend the outright abolition of these agencies.

Underlying forces behind the creation of new administrative agencies have persuaded both Democratic and Republican Presidents to expand the bureaucracy. Richard Nixon came into the White House with a highly conservative orientation and with promises to the people to cut back on the federal government and restore state and local initiatives. Although he was able to cut back on bureaucratic programs in such major departments as HEW primarily by impounding funds, his victories were short-lived and he was able to abolish outright only one agency—the Office of Economic Opportunity—and this took him a long time because of stubborn congressional resistance based on opposition from forces within the constituency of OEO. While President Nixon was striving to integrate and reduce the functions of some administrative agencies, he was expanding in an unprecedented manner the Executive Office. Thus, while operating agencies were being pressured to reduce their programs, staff agencies were being added. With the exception of his de-regulation program, President Ford's attitude toward the bureaucracy was one of benign acceptance. The Presidency, crystallizing an always nebulous public opinion, has provided additional political support for the expansion of bureaucracy generally. This has led some to look upon the administrative process as a primary instrument for the achievement of democratic goals, in terms of implementing the mandates of the people through the President.

THE REGULATORY PROCESS IN EXECUTIVE DEPARTMENTS

Although we have concentrated on the expansion of the independent regulatory agencies, it is a mistake to think of bureaucracy solely in such terms. In many areas of domestic policy formulation these agencies exercise the most important control; however, different economic and political needs have produced administrative agencies exercising vast legislative and adjudicative powers that do not fit the classification "independent regulatory commission." Many executive agencies perform regulatory functions as part of a broader responsibility. Administrative functions, divided into legislative, judicial, and executive categories, are exercised by all types of agencies; however, at the same time agencies may differ with respect to the reasons for their establishment, their principal goals, and organizational structures. These factors are largely determined by political forces which lead to the creation of particular agencies and provide a basis for continuing support.

If one views the executive branch as a whole, it becomes evident that most of the departments exercise significant regulatory power. The reasons for locating such power within these departments are similar to those that led to the establishment of the independent regulatory commissions. Regulatory functions are usually performed by separate agencies within departments, and unlike their commission counterparts they are generally responsible for the regulation of a narrow aspect of private activity, not an entire industry. The Department of Agriculture is a particularly vivid example of many subordinate groups (the Commodity Credit Corporation, Agricultural Marketing Service, Forest Service) engaged in regulation. One of the most significant examples of regulatory functions being performed by a Department is in HEW, where the Food and Drug Administration regulates the giant pharmaceutical industry. The functions performed by the FDA date back to 1906, and were originally lodged in the Department of Agriculture. In the Departments of Agriculture,

Commerce, Defense, Health, Education, and Welfare, Housing and Urban Development, Interior, Justice, Labor, Transportation, and the Treasury, thirty-five agencies perform regulatory functions.

Most agencies exercising regulatory functions within departments possess both legislative and judicial power. Given the similarity of the functions they possess to those of the independent regulatory commissions it is natural to ask why different organizational patterns were employed in different areas. In part the answer is that there is not necessarily any logic to organizational standards in American bureaucracy, or at least not enough logic that people will always agree that a given form of organization should be used when certain functions are to be exercised. True, a formal rationale is always given by Congress and the President in the creation of new agencies and departments. But the rationale that is given does not explain the political forces that are operating. For example, President Lyndon Johnson wanted to create a Department of Transportation in order to reduce the power of independent agencies and give the White House greater control over that segment of the bureaucracy concerned with transportation. Clearly, when a President can integrate independent agencies into a department, his political powers increase, although the reason he usually gives for proposing a department is the need for greater co-ordination in planning and managerial control. The common rationale for departmental status was given by Charles Schultz, the Director of the Bureau of the Budget in 1966, in testimony before the Senate Committee on Government Operations:

Departmental status has been given to those agencies which (1) administer a wide range of programs directed toward a common purpose of national importance; and (2) are concerned with policies and programs requiring frequent and positive Presidential direction and representation at the highest levels of government.[11]

Congress, forever jealously guarding its prerogatives, approved of the new Transportation Department on the condition that the department not be overly centralized. In particular, Senator

11. Committee on Government Operations, U.S. Senate, 89th Cong., 2nd Sess., 1966, hearings on S.3010, "A Bill to Establish a Department of Transportation, and for Other Purposes," p. 81.

Warren G. Magnuson (D., Washington), saw to it that the Department would not interfere with the major responsibilities of the independent regulatory agencies. He agreed to the transfer of the Federal Aviation Agency, an independent agency with regulatory responsibilities created in 1958, only on the condition that it would be transferred intact with its own administrator, and that essentially it would be a legal entity within the Department of Transportation that would operate in a largely independent fashion.[12] When asked how the new Department would affect the role of the Federal Aviation Agency, Senator Magnuson assured the Committee on Government Operations that:

Well, I have just suggested that the FAA be transferred to the new Department in its entirety, as a legal entity, such as the Coast Guard, and then it would work in an autonomous way in the matter of air safety, but that it would correlate its efforts on air safety with other transportation fields.

It [the bill] would not interfere with its [FAA's] absolute independence to establish air safety rules and regulations which it now does. It may have to go through the Secretary of Transportation in other functions, such as where you build airports, how they correlate with cities, or how they correlate with areas, but I hope the independence and the integrity of the FAA would not be violated *at all* by the transfer.[13]

One of the reasons the Department of Transportation bill passed was that it did not make significant inroads into the roles of the independent regulatory commissions, which Congress considers to be its own. What was the logic behind the Department of Transportation? It was both political and practical. It did not upset the political balance of power, but it did provide for a degree of co-ordination of transportation activities.

Although most of the major departments of the government exercise regulatory functions, the fact remains that Congress likes to consider the major regulatory agencies an arm of the legislature, not of the President. In relatively narrow regulatory areas where political conflict is not intense, Congress is perfectly willing to allow regulatory agencies to operate within the purview of the President, usually by locating them within executive

12. See the testimony of Senator Warren G. Magnuson, *ibid.*, pp. 58–77.
13. *Ibid.*, p. 75. Italics added.

departments. But the placement of regulatory agencies within departments may be for other reasons. The political power of the departments themselves and their close alliance with congressional committees may make the location of some regulatory agencies within departments a political necessity. For example, the Occupational Safety and Health Administration was placed in the Labor Department (although checked by an independent Occupational Safety and Health Review Commission) when it was established in 1970 because of pressure from unions, the Labor Department, and their congressional allies. Where regulatory agencies within politically powerful departments have strong congressional backing they operate largely outside of the control of the President, and are considered as much arms of Congress as are independent regulatory agencies.

Political demands, then, dictate the location of agencies. When the independent commissions were established there was enough support both within and without Congress to keep them outside departmental jurisdiction. On the other hand in many instances in which agencies were established to function in a field related to a politically powerful department, there was a strong demand from that department to place the new agency under its control. For example, many new regulatory needs were recognized in the field of agriculture during the 'thirties. By that time the Department of Agriculture was well entrenched as one of the most powerful members of the executive branch; therefore it was virtually impossible to found new agencies in the agricultural field outside the Department. The process of location of agencies is as political as that involved in their establishment. Departments without strong political support in the form of interest groups are likely to be bypassed in the placement of new agencies. The State Department provides an excellent example of this.

EXPANSION OF BUREAUCRACY INTO OTHER AREAS

Department of Defense · American bureaucracy has also developed significant power in many areas that can not be classified as regulatory. First, there has been a tremendous increase in the powers and responsibilities of the Defense Department. This agency, which can not really be considered as a whole but only in terms of subgroups, employs over one-half of all the *civilians* in federal service. Its appropriation amounts to close to sixty per cent of the national budget—over fifty billion dollars. Its responsibilities, shared with the President and Congress, encompass no less than the security of the nation. In the pursuit of this goal the Department exercises powers that affect everyone in the nation directly or indirectly. The reasons for this extraordinary location of power (and we shall see later that the Department is frequently autonomous) are historical, international, and technological.

Congress and the President were to share the "war power" under the Constitution—the former having the power to raise and support armies and declare war, the latter being Commander-in-Chief of the armed forces. Numerous treatises have been written to describe how Congress has lost most of its power in this field to the President because of the latter's superior sources of information and ability to respond rapidly to international events. Although the powers of the President are extraordinary, the military arm will always possess and attempt to employ for its own purposes a high degree of independence. The same factors that led to presidential supremacy over Congress in this area also supported the increasing role of the Defense Department as an autonomous policy force.

The dominant power of the Defense Department, linked with that of the President, has arisen because of the increasing involvement of the United States in the world community, and because of repeated crises that have placed primary emphasis upon the importance of defense and military affairs since the beginning of World War II. At times in the past, as in the Civil War period, the branches of military assumed powers which gave them more than the usual strength, especially in combination with that of the President, over Congress and the courts. Before World War II, however, the military was unable to determine policy for more than brief periods of time. In fact, an examination of congressional-military relations during this period would reveal a dominant Congress turning down repeated and varied military requests. As long as the business of defense was of manageable proportions, and in the absence of strong public demand for stringent measures of military preparedness, it was not difficult to keep the military branches under control.

The generally isolationist attitude in the United States prior to World War II prevented any sustained political support for the military arm of government. Neither Congress, private interest groups, nor the President felt it necessary to establish a large and powerful military branch. In fact, during the period of the 'thirties it was the President who supported substantial reductions in the military budget, not Congress; and beginning in 1936, Congress *added* funds to the budget requests made by the President for the War Department in the face of the continued opposition of the Bureau of the Budget (the President's principal budgetary staff agency). Beginning in 1941, it was common practice for Congress to give the War Department as much money as it initially requested, and in some cases more than it wanted; however, the general practice of the Bureau of the Budget was to cut War Department requests. Beginning with World War II the military branches began to use Congress and private interest groups as a lever against presidential domination.

World War II brought about a change in the relative power position of the military branches to other agencies and departments of the government. Problems involved in military policy formulation became increasingly complex, and in many areas these tended to isolate Congress, and to a lesser extent the President, as effective instruments of control. From time to time presidential decisions have an important effect upon defense policy. Presidents Eisenhower and Kennedy attempted to keep the Defense Department under the presidential thumb by appointing powerful Secretaries of Defense and by taking an unusual interest in the affairs of the Department. Controlling the generals, however, is far from easy, even for an unusually astute Secretary of Defense such as Robert S. McNamara. As the Vietnam war progressed, it became evident that neither President Lyndon Johnson nor Defense Secretary McNamara was able to keep a tight rein on the Defense Department. The Vietnam war illustrated once again how the Defense Department necessarily controls much of the information upon which decisions at a higher level are made.[14] Of course, the military is in a far more powerful position when

14. For a provocative discussion of various aspects of the problem of high-level decision-makers attempting to get adequate information from the military, see David Halberstam, *The Best and the Brightest* (New York: Random House, 1972).

the nation is fighting a war than when it is at peace. But in peace as well as war, the fact is that advances in military technology have made the defense field one in which political actors tend to defer to the experts. This is why Congress almost always recedes into the background, accepting by necessity military estimates of defense requirements and departmental needs.

Although the Vietnam war made Congress more suspicious of the Defense Department, the post-Vietnam era has seen no significant diminution in the ability of the Department to obtain essentially everything that it wants from Congress. Aside from their near-monopoly on technical knowledge of weapons systems, the military leaders and top civilian defense officials have always been skillful in manipulating the patriotic sentiments of Congressmen to gain support for a powerful military establishment. In hearings before the House Armed Services Committee in 1975, half the Committee members burst into applause when Defense Secretary James R. Schlesinger told the Committee that it was about time the country developed a foreign-policy consensus based on military power second to none. Exchanges between the Defense Department and congressional committees tend to be largely rhetorical, with the real final decision-making power remaining in the bureaucracy. The most powerful—and often the most conservative—members of Congress have long since been co-opted by the Defense Department. And although, for example, in the 94th Congress in 1975 Representative F. Edward Hébert (D., Louisiana), the conservative, long-time Chairman of the Committee and strong proponent of Defense Department interests, had been ousted from the Chairmanship, the Committee, under its new chairman Charles Melvin Price (D., Illinois), remained largely an adjunct of the Defense Department.

The development of bureaucratic power is also notable outside the regulatory realm in benefit agencies, public corporations (which may possess regulatory functions), certain staff agencies, and agencies involved in what are essentially public or interagency service functions (as in the case of the General Services Administration, a gigantic agency that is in charge of public buildings, the National Archives, supplies and equipment for federal agencies, as well as public information programs). Although these agencies are not "regulatory" in the sense in which that term is applied to the independent regulatory commissions, they may perform regulatory functions to varying degrees. The growth of bureaucracy in all these areas reflects the increasing demands that are placed upon the national government to assume responsibility for policy development and regulation.

Benefit Agencies · In the benefit field, for example, the primary agencies of importance are the Social Security Administration and the Veterans Administration (VA), both of which were developed to meet public demands for benefits. The VA is of considerable importance because of the large number of citizens who served in the armed forces during the latter part of the nineteenth and in the twentieth centuries. At present this agency dispenses over fourteen billion dollars in benefits each year and affects approximately eighty million persons, in particular twenty-nine million veterans and their families. The Social Security Administration is of equal importance, and dispenses over seventy billion dollars in benefits each year. The growth of government spending on social programs has soared dramatically in the last several decades, necessitating an expansion of the federal bureaucracy. Social Security benefits amounted to a mere eleven billion dollars in 1960, only one seventh of the current level of expenditure. Veterans' benefits in 1960 were three billion dollars, less than one quarter of the current level. Although inflation accounts for part of this increase, the fact remains that government social programs have expanded and are likely to continue to expand in the future at a geometric rate.

It is a mistake to think of the work of agencies such as the Veterans Administration and the Social Security Administration as being merely routine; in fact, a great number of discretionary decisions are made by administrators in these agencies that affect in a very substantial manner individual rights and obligations. Both the VA and the Social Security Administration must adjudicate individual cases and controversies pertaining to levels of benefits. Such adjudication is usually informal, involving conferences and meetings between agency officials and applicants for benefits. The funds for these immense enterprises are supplied through general taxation. It was originally hoped, in 1935, that the Social Security Administration would be a self-sustaining operation, much like a private insurance company, whose expenses for the payment of benefits and administration would come from a special payroll tax. However, over the years Congress found it far easier to expand benefits than to expand payroll taxes to sustain them. The result has been a system that some critics consider to be on the verge of bankruptcy and, above all, one that calls upon general Treasury revenues to pay benefits and administrative costs. Although the Social Security Administration is formally located in the Department of Health, Education, and Welfare, its operations are not in any substantial manner subject to Department controls. The independence of the Social Security Administration merely reflects the fact that HEW is more analogous to a confederation of independent states than a unitary or even federal government.

Government Corporations · The government corporation is an interesting administrative device. It was virtually unknown before the New Deal era, but since that time, and particularly during World War II, it has come to be of importance in the bureaucratic structure. Originally government corporations were given a great deal more freedom of action, especially in the fiscal area, than regular departments and agencies. They were set up to accomplish relatively specific tasks, such as insuring and extending credit to banking facilities (Federal Deposit Insurance Corporation, Federal Savings and Loan Insurance Corporation) and other specialized insurance (Federal Crop Insurance Corporation); regional development (Tennessee Valley Authority and the original St. Lawrence Seaway Development Corporation, established in 1954 but which became part of the Department of Transportation in 1966); managing the Panama Canal (Panama Canal Company); and delivering the mail (United States Postal Service). During World War II, government corporations were created to develop raw materials and to meet other specific wartime needs. At first many of these corporations were much like their private counterparts, operating with independent funds given initially by Congress but sustained through the corporation revenues. But in 1945 the Government Corporation Control Act was passed which, while preserving some of the previous independence of the corporations, sought to make them more accountable to Congress and the President. Government corporations, which were set up at first on an *ad hoc* basis to meet specific problems, have become a permanent part of American bureaucracy. Although there are only about a dozen today, they exercise functions vital to the community as a whole as well as to the particular areas they control.

The most recently created government corporation is the United States Postal Service, which was changed from a government department to an independent corporation in 1970. The Postal Service was originally created in 1775 under the Continental Congress, with Benjamin Franklin as Postmaster General. It did not become a Department until 1872, although the Postmaster General had been a member of the President's Cabinet since 1829. Establishing the Post Office as an independent corporation stemmed from the 1968 report of the President's Commission on Postal Organization. In recommending the creation of a new Postal Corporation, the Commission quoted favorably from President Truman's 1948 Budget Message, in which he expressed the premises of the government corporate structure:

Experience indicates that the corporate form of organization is peculiarly adapted to the administration of governmental programs which are predominantly of a commercial character—those which are revenue producing, or at least potentially self-sustaining, and involve a large number of business-type transactions with the public. In their business operation such programs require greater flexibility than the customary type of appropriation budget ordinarily permits. As a rule the usefulness of a corporation lies in its ability to deal with the public in the manner employed by private business for similar work.[15]

Staff Agencies · Finally, a brief note should be taken of the development of staff agencies. In this category fall those groups that provide facilities for planning and coordination, and act principally in an advisory capacity to operating departments. All agencies, of course, have their staff divisions; in addition to intra-

15. Quoted in the Report of the President's Commission on Postal Organization, *Towards Postal Excellence* (Washington, D.C.: U.S. Government Printing Office, 1968), p. 54.

agency staff groups several significant agencies have developed whose sole purpose is to provide operating departments with planning assistance. In particular the Office of Management and Budget should be mentioned as an important budgetary and legislative coordinating and planning agency in the Executive Office of the President.[16] This type of bureaucracy arose in response to the need to provide adequate staff facilities and to coordinate bureaucratic operations in the sprawling maze of agencies.

The Constitutional and Political Aspects of Bureaucratic Organization

In terms of the impact the bureaucracy has upon the governmental process as a whole, it is important to point out the way in which political considerations intrude into its organization as well as its functions.

CONSTITUTIONAL FACTORS AFFECTING ADMINISTRATIVE ORGANIZATION

The Constitution has profoundly affected the structure of American bureaucracy; it explains in many instances differences between administrative organization in America and many other countries. This statement may seem, at first, inconsistent with the discussion of the Constitution in Chapter 1, in which it was pointed out that our constitutional system was necessarily constructed without thought to the kind of bureaucracy we have today. If bureaucracy is not mentioned in the Constitution in any important way, how has the resulting system of government affected bureaucratic organization?

First, the Constitution was actually ambiguous as to who was going to control the small executive branch of the new Republic. This ambiguity stemmed from the general separation of powers rather than from specific provisions designed to fragment control of the executive branch. In fact Alexander Hamilton articulated a concept of presidential responsibility for the administrative

16. See Chapter 5 for a discussion of the Executive Office of the President, pp. 206–247.

branch, as it was then known, in *The Federalist*, although his definition of administrative activity was confined to "mere execution" and "executive details," and in no way encompassed what was to develop later. In *Federalist 72*, after defining administration in this narrow way, Hamilton stated:

> . . . The persons, therefore, to whose immediate management these different [administrative] matters are committed, ought to be considered as the assistants or deputies of the chief magistrate, and on this account, they ought to derive their offices from his appointment, at least from his nomination, and ought to be subject to his superintendence. This view of the subject will at once suggest to us the intimate connection between the duration of the executive magistrate in office and the stability of the system of administration. To reverse and undo what has been done by a predecessor, is very often considered by a successor as the best proof he can give of his own capacity and desert; and in addition to this propensity, where the alteration has been the result of public choice, the person substituted is warranted in supposing that the dismission of his predecessor has proceeded from a dislike to his measures. . . .

In other words, the President is to be responsible for administrative action as long as he is in office. These statements of Hamilton, combined with his expressed belief in the necessity of vigor, energy, and *unity* in the Presidency, led the early administrative management theorists to say that it was the intention of the constitutional system to place the entire administrative branch under the President. Whether or not this was, or might have been, the intention of those who framed the Constitution had they foreseen the nature of bureaucratic development, the fact is that the system they constructed supported in many particulars bureaucratic organization and functions independent of the President. It was the role they assigned *Congress* in relation to administration that assured this result, as well as the general position Congress was to occupy in the governmental system.

Let us, briefly, juxtapose the powers of Congress and the President over the bureaucracy as they are derived from the Constitution. First, with respect to the organization of bureaucracy, Congress retains the primary power. It may create and destroy agencies, and it determines where they are to be located, in the executive branch and outside it. This is one of the key powers of Congress regarding administrative organization, enabling it to create a highly autonomous bureaucracy. In addition, Congress has the power of appropriation, and in this way too it is able to exercise a great deal of control over the administrative arm. Congress can not only set up an administrative agency on an independent basis, but it can see to it that the agency remains independent. Moreover, Congress has the power to define exactly what the agency may or may not do, that is, its general jurisdiction. Finally, the Constitution gives Congress the power to interfere in certain presidential appointments, which are to be "by and with the advice and consent of the Senate." Congress may, of course, extend the sharing of the appointive power when it sets up new agencies. As a result of these powers, Congress has virtually complete authority to structure the administrative branch and determine where formal lines of accountability shall be placed. It may or may not decide to let the President exercise various types of controls.

Turning to the powers of the President over the bureaucracy, especially as they relate to bureaucratic structure and lines of control, it is evident that the Constitution gives him a relatively small role. Not only did the Constitution purposely pit Congress against the President in the governmental system generally, it gave Congress greater reign over the bureaucracy. One of the primary purposes of the constitutional system is to motivate the branches of government to oppose each other; therefore Congress and the President are adversaries. The effect of this upon bureaucratic structure is that Congress does not wish to increase the President's power over administrative agencies any more than necessary. For this reason there is a positive desire on the part of Congress to give many agencies independence. Simply because an agency is engaged in administrative functions does not mean that it should be placed within the executive branch, according to many past and present members of Congress. This view is emphasized because administrative *functions* are not so much executive as they are *legislative* and *judicial*. Insofar as they are legislative, it is natural for Congress to consider the agencies as an extension of itself; insofar as they are judicial, Congress feels in many instances that administrative independence is desirable, to avoid partisan influence over judicial proceedings.

The Constitution, then, has left a great deal of ambiguity regarding exactly where agencies are to be located, and to whom they are to be accountable. Although there is little doubt that Hamilton might have wished the bureaucracy to be under presidential control, the system established did not indicate this. Thus, to say that it is the constitutional responsibility of the President to control the administrative branch is not accurate, because he was not given the tools to do so. Considering many agencies as arms of Congress is as much in accord with the Constitution as maintaining that the bureaucracy is the responsibility of the President.

Finally, federalism has had a profound effect on bureaucratic organization in that it has necessitated various devices to aid the administrative branch in carrying out its programs in areas involving federal-state cooperation. Frequently, for example, federal and state agencies must cooperate in program implementation if national policy is to be effective. In addition to other factors such as geography, economic dispersion, and sectionalism, such cooperation has fostered a decentralized federal bureaucracy, and an emphasis upon field organizations. In turn, this development has caused various problems of control in the federal bureaucracy, for a field agency always has a certain amount of autonomy resulting not only from such factors as distance, but also from local political support for program implementation that may or may not accord with central directives and policy. The fact that the states and their agencies possess a great deal of independent power under our constitutional system explains the existence of a variety of organizational patterns in the bureaucracy, as well as many problems of congressional or presidential control of the administrative branch.

The effect of the Constitution is to fragment the bureaucracy. Lines of control are blurred, organizational patterns are diverse, and in general unity is absent. The Constitution has fragmented our political system generally, and the bureaucracy is no exception. In the same way that we have pluralism in our society, we have it throughout the government and in the administrative branch in particular. If the Constitution had structured our government as a whole to operate on a principle of fusion of power between executive and legislative branches, and had possibly provided a unitary rather than a federal form in relation to the country as a whole, the bureaucracy, reflecting this unity, would be more cohesive both in terms of organization and operation.

POLITICAL FACTORS SHAPING AMERICAN BUREAUCRATIC STRUCTURE

The Constitution alone is not responsible for lack of unity in our political system, and a change in the constitutional system would not by itself provide a cure. The great variety of interests throughout the country is reflected politically, and results in the exertion of diverse pressures on the bureaucracy by groups of all kinds. This kind of pressure is made more significant because of the lack of administrative unity and because the bureaucracy is deeply involved in the policy process. There is no single focal point of control for the administrative branch, and the way is cleared for disjointed control by interest groups in proportion to their political power.

Political pressure is largely responsible for the creation of administrative agencies in the first place, as we have seen; in addition once an agency has been established it begins to develop what is in effect a *constituency,* that is, a number of groups and individuals over which it has, in some instances, jurisdiction, and with which it interacts in a variety of ways. In the broadest sense the constituency of an agency includes those groups, both governmental and nongovernmental, whose interests must be taken into account, and because they must be taken into account the agency is by definition responsible to its constituency. In terms of this definition, administrative constituencies include those private groups within the jurisdiction of the agency, congressional committees, other administrative agencies, the judiciary, and the Presidency. At this point we may assume that the "public" is subsumed within these designated groups composing the administrative constituency. Although at first statutory provisions have a lot to do with defining administrative constituencies, soon extralegal factors come into play. Constituencies are fluid over a period of time, and in addition change as the issues requiring administrative decision change. There is always a core element of a constituency that can be identified as being relatively stable; however, the concept of administrative constituencies is dynamic, not static.

It is administrative constituencies that determine organizational patterns. The groups within constituencies must, of course, operate within our constitutional framework, and their attitudes are in part shaped by their role within the constitutional system. Not only do administrative constituencies determine structure, but the structure of an administrative agency should in the broadest sense be considered to include its constituency. Congressional and presidential constituencies are frequently considered an integral part of those institutions, and the same should apply to the administrative branch.

Administrative constituencies are composed of diverse groups with divergent attitudes. The agency is the focal point of the constituency structure, and it seeks to maintain a balance of political support over opposition. In any given situation, and in some cases generally, there will be interests opposed to particular agencies. Because they are in opposition does not, of course, affect the fact that they form part of the agency's constituency. This raises the question of why agencies respond to governmental and private interest groups in the process of making decisions. In some instances they are compelled to because of statutory mandates. For example, the statutes governing their activities may state that under certain circumstances the decisions of an agency are subject to judicial review. This type of provision immediately places the judiciary within the constituency of the agency involved, with respect to a particular decision making area. In a similar way statutes set up lines of control and authority from agencies to other administrative groups, to the President, and to Congress. The diversity of the constituencies of administrative agencies based upon statutory provisions stems in part from the ambiguity of constitutional provisions as to who is to control administrative activity.

Statutory provisions also help to define private constituencies for administrative agencies by setting up their jurisdiction. In other words, statutes define the areas over which agencies are to have control, and in this way the groups that will be affected by agency action are determined. These groups become part of the agency's constituency.

What groups oppose and what groups support administrative agencies? This, of course, depends upon a number of factors, including the constitutional and statutory position of the groups within the administrative constituency. Within the stable core of the constituency, agencies frequently have strong support from private groups in the industry that is being regulated, which in turn may be reflected in support from particular congressmen and congressional committees. In such instances the agencies tend to be relatively autonomous, regardless of the existence of legal lines of authority from the agency to superiors in the administrative branch, such as the President or a department head. For example, the Army Corps of Engineers is placed by statute within the Department of the Army, which is in turn in the Defense Department. From a legal point of view the Corps is subject to control by the Secretary of the Army, the Secretary of Defense, and the President. Also, the President's authority over the Corps is strengthened by the constitutional provision making him Commander-in-Chief of the Armed Forces. From a statutory and constitutional standpoint nothing could be clearer than the fact that this administrative agency is subject to many lines of control from superiors. The fact is, however, that the Corps has developed exceptionally strong *political* support from outside groups, many of which have a local orientation that is reflected in Congress. Thus, Congress is intensely interested in preserving the Corps on an independent basis in order to enable it to act in congressional interests. The dominant forces in its constituency are private and congressional, and hence the decisions of the Corps are oriented in this direction.

Administrative agencies tend generally to act in accordance with the dominant interests in their constituency, and to some extent the attitude of the "constituents" towards the agency is determined by the extent to which they can influence its behavior. An agency, for example, which consistently acts in opposition to the private groups within its jurisdiction is likely to incur their wrath. This tends to be reflected in Congress and generally results in congressional opposition to the agency. If an agency is to survive it must be able to obtain enough political support from non-opposing groups to offset adversary groups. Such support may, and frequently does, come from the President and other administrative agencies. Both government and private allies are necessary to sustain most agencies, and rarely will there be significant government support unless there is private support.

A major reason why regulatory agencies cannot be reformed is their political support, reflected in Congress. From the report of the President's Committee on Administrative Management in 1937 to the recommendations of President Ford to reform the regulatory process, the agencies have remained largely intact. The cozy relationships these agencies have developed with the industries they regulate have been reflected in Congress, which, in turn, has refused to abolish them by merging their functions into executive departments. The only significant exception to this occurred with the establishment of the Department of Transportation in 1966, which incorporated the Federal Aviation Agency. However, since it was the clear intent of Congress that the FAA remain a legal entity, its independent regulatory powers remained undiminished with the exception of its safety functions, which were transferred to the National Transportation Safety Board within the Department. This Board also assumed the safety functions of the CAB and the ICC, a transfer of responsibilities that did not in any way significantly diminish the independent regulatory powers of those agencies. The independent regulatory commissions and boards have repeatedly been able to resist significant changes in their status.

Other examples abound of the ways in which political forces affect administrative organization, policies, and procedures. When President Nixon, beginning in 1972, mounted a concerted effort to abolish the Office of Economic Opportunity, located within the Executive Office of the President, he ran into strong opposition from the agency and its supporters. Anti-poverty workers and community-action groups succeeded in stalling the abolition of the agency and in saving the programs it administered. The agency was finally abolished in 1975, to be replaced by an independent Community Services Administration. Most of the programs formerly administered by OEO have been transferred to the Departments of HEW, Housing and Urban Development, and Labor. Over the course of the controversy, President Nixon was forced to fire OEO director Alvin J. Arnett in July, 1974, for his persistent lobbying to continue his agency's programs. The

OEO story illustrates how agencies even within the Executive Office, which are presumably directly under the President's control and which often must rely upon him for political support, can develop powerful outside support that may be used in resisting presidential demands. The Office of Emergency Preparedness, also formerly within the Executive Office of the President, did not have the kind of political support possessed by OEO, and it was abolished without a whimper by a Presidential Reorganization Plan in 1973, its functions being transferred to the Department of the Treasury, the Department of Housing and Urban Development, and the General Services Administration. OEP was a planning agency that did not have the opportunity to gain pressure-group support from the outside because it did not administer programs that affected private or governmental interests in a significant way. It could continue to exist only at the pleasure of the President. The same story was true of the Office of Science and Technology, also within the Executive Office, which was abolished by President Nixon in 1973, its functions being transferred to the National Science Foundation, an agency with considerable political clout. The scientific community succeeded in persuading Congress to create a new White House Office of Science and Technology Policy in 1976.

President Ford, like President Nixon, also found that he could not unilaterally decide the fate of agencies within the Executive Office of the President. When he assumed the presidential mantle in August, 1974, he almost immediately sought to reduce the power of the OMB on the basis of recommendations made to him by a team of advisers he had appointed to smooth the transition between administrations. He and his closest advisers felt that the OMB had become a super-agency with too much power not only over the bureaucracy, but also over the White House itself. As one White House insider put it, the OMB "had become an advocate of policy rather than a politically neutral analytical tool."[17] Critics of the OMB charged that it had become too politicized, attempting to impose its preferences upon other parts of the bureaucracy. In the fall of 1974, the OMB was careful not to assert itself independently of the President. It responded to

17. Philip Shabecoff, "Budget Office Withstands Moves to Cut Its Power," *The New York Times*, November 11, 1974, p. 16.

criticism of the President and his advisers by becoming less intrusive in the affairs of the various departments and agencies. In this way it avoided a confrontation with the White House and any formal cuts in its powers. The OMB, like its predecessor the Bureau of the Budget, had become a dominant force in government. Control over the budgetary process invariably means control over important aspects of policy-making. The OMB's success in resisting formal encroachments upon this important preserve of its powers guaranteed that it would continue to be a significant political force.

The pluralistic nature of the bureaucracy is fortified by the fact that administrative organization and action is so responsive to differing constituent interests. A unified bureaucracy could only exist if there were a unified constituency for the entire administrative branch. Intense bureaucratic infighting is often a reflection of conflicting outside pressures. For example, the anti-trust division of the Justice Department often finds itself in head-on conflict with regulatory agencies over the meaning of the anti-trust laws. Both are responsible for the administration of anti-trust policy; however, the regulatory agencies are far more likely to be lenient in permitting business mergers that the Justice Department would consider a clear violation of the anti-trust laws. The anti-trust division is far more oriented toward preventing business combinations in restraint of trade than the regulatory agencies are, which, in contrast, tend to promote the interests of the industries under their jurisdiction. The Justice Department cannot prevent mergers within regulated industries, but can intervene in the proceedings before regulatory agencies to make its views known.

Other examples of inter-bureaucratic rivalry stemming from the contrasting constituencies of administrative agencies include the chronic conflict between the Army Corps of Engineers and the Bureau of Reclamation within the Interior Department. Both agencies have statutory responsibility for the development and utilization of water resources, with the Bureau of Reclamation being limited in its jurisdiction to seventeen contiguous western states. The Corps of Engineers is highly responsive to local interests, while the Bureau of Reclamation tends to rely more upon the Secretary of the Interior and the President for political backing. These differing political inputs may cause the two agencies to go in opposite directions in planning water-resource development.[18]

The long struggle over whether to permit a license for the High Mountain Sheep Project, that would have created a new dam on the Snake River in Hells Canyon, Idaho, witnessed conflicts between the Federal Power Commission and the Interior Department. The FPC originally authorized the dam in 1964, at a time when it was highly responsive to private power interests. The Supreme Court, however, returned the case to the FPC on the grounds that it had not sufficiently considered the possibility of federal construction of the dam. The increasing strength of environmental pressure groups was felt as the dispute continued, and these interests succeeded in stalling any further FPC action and, at the same time, supported legislation that would prohibit the building of any more dams in that section of the river. The struggle witnessed a dispute between the FPC and officials of the United States Fish and Wildlife Service in the Interior Department. One Interior Department official was quoted as saying in reference to the Hells Canyon Project that "it is imperative that this free-flowing segment of the Snake be preserved if we are to succeed in our efforts to raise these [fish] runs to anything approaching their former magnitude."[19] The issue was resolved when Congress included the part of the Snake River in dispute in the National Wild and Scenic River System, which precluded the licensing of any new dams in the area.

Agencies jealously guard their own preserves of power and, if they can get away with it, will happily venture into the jurisdictions of other agencies in order to increase their power. It is where jurisdictional lines between agencies are blurred that bureaucratic infighting becomes most intense.

18. A classic case describing conflict between these two agencies is "The King's River Project," in Harold Stein (ed.), *Public Administration and Policy Development* (New York: Harcourt, Brace and Co., 1952), pp. 533–572.
19. This is reported by Richard D. James, *The Wall Street Journal*, July 29, 1975, p. 38.

Conclusion

Political forces have led to the creation of administrative agencies, helped to shape their organization, and continue to determine their behavior. These forces have a clear impact on a proper performance of administrative functions and on the constitutional role of the bureaucracy. The organization of bureaucracy relates directly to the problem of control. The organizational patterns provide the environment within which administrative agencies perform legislative, executive, and judicial functions. Thus, for example, one of the justifications for the independent regulatory commission is that its independence gives it greater impartiality in the performance of judicial decision-making, a desirable goal to many theorists. Similarly, agencies are frequently thought appropriately placed within executive departments because their functions fit the "executive" category more than anything else.

The exercise of administrative functions involves several important problems. First, when administrative agencies formulate legislation, either through rule making or through direct influence on Congress, democratic theory requires at least limited control by the people. Congress as a whole does not control the bureaucracy, nor does the President. The question naturally posed is to what extent can the administrative branch, in terms of present organization, be considered democratic? In general it is possible to state as a minimum that the bureaucracy can be controlled from a variety of sources, which, when put together, constitute a form of democratic control. The fragmentation of administrative organization may preclude the possibility of control by any one governmental or nongovernmental group, but this does not prevent meaningful control entirely. The fact is that in the American system of government there is no cohesive majority and hence no possibility that one group will represent the "will of the people," whatever that term may mean. Bureaucratic organization is but a reflection of the pattern of American government; thus it may not be justified to criticize the bureaucracy because of its relatively autonomous position, and because of lack of unified control. The former is characteristic of all branches of government, and unity does not exist anywhere in the American system. In this regard the legislative functions of administrative agencies are in harmony with organizational patterns, i.e., administrative organization does not by itself prevent a proper performance of these functions insofar as democratic control is involved. This does not mean, of course, that there may not be other factors limiting adequate democratic control.

Second, administrative policy formulation necessitates some degree of planning and coordination. The proper nature of such planning and coordination is subject to debate, and there is little agreement about these areas in public administration. Criticisms have been made of the administrative process that the lack of central direction, either within agencies or from a source outside the bureaucracy, results in a serious lack of planning and coordination. Planning involves, and in the minds of many, necessitates, inter-agency coordination. The independence of agencies, often a statutory independence, acts as an impediment to the attainment of this goal. The Interstate Commerce Commission, for example, does not have to coordinate its activities with the Justice Department in the field of railroad mergers; hence it may frequently be working at cross purposes with the anti-trust division of the Justice Department. Agency constituencies, which determine to a large extent administrative decisions, differ and place different demands upon various agencies; this is the basic reason for the lack of agency coordination of policy. Administrative organization is not conducive to securing inter-agency cooperation.

There are other implications of agency organization that should be noted with regard to problems of policy formulation, planning, and coordination. The independent regulatory commissions have been accused of having organizational structures that place too many demands upon top agency officials in the adjudicative process, leaving them too little time for planning and proper policy formulation. From the report of the President's Committee on Administrative Management in 1937 to the present day, proposals have been made to separate the performance of legislative and judicial functions. The most drastic recommendations are for the establishment of administrative courts to take over the adjudicative responsibilities of administrative agencies. Policy-making would remain as the primary responsibility of agency heads and commissioners, who would presumably have greater time for long-range planning after being freed from the details of day-to-day administration, and particularly adjudication. Proposals of this kind relate directly to the problem of whether or not—or to the extent to which—the judicial functions of administrative agencies can be separated from their legislative role.

Proponents of the separation of legislative and judicial functions see this as a way to achieve administrative justice. We will see in the next chapter on administrative law that in the area of administrative adjudication there are many standards for administrative justice considered essential to the maintenance of constitutional government. One criterion for the realization of due process of law is that the judge must be impartial in decision making. Agency organization frequently tends to orient decisions in the direction of particular constituencies, and sometimes in favor of particular constituents. Although the agencies may not be partisan in the sense of favoring one political party over another, they are highly political. This aspect of their organization does not foster detachment. Before the rise of the bureaucracy, American constitutional practice separated legislative and judicial powers. But the present role of the bureaucracy in our constitutional system makes such a proposal far less feasible today than in the past.

Finally, with respect to the proper performance of many executive functions, there are those who feel that efficiency demands that the agencies be placed under some form of central control. The problems that arise in accounting and supply, for example, are quite different from those that are present in the legislative and judicial areas of administrative activity. Centralization, and even coordination, might seem clearly appropriate organizational devices to achieve goals of executive efficiency in the former, but are in fact far more questionable in the latter areas. To some extent the political aspects of public administration and administrative organization make the efficient management of executive details more difficult. This is assuming, for the moment, that "efficiency" is desirable in the executive field.

Administrative organization may or may not aid in the implementation of a given definition of what should constitute proper performance of administrative functions. The functions of administrative agencies fall into legislative, judicial, and executive categories. An organizational pattern that may facilitate one's definition of proper performance, say, in the legislative area may hinder the achievement of performance goals in the judicial or executive areas. The problem of relating, even in theory, functional goals with organization is difficult.

It has been suggested that the organizational patterns of American bureaucracy are more or less "set" in terms of our constitutional and political system. In other words, given our system of government it is very hard to see how bureaucratic organization can be substantially changed. This does not mean, of course, that particular agencies can not be moved about from one part of the organization to another; however, regardless of where agencies are located they will tend to act in terms of their constituencies, and the bureaucracy generally will present a picture of fragmented power. Any discussion of how administrative functions should be performed must recognize the organizational context of the bureaucracy and must take note of the fact that organization shapes the performance of function to a substantial degree. Many proposals for change in American bureaucracy recommend structuring the agencies in a way that is entirely unrealistic in terms of the political context within which they function.

Chapter 3 Administrative Law and the Courts

THE VAGUENESS of congressional standards governing agency operation necessarily leaves a great deal of discretion in the hands of the administrative branch. Because of this it is generally accurate to think of the process of agency rule making as one of filling in the details of vague laws. The term "administrative law" embraces both the legislative and judicial aspects of administrative activity, because administrative agencies implement policy, or legislation, through a process of bringing and settling specific cases. Administrative law initially involves agency rule making, which is the establishment of regulations (laws) pertaining to the community and governing the activities of those groups falling within their jurisdiction. In terms of this definition administrative law becomes the law that is established by the administrative branch. Agency rules also govern internal administrative procedure, but for the moment we are interested only in rules that pertain to groups outside of the agencies themselves.

When administrative law is equated to agency legislation (or rules) it is generally referred to as "substantive law." Some idea of the volume of substantive agency legislation may be seen in the Code of Federal Regulations, which contains agency rules that have been previously published in the Federal Register. In the Code the agencies interpret for the public, and more specifically for the groups falling within their jurisdiction, the general standards established by Congress.

Apart from the substantive element in administrative law, there is an area which encompasses the procedures used by agencies in deciding cases and controversies, that is, administrative adjudication. The term "administrative law" is more frequently than not equated with it. The field of administrative law also encompasses the many cases that reach the courts on judicial review of agency decisions. Law students first learn about the field by studying almost exclusively formal court cases in administrative law. Lawyers who eventually specialize in the field become experts not only in cases resulting from judicial review, but also in the rules and procedures of particular agencies. Both from the standpoint of the agencies and private litigants, administrative law requires the services of skilled practitioners. As formally taught in law-school curriculums, the emphasis is on protecting the rights of individuals and groups (usually corporations) involved in administrative litigation. However, litigation always has two sides, and administrative adjudication is no exception. Agencies are charged by law with doing a certain job, usually protecting the public interest, and in litigation it is the responsibility of government lawyers to protect and advance the positions taken by the agencies against private parties. Therefore, lawyers become advocates for the government as well as for private interests. Their formal training, however, fits them better for acting as advocates of private rights than of the public interest, at least of a public interest defined separately from the rights and needs of private parties. Administrative lawyers are formally trained in how to prevent government from acting arbitrarily against private interests, rather than in how to make a government action more effective in the public interest.

The Nature of Administrative Adjudication and Rule Making

"Adjudication" refers to the specific disposition of a case and controversy, and may be contrasted with such terms as "law making" or "rule-making," that involve the formulation of general standards applicable to an entire community. Rule-making is based on the consideration of general facts, and rules do not become operative against groups and individuals until defined in further adjudicative proceedings resulting in administrative orders. In contrast, administrative adjudication takes into account facts relating to the specific parties involved, and orders issuing from the adjudication have immediate rather than future effect. Rule-making is based on judgments about future events and results, whereas adjudication involves the determination of past facts and events. It is in this sense that rule-making is called prospective and adjudication retrospective. Rule-making may involve only a very limited class of persons and, theoretically, could pertain to a single party; however, the class involved in rule-making is always capable of opening up to new members, whereas the parties in adjudicative proceedings are fixed and invariable. Because of the different determinations involved in rule-making and adjudication, different types of proceedings are considered appropriate. Rule-making proceedings need not be patterned along judicial lines, whereas in adjudicative proceedings trial-type procedures may be desirable. This is because trial-type procedures are designed to elicit facts ("adjudicative facts") from the parties directly involved. But rule-making must elicit "legislative facts," which are general in nature and pertain to a broad rather than a narrow group.

Because rule-making usually does not have concrete effect until the initiation of further adjudicative proceedings, it is not considered properly subject to judicial review. This is not always the case, however, because administrative rules may have an effect similar to an administrative order and may raise legal issues that can appropriately be decided by a court before enforcement of the rules takes place. For example, *Abbott Laboratories v. Gardner* involved the issue of whether or not comprehensive rules of the Department of Health, Education, and Welfare made on the basis of recommendations of the Commissioner of Food and Drugs within the Department could be subject to judicial review before any enforcement action under the rules had taken place.[1] The majority of the Supreme Court, in a complicated opinion, held that the rules were reviewable because (1) there was no statutory preclusion of judicial review of the rules before they were enforced; (2) the rules had been formally promulgated and thus constituted final agency action (the absence of final agency action would have precluded judicial review because administrative remedies would not have been exhausted); (3) the rules had a profound adverse effect on the pharmaceutical industry at the pre-enforcement stage in terms of potential penalties, business uncertainty, and the expense of complying with the rules; (4) the question presented

1. 387 U.S. 136 (1967).

by the rules was legal in nature, involving the authority of the Commissioner of Food and Drugs to issue the regulations and, as such, a proper matter for judicial resolution; (5) further administrative proceedings would not clarify the issue any more than it had already been clarified. On the basis of all of these considerations, the Supreme Court considered the matter "ripe" for judicial review.[2]

Whenever administrative agencies exercise judicial power through the issuance of orders, there are always policy considerations in the background. However, agency policies are not necessarily contained in formal statements that have resulted from prior rule-making proceedings. This means that the parties involved in administrative adjudication may not know exactly what policies the agency will be implementing in their case. This causes a great deal of uncertainty, and prevents the parties from making effective presentations before the agencies to refute what, in effect, are agency positions taken after the proceedings are completed. Prominent scholars and judges in administrative law have repeatedly called for a greater emphasis on the need for administrative rule-making and the development of administrative policy standards prior to the adjudication of specific cases.[3]

Most administrative policy, particularly in the regulatory realm, is developed on an *ad hoc* basis through individual cases and controversies—an inductive rather than a deductive process. More often than not, agencies are simply unable to agree on what *general* policy should be developed to fill in the details of vague legislative delegations of authority to them. This is understandable in novel situations where the agency is confronting for the first time a particular policy dilemma, but it is less acceptable where the agency has been dealing with a policy area for many years, even decades.[4] Moreover, when

2. The case was remanded to the Court of Appeals for the third circuit to review the District Court's decision in the case, which had held that the regulations promulgated by HEW were beyond the authority of the Commissioner of Food and Drugs.

3. See, for example, Kenneth Culp Davis, *Discretionary Justice* (Baton Rouge: Louisiana State University Press, 1969); Henry J. Friendly, *The Federal Administrative Agencies: The Need for Better Definition of Standards* (Cambridge: Harvard University Press, 1962).

4. *SEC v. Chenery Corp.*, 332 U.S. 194 (1947).

agencies do develop general policies, they are often stated in terms as vague as the statutes under which they are promulgated. One is very hard pressed to find exactly what the policies are of such agencies as the Civil Aeronautics Board, the Federal Communications Commission, and the Interstate Commerce Commission. Those within the jurisdiction of such agencies simply do not know what is expected of them from one day to the next nor how the agency is likely to act in dealing with their interests.

The fact that agencies rely on the case-by-case approach to the development and implementation of policy adds to the confusion caused by vague rules or lack of rules. Members of agencies do make general policy statements, but these are often not formalized in agency rules. For example, the Federal Communications Commission might issue a general statement opposing concentration of ownership of newspaper, television, and radio media, but may not take steps to formalize such a policy in an agency rule. This would mean that when specific cases arise before the agency, there would be no formal substantive policy rules to guide private parties, the administrative law judges that conduct the initial hearings, or the agency upon final review. Moreover, if a case reaches the courts, the judges would not have a formal policy statement of the agency to guide them. Under such circumstances, it is difficult for the courts to determine *ultra vires* (beyond the legal authority) action by the agency, and they have to fall back upon procedural considerations to decide whether or not the agency has acted properly.

The FCC's actions in the area of media concentration provide an excellent case study of the dilemmas of regulatory policy development. For well over a decade the Commission has grappled with the problem of what specific policy it should implement in the media-concentration area. But, during all this time it has never issued a comprehensive set of formal rules governing media concentration.[5] FCC Commissioners have had strong and opposing points of view on the issue, making it almost impossible to arrive at agreement on a formal rule. In

5. An excellent case study of this problem may be found in Stephen R. Barnett, "The FCC's Non-Battle Against Media Monopoly," *Columbia Journalism Review* (January/February, 1973).

the meantime, using the case-by-case approach, the Commission has allowed differing degrees of media concentration from one city to another. In only one case throughout the nation—that of the late Boston *Herald-Traveler*—did the FCC require a newspaper to divest itself of a television station in the same city because of undue media concentration. The *Herald-Traveler* case is an excellent illustration of the dilemmas that arise when a hesitant and uncertain agency fails to develop explicit policy standards.

The Boston *Herald-Traveler* case began before the FCC in 1957, and was not finally settled until 1970, when the newspaper lost its plea in court to overturn the Commission's 1969 decision to take away Boston television Channel 5 from the *Herald-Traveler*. In its opinion requiring divestiture, the FCC said in passing that "it is important in a free society to prevent a concentration of control of the sources of news and opinion." But at no time before the Boston decision had the Commission adopted a formal rule setting forth its policy on media concentration. It had issued a "policy statement on comparative broadcast hearings" in 1965, in which it stated that a desirable objective in determining broadcast licenses was the "maximum diffusion of control of the media of mass communication."[6] It went on to state that "division of concentration is a public good in a free society, and is additionally desirable where a government licensing system limits access by the public to the use of radio and television stations."[7] But the 1965 policy statement made it quite clear that the Commission was to have discretion in determining when and how it was to require media diversification. Presumably the facts of each particular case would decide Commission policy. There was no hint in the 1965 policy statement of exactly what facts would persuade the Commission to refuse a license on the basis of lack of sufficient media diversity. Only very vague and general guidelines were offered in the 1965 statement.[8] The Commission clearly felt that its policy statement set only general guidelines which might or might not govern future cases according to the discretion of

6. 1 FCC2d 393, at 394 (1965).
7. *Ibid.*
8. *Ibid.*, pp. 392–395.

the agency.[9]

When the FCC moved against the Boston *Herald-Traveler* in 1969 it acted without a policy and without precedent. The most outspoken critic of the broadcasting industry ever to sit on the Federal Communications Commission, Nicholas Johnson, even admitted it was an experiment in media diversification in his concurring opinion. But, as Louis Jaffee of the Harvard Law School pointed out, the criteria for selecting the victim of such an experiment was anything but clear.[10] If the Boston case were to establish a general principle, it would mean that in the future all television licenses owned by newspapers within the same city would have to be forfeited. This has not happened, and the Boston case remains an anomaly.

The fact that administrative agencies often develop and implement policy through adjudication on a case-by-case basis rather than through general rule-making may, as in the Boston *Herald-Traveler* case, result in unequal treatment of those within the jurisdiction of the agencies. Which policy principles, if any, are to apply to whom will remain unclear under such circumstances. The courts might aid in the process of clarification by requiring uniform policy standards to be applied by the agencies. However, although the latter 1960s and 1970s have witnessed a resurgence of judicial activism in many areas, in administrative law there still remains a tendency to defer to the judgment of administrative agencies unless procedural irregularities can be demonstrated. As the court held in the Boston case when it received an appeal from the *Herald-Traveler* in 1969 to overturn the FCC's action, "the importance of avoid-

9. When the Commission issued a "Policy Statement on Comparative Hearings Involving Regular Renewal Applicants," 22 FCC2d 424 (1970), it attempted to avoid judicial review of the statement on the grounds that it was not a formal rule, but only a general guideline for the agency which it might or might not choose to follow. Part of the policy statement provided that in renewal proceedings, existing licensees would be preferred if they demonstrated substantial past performance without serious deficiencies. The Court of Appeals for the District of Columbia allowed judicial review of this section when it was challenged by two non-profit organizations on the basis that the legal rights of these organizations were affected by the statement. See *Citizens Communications Centers v. Federal Communications Commission*, 447 F.2d 1201 (D.C. Cir. 1971).

10. Louis L. Jaffee, "WHDH: The FCC and Broadcasting License Renewals," 82 *Harvard Law Review* 1693, at 1698 (1969).

ing concentration of control in communications is such an important objective that the Commission must be accorded discretion in choice of measures for its fulfillment."[11] The court is claiming that it approves of the Commission's policy of avoiding concentration in communications, but at the same time it is granting the FCC total discretion in determining how it is to apply that policy. In effect, this means that the court has retreated from meaningful judicial review of the media-concentration policy of the agency. The Court of Appeals for the District of Columbia, to which appeals from the FCC go by law, has urged the Commission to adopt a general rule outlining its media-concentration policy. The Commission, in turn, has initiated rule-making proceedings but has never completed them. Meanwhile, in case after case, the FCC has permitted media concentration that directly contradicts its Boston *Herald-Traveler* decision, and the Court of Appeals has upheld the Commission in every case.[12]

The struggle of the Federal Communications Commission over media concentration illustrates how the procedural policy of an agency profoundly affects the content of the substantive policy that is finally implemented. The case-by-case approach emphasizes the relatively narrow inputs of individual interests. Since each case is likely to present a relatively unique set of circumstances, it is difficult for an agency to carry out consistent policy when the case-by-case method is employed. An important theoretical reason for establishing administrative agencies in the first place was to enable them to carry out policy without having to adhere to the strict confines of judicial procedure. The judiciary had proven itself to be an inadequate instrument of policy formulation in the new regulatory areas that the government was entering. Almost all regulatory agencies are authorized

11. 444 F.2d 841, at 860 (D.C. Cir. 1970).
12. In several important cases, the Court of Appeals upheld the FCC solely on the basis that the agency was seriously engaged in rule-making proceedings to clarify its media-concentration policy. Pending the outcome of such rule-making by the agency, the Court was reluctant to intervene in specific cases. Proposals for rules to govern this area began as early as the 1950s, but by the mid-1970s no formal Commission rules had been promulgated. In effect, the Court of Appeals is permitting the Commission to maintain a policy that is directly contradictory to the local diversification that has verbally been supported by both the agency and the Court.

by law to formulate general rules through flexible, non-judicial procedures. Rarely are agencies required to hold formal hearings before the issuance of regulations. Where no specific statutory hearing is required, the Administrative Procedure Act simply requires that "general notice of proposed rule making shall be published in the Federal Register, unless persons subject to thereto are named and either personally served or otherwise have actual notice thereof in accordance with law."[13] In rule-making, agencies can take into account a far broader range of constituent interests than in adjudication. While agencies must always heed the balance of power within their constituencies when they formulate policy, a broader, more consistent, and more readily enforceable definition of the public interest is likely to emerge from rule-making than from adjudication. In some instances, as in the trade-regulation rules of the Federal Trade Commission, agencies not only set general policy guidelines but also stipulate that certain actions constitute per se a violation of the law. In 1964, for example, the Federal Trade Commission issued a rule which stated that

In connection with the sale, offering for sale, or distribution in commerce . . . of cigarettes it is an unfair or deceptive act or practice within the meaning of Section 5 of the Federal Trade Commission Act . . . to fail to disclose, clearly and prominently, in all advertising and on every pack, box, carton or other container in which cigarettes are sold to the consuming public that cigarette smoking is dangerous to health and may cause death from cancer and other diseases.[14]

In the absence of such a rule, the FTC would have to show in each individual case that failure on the part of a cigarette company to include the specific warning labels delineated by the Commission in its rule constituted a violation of section 5 of the Federal Trade Commission Act. Such a procedure would be

13. U.S.C. §553. 80 Stat. 378 (1966) codified the Administrative Procedure Act of 1946, 60 Stat. 237.

14. 29 Fed. Reg. 8325 (1964). An excellent discussion of the controversy surrounding the entry of the Federal Trade Commission into the area of "prescriptive" rule-making may be found in A. Lee Fritschler, *Smoking and Politics* (2nd ed., Englewood Cliffs, N.J.: Prentice-Hall, 1975), pp. 70–82, 88–100. See also David L. Shapiro, "The Choice of Rule Making or Adjudication in the Development of Administrative Policy," 78 *Harvard Law Review* 921, at 958–967 (1965).

cumbersome and slow, to say the least, and would allow the cigarette companies to fight the Commission to a standstill by taking a firm stand in each case before the agency and by challenging any adverse agency decision in the courts. In such rule-making, the companies are given their "day in court" when they are afforded the opportunity to rebut the rule before the Commission.

In the case of the cigarette-advertising rule of the FTC, the cigarette companies were given far more than a normal day in court. Both before and after the rule was promulgated by the agency, the companies were afforded an opportunity to comment. Recognizing the political and economic consequences of the rule, the Commission postponed its implementation with regard to cigarette packages until January 1, 1965, and with respect to advertising until July 1, 1965, more than a year after its promulgation (June 22, 1964). Through the exertion of extreme political pressure on Congress, the cigarette companies, with the aid of many able attorneys (including Abe Fortas, who was later appointed to the Supreme Court by President Lyndon B. Johnson), succeeded in putting off Commission action through the substitution of a far less stringent Congressional Cigarette Labeling and Advertising Act passed in 1965. Not only did the Act require a less stringent warning on cigarette packages than required by the agency rule, but also eliminated altogether the agency requirement for a health warning in cigarette advertising. Morever, under the provisions of the law, the FTC was banned from exercising rule-making power in the cigarette-advertising field until July 1, 1969.[15] After the ban ended, the House Interstate and Foreign Commerce Committee reported out a bill in June, 1969, that was passed by the House that would have extended until 1975 the ban on the FTC as well as the Federal Communications Commission, the latter having entered the controversy over cigarette advertising by proposing a rule in February, 1969, to ban cigarette advertising from radio and television. The Senate passed a different version, and in March, 1970, House and Senate conferees banned radio and television advertising for cigarettes beginning January 2,

15. The entire story of the cigarette controversy is told in Fritschler, *op. cit.*

1971. The ban on the FTC was extended until July 1, 1971, after which it would be permitted to engage in rule-making proceeedings to establish policy over printed cigarette advertising. Congress kept a tight rein on the FTC, however, by requiring that the Commission must give it six months' notice of pending rule-making proceedings concerning cigarettes. The Act also required a more stringent warning on cigarette packages. Congress did not extend the ban on FTC action beyond 1971, and when the ban ended, the agency immediately took action to require a health warning on all cigarette advertisements. The major cigarette companies agreed to issue such warnings in advertising under a consent order of the agency.[16] Because of congressional action requiring the labeling of cigarette packages, the FTC has not engaged in further rule-making on this matter. This is entirely appropriate, for the agencies are, in reality, agents of Congress. Where Congress has explicitly stated what the law should be in an area administered by an agency, it is the responsibility of the agency to carry it out to the letter. Congress always pre-empts a policy field when it chooses to act.

The initial context of administrative adjudication and rule-making is determined by Congress in the various statutes that govern the organization, jurisdiction, and procedures of the agencies. A typical statute setting up an administrative agency outlines in general terms the power that the agency is to possess, the procedures it is to employ in administering the law (which include both adjudication and rule-making), and usually appropriate methods that may be used to obtain judicial review, as well as the courts having jurisdiction over the agency. Statutes determine the *formal* limitations that are placed on the bureaucracy, the nature and scope of the powers of the agencies, and lines of accountability to Congress, the President, and the Courts.

Congress determines the authority of each agency and the policy standards that are to guide it. No agency can engage in

16. An FTC consent order requires private parties to cease and desist from engaging in certain activities, but does not require them to admit violations of the law. The FTC had threatened to sue the companies for misleading advertising under the Federal Trade Commission Act if they did not agree to the order.

adjudication or rule-making without congressional authorization. And, theoretically, agencies are to adhere to the intent of Congress in all decision-making that shapes public policy, whether through rule-making or adjudication. Although formal statutory standards are supposed to confine the agencies, in fact they are usually so vague in the regulatory realm that the agencies have the legal authority to proceed as they wish. The real checks upon agency activity are political and do not stem from the formal provisions of statutory law. The main way in which statutes limit agencies is by confining their jurisdiction, not by the careful delineation of policy guidelines in the statute. For example, the Federal Communications Commission has been given the authority to license television and radio stations and to determine telephone and telegraph rates in interstate commerce. The Commission clearly cannot exceed this authority and take under its jurisdiction areas outside of broadcasting and the telephone and telegraph industry. While the jurisdiction is clear-cut, the policy that the Commission is to implement is only vaguely suggested in the statute. For example, section 309 of the Communications Act of 1934 as amended provides that if upon examination of any application for a radio or television license a Commission "shall find that public interest, convenience, and necessity would be served by the granting thereof, it shall grant such application." Section 201 of the Act provides that with respect to such common carriers "all charges . . . shall be just and reasonable, and any such charge . . . that . . . is unjust or unreasonable is hereby declared to be unlawful." The extraordinary discretion of the FCC comes from these vague and undefined statutory standards, not from the jurisdictional grant of authority. Congress really seems to be saying that here is a tremendous job to be done, requiring a great deal of specialized knowledge, a job that is most appropriately carried out by a Commission vested with adequate powers. The FCC is not an unusual case; and in most regulatory areas, what substantive policy is to be carried out in adjudication and rule-making is generally within the discretion of the agencies.

The Administrative Procedure Act of 1946 sets forth elaborate procedures to be followed by the agencies in adjudication, but only where there is a prior statutory requirement that the agency must hold hearings in particular case categories. The APA's guidelines for rule-making are far less stringent than those for adjudication, essentially requiring general notice of proposed rule-making and an opportunity for interested persons to make known their views on the proposed rule. Agencies can meet the requirements of the APA in rule-making through a variety of informal procedures, whereas where their is prior statutory requirement for formal adjudicative hearings, the agencies must institute formal judicial-type procedures to meet APA standards. The effectiveness of the APA in controlling administrative procedure is severely limited by the inclusion of a wide variety of exemptions in the Act. Moreover, an even more important limitation on the APA is its failure to establish guidelines for informal administrative adjudication and discretionary agency actions.[17]

The pervasiveness and importance of informal administrative adjudication, and the wide range of discretionary actions that administrators constantly take, cannot be changed by legal provisions governing administrative procedure and judicial review. Administrative discretion has greatly broadened because administrators are reluctant to formalize their policies through rule-making. But even where substantive standards in legislation and in agency rules are relatively clear, as in the case of the Internal Revenue Service, informal procedures used by the agency may lead to unequal and unfair agency action. Dominance of the informal decision-making process in all agencies permits few cases to reach the courts. From a quantitative standpoint, well over 90 per cent of all administrative adjudication is handled informally. This is not to deny the fact that most of the major policy-decisions affecting powerful interests and the community are the result of formal rather than informal proceedings. Where the stakes are high, the time and expense of the formal administrative process does not deter powerful interests from challenging agency decisions both in formal hearings before

17. For a description and analysis of the vast area of informal administrative adjudication see Peter Woll, *Administrative Law: The Informal Process* (Berkeley and Los Angeles: University of California Press, 1963). The scope and implications of discretionary administrative actions are discussed in Kenneth Culp Davis, *Discretionary Justice* (Baton Rouge: Louisiana State University Press, 1969).

the agency and, if necessary, in the courts. The informal process tends to operate more directly on individuals than groups, and administrative discretion is greatest in dealing with the "little guy."

The informal process is used by individuals and groups where considerations of time and expense are paramount and where it is desirable not to strain relations with the agencies. Further, very little publicity is given to informal proceedings; therefore, many business interests that consider good will an important asset prefer this form of adjudication because the public need never know that they have been involved in illegal or questionable activity of any kind. The same factors that keep private parties away from the formal hearing process result in limiting judicial review. The courts are available, but all too frequently taking a case to them is self-defeating. Moreover, the courts themselves have adopted doctrines of review that give the agencies maximum discretion.

The environment of administrative adjudication is determined directly by the types of cases handled; hence, it varies within and among agencies. Some examples will be illustrative. One of the most powerful and significant agencies with judicial power is the Internal Revenue Service. Elaborate substantive regulations are prescribed by the agency in the Internal Revenue Code relating to corporate and individual income taxes. Because of the complexity of the regulations and a necessary lack of absolute precision in many fields, such as deduction categories, which depend a great deal upon changing circumstances, the Internal Revenue Service has a large amount of discretion in the way it carries out the law. Its interpretation of the law may be challenged formally in the Tax Court or in the judiciary; however, the chances are excellent that these appellate authorities will uphold the Internal Revenue Service. There is a presumption in favor of the agency, and this is well known to those groups and individuals within its jurisdiction. In this respect the Internal Revenue Service is like most administrative agencies.

A second important fact determining the nature of Internal Revenue Service adjudication is that the decision process involves individuals as much as it involves groups. There are at present sixty million individual income tax returns, plus one million corporation returns that must be processed each year, and over twice as much money is collected from individuals as from corporations. Further, the number of cases that must be *adjudicated,* i.e., where there is a case and controversy, is far greater for individuals than for corporations. What effect does this have upon the exercise of judicial power by this agency? It gives the Internal Revenue Service far greater power than would otherwise be the case, because the resources of individuals faced with the problem of challenging an adverse agency decision are proportionately far less than those of corporate groups. Added to the individual's lack of time and money is a fear of the Internal Revenue Service; some people believe they will immediately go to jail for failure to pay their taxes in accordance with the wishes of the agency. For these reasons, the atmosphere is simply not conducive to any kind of an adversary proceeding, and even initial agency decisions go unchallenged as a rule. On the other hand, when corporations are involved, the element of wealth and power enters the adjudicative process. Expensive legal advice is readily available to fight the government all the way to the Supreme Court if necessary, and corporations are able to secure such advice. In administrative law, as in private law, if parties are adversaries, fair adjudication is best achieved when the economic resources of the parties are more or less equal. This is true regardless of the type of procedure employed in adjudication, although it has greater validity in the formal hearing process.

When the Internal Revenue Service decides, after reviewing (auditing) an income tax return that certain claims made by a private party do not conform to regulations, it will inform the individual or group involved that a deficiency exists and that a certain amount is owed to the government. The case and controversy is between the agency on the one hand, and the private party on the other. After a notice of tax deficiency has been made, the agency will attempt to settle the case informally through negotiation with the party concerned. The same type of procedure is employed by other agencies when they make complaints against private parties. Informal procedure saves time and expense, and in this respect benefits the government agency as much as the private party, for, contrary to the views of many observers, the resources of the bureaucracy are limited. Through informal procedure the agencies hope to achieve the greatest amount of enforcement with the least expense. In this area of administrative law over 90 per cent of the cases are settled informally, which is true both for corporations and individuals.

Administrative adjudication may involve cases that are not contested, in the usual sense of that term. For example, if the Internal Revenue Service finds a deficiency in a tax return that the taxpayer does not wish to contest, it can be regarded as an instance of adjudication. This may be difficult to grasp, particularly for those accustomed to thinking of adjudication in terms of traditional court procedure. First, although there may be no contest there may be a case, because the rights and obligations of a particular party are involved. Second, although there may be no contest there is a "controversy" because the agency is challenging the action of an individual or group. The fact that the agency is making a specific determination contrary to the wishes of a private party, and defining the rights and obligations of that party under the law, is sufficient to call the action "adjudication." Administrative adjudication is often uncontested because of factors adverse to the private parties involved, such as expense and the existence of administrative sanctions.

The activities of the Internal Revenue Service illustrate only one area of administrative adjudication, though a very important one. The kinds of cases handled by this agency have been called "complaint cases" because they involve the resolution of a complaint initiated by the government. Complaint cases arise from private activity which is considered a violation of administrative regulations. Complaints may be made to regulatory agencies by private parties, although formal initiation of a complaint is usually made by and in the name of the agency. Individuals or groups often bring possible legal violations to the attention of the relevant agency, which then must decide whether or not this outside complaint is valid and whether proceedings should be initiated against the party in question. The agencies also use their own staffs to investigate business or other private activity within their jurisdiction. If the staff finds something questionable, the agency will be alerted and proceedings may be started to stop the private activity in question. Usually voluntary settlement is secured through informal negotiation, as is illustrated by the Internal Revenue Service process of settling tax cases. Complaint

cases fall into the category of adjudication because they relate
to specific parties and involve a controversy concerning the extent of legal violation. Further, the agencies have legal authority,
given to them by Congress, to render final decisions in this area
within narrowly defined limits of judicial review. In actual practice they generally have the power, which is based upon legal
authority but goes beyond it, to make final decisions without outside review of any kind.

Examples of complaint cases include: Federal Trade Commission proceedings in alleged cases of deceptive business practice;
Civil Aeronautics Board cases involving complaints about airline service; Federal Communications Commission cases concerning complaints against broadcasters and radio operators; Interstate Commerce Commission cases relating to complaints about
service, charges, etc., on the part of railroads and truckers; Securities and Exchange Commission cases involving complaints
against brokers, and business advisory services; and unfair labor
practice cases before the National Labor Relations Board.

Complaint cases may reflect a purely governmental interest,
as in the case of the Internal Revenue Service, in securing ad-
herence to the law. Or such cases may reflect agency concern
with a broader public interest, which is illustrated by the actions
of most regulatory agencies in the complaint-case area. Regulatory agencies have always received complaints from the general public to take action in particular areas—for example, to
force airlines to provide better service to customers. Until the
rise of consumerism in the middle and late 1960s, there was little
public pressure on the agencies to pursue vigorously complaints
from the outside. Most public-interest complaint cases were
originated within the agencies themselves, and unless there
were internal agency incentives to pursue complaints, no action
was taken at all. But the consumer movement saw the rise of
public-interest pressure groups, led by Ralph Nader and other
activists. These groups were able to marshal a great deal of
public support and had the resources, although limited, to use
both the formal administrative processes and the courts as well as
informal agency proceedings to gain their goals.

As the consumer movement became more and more politically
active, the regulatory agencies responded by establishing special

consumer units to handle complaints. No longer were complaint letters from the public buried in an agency file, never to surface. For example, the extremely active Aviation Consumer Action Project, an affiliate of Ralph Nader, has prodded the Civil Aeronautics Board to pay close attention to the complaints of airline travelers. This has resulted in a more active CAB in the complaint-case field. Similarly, another organization backed by Ralph Nader, the Health Research Group, looks out for the interests of consumers in the health field and prods agencies such as the Food and Drug Administration to take action to protect the public against dangerous food and drug products. These consumer groups, represented by highly effective public-interest lawyers, have caused regulatory agencies to become far more active in overseeing private industry, which, in turn, has been responsible in part for the barrage of complaints from small businessmen and industry groups about over-regulation.

Apart from complaint cases, administrative adjudication relates to what may be called "application cases." In many fields individuals and groups wishing to engage in particular types of activity must secure permission from the government agency that regulates their area of interest. They first submit an application presenting their "case" to those having the power of decision. Then, the agency must decide whether or not, and on what condition, it will grant the application. Such an action is adjudication because it involves a specific case and also a "controversy" between the applicant and the agency. If there were no controversy, and all applications were granted automatically, there would be no need for an agency in the first place. In determinations concerning applications, agencies apply very broad standards which usually demand that the "public interest, convenience, and necessity" be served.

Examples of application cases include Securities and Exchange Commission determinations concerning registration statements and the listing of securities, and decisions by the Civil Aeronautics Board, Federal Power Commission, Federal Communications Commission, Nuclear Regulatory Commission, and Interstate Commerce Commission on license and rate applications. In all of these areas, private parties must apply to the relevant agencies for approval of their activities. Although opportunity for formal hearings must be given in many of these application cases, a significant proportion is settled informally, especially in rate-making. Just as public-interest pressure groups operate in the complaint field, they also are active with regard to application cases. For example, the Citizens Communication Center, a public-interest pressure group in the communications field, actively seeks representation of blacks, Chicanos, and other minority groups in FCC licensing proceedings. Applications to the Nuclear Regulatory Commission for licenses to build nuclear generating plants are frequently delayed because of intervention by public-interest lawyers who argue for stringent safeguards to protect the public and the environment against nuclear pollution.

While most application cases deal with licenses, certificates of public convenience and necessity (a form of license), and rate-making, there is an additional area of tremendous importance that falls into the application-case category that involves the adjudication of applications for Social Security and Veterans Administration benefits as well as for benefits in other areas of government welfare such as food stamps. The Social Security Administration within the Department of Health, Education, and Welfare and the Veterans Administration are the primary benefit agencies, handling millions of cases and dispersing billions of dollars each year. This area of adjudication is characterized by a large volume of highly technical cases. For example, many involve application of medical criteria to individual cases to determine the nature and extent of physical and mental disabilities. The agencies have been directed not to take an adversary position with respect to applicants. They are to adjudicate in a friendly manner. Nevertheless, this type of decision making is classified as "adjudication" not only because specific parties are involved, but also because the agencies have a great deal of discretion in many case categories in the way they carry out the law. One example of this occurred in 1974, when the Social Security Administration was accused by members of Congress with not following the intent of the Legislature in administering supplemental security income benefits for the aged, blind, and disabled. At that time, various offices of the Social Security Administration that were in charge of adjudicating benefit cases in the Supplemental Security Income Program were anything but friendly to the applicants, and many cases were turned up of failure to expedite cases for extremely needy individuals.

The benefit laws passed by Congress are far more specific in setting standards to guide administrative action than regulatory legislation. A major reason for this is that there is far less political conflict over the creation of benefits than over the establishment of a regulatory agency. Congress receives credit for the granting of benefits, whereas it usually ends up being criticized on all sides for its regulatory laws. Therefore, it is far more likely to be specific in benefit legislation, giving explicit standards for eligibility for government largesse, than it is in setting regulatory standards. The incentive in the regulatory area is to pass the buck to administrative agencies to handle the political conflict rather than to attempt to resolve it in Congress. But regardless of the relative specificity of standards for government benefits, the laws remain highly complex and require administrative interpretation which occurs in case-by-case adjudication. Agency discretion applies more in relation to procedural than substantive standards—that is, the agency determines how one is to establish eligibility for benefits under the law. A major exception to this is disability cases, where benefits are geared to the level of disability. This requires the agency (the Social Security Administration and the Veterans Administration, both of which deal with disability cases) to set standards to measure extent of disability. But here, as elsewhere, the real discretion of the agency comes in the interpretation of agency or congressional standards by administrators involved in case-by-case adjudication.

The nature and scope of administrative adjudication clearly differs substantially from court adjudication. The environment of administrative decision-making is quite distinct, and the scope of adjudication is as broad as government itself.

ADMINISTRATIVE SANCTIONS AND ADMINISTRATIVE ADJUDICATION

The existence of administrative sanctions is a key distinction between administrative law and other areas of law, particularly in the effect these sanctions have upon the decision making environment of the agencies as opposed to that of the courts. With reference to bureaucracy the term "sanction" includes particular powers possessed by administrative agencies that may be employed against individuals and groups to bring them into line with administrative policy. Sanctions may be specifically stated in statutory law, or they may derive from the general regulatory powers of the agencies. For example, the Federal Communications Act of 1934, governing the operations of the FCC, states that the Commission may revoke a station's license upon finding that the licensee has violated administrative standards.

The fact that these standards are rarely stated explicitly increases administrative discretion. The owners and managers of television and radio stations constantly have to guess which standards the FCC will enforce in such areas as programming in the public interest, equal time for political candidates, and media concentration. One of the reasons that the power of license revocation has virtually never been used is because those subject to the Commission's jurisdiction are very careful not to take any action that would be considered improper. In the area of requirements for equal time, stemming from a provision in the Communications Act of 1934, station owners have generally refused to allow political candidates free air time on regularly scheduled programs unless they have prior clearance from the FCC or, as for the 1972 elections, a congressional law is passed specifically exempting the stations from having to grant equal time to anyone other than major political candidates. The FCC is typical of regulatory agencies, all of which possess formal sanctions that are highly effective because they can put a stop to profitable private activity. Regulation by sanction has been called the "raised-eyebrow" technique because the mere hint of possible agency action immediately puts a stop to private action. Private parties subject to administrative jurisdiction do not wish to offend the bureaucracy any more than is absolutely necessary and will, in many instances, voluntarily acquiesce to agency directives because of potential action that might be taken against them.

The FCC is not the only agency that applies sanctions that profoundly affect the exercise of its judicial functions. In fact, it is one of the weakest in this respect. Station owners and networks can and do ignore the Commission when the Commissioners themselves fail to agree on what action should be taken. The FCC frequently threatens action and dire consequences, but the threat more often than not comes from a minority of the Commissioners. When the Commission is united its sanctions are imposing. In 1961, it ordered a Miami television station off the air and revoked its license, because of misconduct on the part of the owners in securing the license. The misconduct, which consisted of improper political pressure, was also a factor in three other applications for this license that the Commission disqualified from further consideration. The FCC action relating to Channel 10 in Miami came at the end of a long series of public disclosures and attacks concerning the Commission's previous decision in this case; hence, it was unusually severe and designed to prove to critics that the FCC could operate with integrity. The refusal of the Commission to grant a license renewal to the Boston *Herald-Traveler* in 1969 was another extraordinary and unusual case.[18] Although the Commission ostensibly refused to renew the *Herald-Traveler*'s license because of undue media concentration, in fact there had been allegations of improper influence being exercised by the *Herald-Traveler* in obtaining the license in the first place in 1957. Evidence was presented that the then-Chairman of the FCC had met secretly on several occasions with a Herald-Traveler Corporation Vice-President while the newspaper's application for the license was pending before the FCC. Although the *Herald-Traveler* was subsequently cleared on two separate occasions by independent hearing examiners of having exerted improper influence, the incident was embarrassing to the agency, especially when it was first disclosed by the House Legislative Oversight Subcommittee in 1958. Although formally cleared of the charge of having exerted improper ex parte (representation from one side only, outside of the formal record of the proceedings) influence, the *Herald-Traveler* was undoubtedly at a disadvantage because of the incident in its long fight to maintain its license.

A notable example of an agency with powerful sanctions is provided by the Securities and Exchange Commission (SEC).

18. For a discussion of this case, see pp. 81–83.

This independent regulatory agency has jurisdiction over the stock exchanges and over the investment business generally. Various formal sanctions are written into the statutes that grant the SEC power; however, it rarely employs these formal sanctions. Decision-making by the SEC is almost uniquely affected by the area of its jurisdiction, since the stock markets are by their nature responsive to the behavior and mood of the individual investor. One of the principal jobs of the Commission is to make certain that public information about securities, which includes the kinds of information given the investor by so-called advisers or advisory services, is accurate. The Commission is supposed to protect the public from deceitful practices on the part of those selling or marketing securities. The Securities Act of 1933 requires that companies wishing to sell securities to the public must file with the SEC a registration statement which presents an accurate picture of their financial status. On the basis of this statement a prospectus is issued to potential investors so that they can make up their own minds as to the worth of the securities in question. SEC adjudication involves deciding the basis on which private parties may market securities.

The SEC has potent administrative sanctions because of its ability to delay the marketing of securities, and to publicize anything questionable about the parties involved. The Commission must take positive action to *accelerate* even a normal application that requires very few changes, or amendments. This is because the law requires a twenty-day waiting period after each amendment to a registration statement is made before the issue can be marketed. Unless the Commission agrees to waive this requirement, delay is automatic. This power constitutes an extraordinarily effective sanction; security issues are always hopefully timed to reach the market during a favorable period, and delay results in uncertainty and possible adversity in the stock and bond markets.

Even more important than the Commission's power to delay the issuing of securities is its power to cast a shadow on the reputation of the parties involved by issuing a "stop order," which forbids sale of the securities pending a hearing. Such a hearing automatically raises doubts in financial circles about the soundness of the securities, and does far more harm to a successful sale than Commission delay of the effective registration date. In this type of administrative activity, formal hearings would virtually preclude a fair judgment because they automatically invoke sanctions adverse to the interests of the private parties.

The net result of the sanctions possessed by the Securities and Exchange Commission is that companies making application for permission to sell their securities will rarely question Commission decisions, which are normally made by the staff, concerning the necessary components of registration statements. The adjudicative process generally prevents the applicant from taking an adversary position; the word of the Commission becomes law. *Formally* a challenge may be made, but practically it is an extremely risky course of action. This is not so much because of the possibility of adverse action by the SEC, but because of unfavorable public reaction. In this respect the sanctions of the SEC differ from those of the Federal Communications Commission.

Administrative sanctions exist because the bureaucracy combines the ability to initiate action with the power to decide particular cases. In other words the problems that arise from sanctions in the exercise of judicial functions by the bureaucracy stem directly from the fact that administrative agencies have regulatory power that combines not only the legislative and judicial powers, but also requires as a result of the combination of these powers that agencies initiate action in the public interest as they define it, and decide cases on the basis of policy standards. In controversies in the courts, parties are placed in adversary positions, and the judge (and sometimes a jury) acts as a third party. In administrative proceedings the "third party" nature of the deciding authorities is frequently absent, because they must function in the interests of broad regulation based upon subjective policy requirements they themselves define. The judicial function becomes a critical part of the enforcement process in the bureaucracy, and cases arise directly as a result of the regulatory power of the administrative branch.

Where sanctions exist they are generally significant only in the sphere of particular agencies. The lack of unity in American bureaucracy generally prevents the possibility of sanctions by one agency from affecting the nature of judicial proceedings before another. A united bureaucracy would present an imposing threat to fair adjudication, which may be illustrated by several incidents that took place during the first years of the Kennedy administration. In 1961 the General Electric and Westinghouse Electric corporations, along with a number of smaller concerns, were convicted for price fixing in a broad range of electrical equipment. Since the case involved a violation of the Sherman Act and the anti-trust laws, it fell within the jurisdiction of the Justice Department to secure the convictions. The executives of these companies were accused of being aware at all times of the flagrantly illegal practices on the part of their subordinates, and some of the executives of both companies were given jail sentences in an unprecedented judicial action in a Federal District Court in Philadelphia. Normally the case would have ended at this point, apart from the damage suits against the companies, and other administrative agencies would have had little if any interest in the situation.

But some months after the General Electric and Westinghouse convictions, the FCC issued a statement to the press which was also sent to the two companies to the effect that the prior activities of their executives in fixing prices for electrical equipment raised serious doubts about the capabilities of the companies to operate the rather large number of television and radio stations they owned. The FCC challenged them to prove that continued operation of their stations would be in the public interest. The companies were told to submit evidence concerning their broadcasting activities, and the Commission indicated that such evidence had to outweigh their record of unlawful conduct.

Although the FCC has some responsibility in the anti-trust field, it was really raising a rather extraneous issue against these large and diversified corporations whose station licenses were up for renewal. It was serving notice that illegal activity under the jurisdiction of outside agencies would be taken into account in its own consideration of whether or not to grant or renew a license, which is of course a judicial decision. In this way the sanctions of the FCC were being used to reinforce those of the Justice Department.

The development of inter-agency cooperation in the anti-trust field was not, in itself, dangerous. Nevertheless, if the practice were to spread to other bureaucratic activities it could in many instances have the effect of inhibiting private individuals and groups from challenging administrative decisions, and hence would distort the decision process in a way that would certainly be considered unfair in terms of the judicial model, and probably in terms of a more flexible model that sought to achieve a fair balance between the rights of the individual and the powers of government.

The sanctions of administrative agencies are particularly dangerous if used for political purposes. The Committee for the Re-Election of the President (CREEP) in 1972 was particularly adept at threatening corporate executives with adverse administrative action if they did not make contributions to the Nixon campaign. The false implication given was that the President could control the actions of regulatory agencies such as the Civil Aeronautics Board, and that if contributions were not forthcoming from the airlines they would not receive favorable treatment on route applications and other matters of vital concern to them. Similar threats were made to other business executives whose businesses were regulated by government agencies. Well before the 1972 campaign, President Nixon and his advisers used various units of the bureaucracy to advance their political goals. Of particular concern was the establishment in 1969 of a secret unit within the Internal Revenue Service called the Special Service Staff, or SSS, that kept secret files on thousands of individuals and organizations with a view to applying administrative sanctions against those not conforming to the wishes of the President. The President had expressed concern to the Commissioner of the Internal Revenue Service that tax-exempt funds were being used by activist groups to stimulate unrest. The clear implication was that the IRS should remove the tax-exempt status from such organizations, a move that would have resulted in IRS action for strictly political purposes and in clear violation of its own charter as well as of the First Amendment of the Constitution. The second Article of Impeachment reported out of the House Judiciary Committee in 1974 accused the President of impeachable conduct because

He has, acting personally and through his subordinates and agents, endeavored to obtain from the Internal Revenue Service in violation of the Constitutional rights of citizens, confidential information contained in income tax returns for purposes not authorized by law; and to cause, in violation of the Constitutional rights of citizens, income tax audits or other income tax investigations to be initiated or conducted in a discriminatory manner.

The same Article of Impeachment also accused him of misusing the FBI, the Secret Service, and the Central Intelligence Agency for political purposes. The use of the IRS by a President for political harassment was not new with the Nixon administration. President John F. Kennedy had ordered the IRS to investigate the tax exemptions of approximately fifty right-wing groups. Political investigations by the IRS were continued during the Johnson administration, but apparently dropped. Interestingly, the secret IRS unit that was created during the Nixon administration was not established upon direct order by the President himself, but apparently stemmed from pressure from the Chairman of the Federal Reserve Board, Arthur Burns, acting in behalf of the President, and from Senator John McClellan (D., Arkansas), Chairman of the Government Operations Committee and of its Permanent Investigations Subcommittee. Using the threat of agency sanctions for political purposes is a clear subversion of fair and just procedures.

PROBLEMS IN OVERLAPPING AGENCY JURISDICTION

Bureaucratic pluralism often causes an inconsistent administration of the law and confusion about administrative intent which is infuriating. In 1975, for example, the Equal Employment Opportunity Commission (EEOC) took a position that men and women employees of the same status must get equal monthly pension payments after they retire. Because of the greater funding needs for women, the EEOC plan would require employers directly or indirectly to collect greater monthly contributions from women than from men if each group is to be treated equally. At the time the EEOC promulgated its policy, the Office of Federal Contract Compliance in the Department of Labor issued concurrent guidelines which required that monthly contributions for men and women in retirement plans must be equal for employers having contracts with the federal government. Meeting the conditions of the Labor Department's guidelines while adhering to EEOC policy would effectively discriminate against men as a class because more funds would be collected from men than would return to them, the difference being taken up by the women, who outlive them. This confusion prompted the president of Colby College in Maine to write to the EEOC that "Colby is prepared, as we have always tried to do, to comply with the law of the land, but first it would be helpful to know what the law of the land is." The EEOC policy was challenged in court by several associations representing private colleges.

In 1975, the newly formed Federal Election Commission not only had to defend itself against congressional attacks, but also from Justice Department threats to restrict its authority. The powers of the Justice Department as a prosecutor overlap the jurisdictions of many other agencies. In many cases, agencies have primary jurisdiction to find legal violations, but their prosecution is left to the Justice Department. This means that if the Justice Department interprets the law differently from an agency it may not wish to proceed to prosecute on the basis of agency advice. The Justice Department essentially told the Federal Election Commission in 1975 that it was not going to pursue cases where its interpretation of the campaign law differed from that of the Commission. This stance of the Justice Department prompted the general counsel of the FEC to proclaim that the Justice Department did not have discretionary authority to interpret the campaign-practices law, and that primary jurisdiction in interpreting the Act rested with the Commission itself. The Justice Department, he held, had a responsibility to prosecute on the basis of Commission determinations that the law had been violated. Contradictory agency statements and overlapping jurisdiction meant that those subject to the law could only guess at which interpretation, that of the Federal Election Commission or of the Justice Department, would prevail where conflict between the agencies existed.

One powerful agency that is constantly embroiled in conflict with the rest of the bureaucracy is the Environmental Protection Agency, created by an Executive Order of the President in 1970. By the mid-1970s it had become the largest regulatory agency, employing 9,000 people and operating under a two-million-dollar-a-day budget. When the EPA was created, it assumed authority in a variety of areas that had been under the jurisdiction of old-line departments and agencies. For example, it took over regulatory control of pesticides that had been within the Department of Agriculture, and the Department of Agriculture is still trying to regain its former power in the pesticide field. The pesticide industry clearly feels it has more clout in the Department of Agriculture than before the EPA, and is pressuring Congress to restore the Department of Agriculture's jurisdiction over pesticide regulation. The basic political constituency of the EPA consists of the active environmental groups that came on the scene in the later 1960s and successfully pressured government in the courts to support more stringent regulation of the environment. All of the old-line departments and agencies, on the other hand, have constituencies consisting of particular sets of economic interests. The creation of the EPA helped to place governmental control of the environment in more disinterested hands than had previously exercised regulatory power. Environmental policy is not exclusively under the jurisdiction of the EPA, however, since it has shared responsibility with other agencies in a number of fields. For example, it sets general environmental radiation levels, but the Nuclear Regulatory Commission sets specific limits on radiation emissions from nuclear power plants. It has only advisory power in the area of noise control, sharing responsibility with such agencies as the Federal Aviation Administration, which sets permissible limits for airport noise, and the Occupational Health and Safety Administration (OSHA), which has primary control over noise levels in factories and business establishments. The Environmental Protection Agency was created to bring about rational co-ordination of federal policies, but intense inter-agency infighting continues in this crucial policy field.

The fight that began in 1974 between the EPA and OSHA over permissible noise levels in the work places of the nation is an interesting example both of inter-agency conflict and of the way in which agency rules are promulgated. Under the Occupational Safety and Health Act of 1970, OSHA has final authority to promulgate rules regulating occupational safety and health.[19] But Congress has also created an Office of Noise Abatement and Control within the Environmental Protection Agency, which has

19. 84 Stat. 1590 (1970).

statutory responsibility to "carry out . . . a full and complete investigation and study of noise and its effect on the public health and welfare in order to . . . determine . . . the psychological and physiological effect [of noise] on humans."[20] Recommendations for action based upon EPA studies are to be forwarded to the President and Congress. But the EPA has gone further than this, and has actively intervened in proceedings before other agencies concerning regulation of noise.[21] One such intervention occurred before OSHA in 1975 when it was conducting twenty-two days of hearings on proposed noise standards to govern occupational establishments. The EPA strongly objected that the proposed criterion of OSHA was not adequate to protect the health of employees. In extensive post-hearing comments, the EPA summarized its position that the OSHA proposal to allow a ninety-decibel noise level for eight hours was inadequate, concluding that

Millions of Americans lose their hearing because of occupational noise. OSHA can take the lead and work toward a society where senior citizens are no longer repaid for a life of labor by being hard of hearing. As more data are unfolding, it becomes clear that there is even more at stake than hearing loss. In a few years, OSHA will be praised for its vision, if the right choices are made today.[22]

The EPA's extensive report was cited by Senators and Representatives favoring more stringent noise-control levels.[23] In 1976, as the issue was moving toward resolution, OSHA maintained its position in opposition to EPA's recommendations.

Where more than one agency has law-making and enforce-

20. U.S.C.A., § 1858a (1970 ed.).

21. In addition to OSHA and the EPA, primary regulatory authority over noise has been delegated to the Secretary of Transportation, who is to take into account adverse environmental effects of noise resulting from proposed highway projects in the federal-aid highway system, and is, moreover, to consult with the Federal Aviation Administration on airport noise and to the Secretary of Health, Education, and Welfare, who has been given statutory responsibilities to establish mandatory noise levels for underground coal mines. See 23 U.S.C.A. § 109h (1); 49 U.S.C.A. § 1431a; 30 U.S.C.A. § 846.

22. Before the Occupational Safety and Health Administration, U.S. Dept. of Labor, post-hearing comments, Docket No. OSH–11, Sept. 15, 1975.

23. For example, see Vol. 122 Congressional Record, 94th Cong., 2nd Sess., February 18, 1976, p. S1842.

ment powers in a particular field, inconsistent sanctions may be employed against private parties. What is legal before one agency may be considered illegal by another. The problem especially arises in the anti-trust field, where the Justice Department shares jurisdiction with the regulatory agencies for the administration of the anti-trust laws. The Justice Department operates through the courts, whereas the regulatory agencies have independent authority to approve or disapprove of mergers. Both Justice Department and regulatory agency decisions, of course, may eventually be challenged in the courts. However, the real dilemma is that members of regulated industries are subject to three masters—the Justice Department, regulatory agencies, and the courts—who may disagree on the application of the laws. While the "doctrine of primary jurisdiction," a judicial invention, attempts to resolve potential disputes between the Justice Department and the agencies by granting primary jurisdiction to the regulatory agencies, this does not always prevail, nor does it satisfactorily eliminate the dilemmas caused by overlapping agency jurisdiction. The failure of the Justice Department and the regulatory agencies to co-operate in their administration of the anti-trust laws produces uncertainty and inaccurate expectations on the part of private companies that may find they have spent a great deal of money and time on a merger proposal they think will be approved by one agency, only to have it attacked or turned down by another.

Confusion in agency jurisdiction has the obvious result of encouraging the large and powerful private interests to play one agency off against another to secure approval for a particular action. This adds a new dimension to the adversary process, bringing in opposition between agencies, alongside opposition between private interests and between private and governmental groups. Lack of cooperation in the bureaucracy is to the advantage of large interests with financial backing, but may be quite detrimental to small groups and individuals with limited resources. The former will play the game to their advantage; the latter will not know where they stand in relation to the agencies that have jurisdiction over them. It is quite possible that one administrative agency will take action against an individual or group that has been acting in accordance with the wishes of another agency, the very reverse of the situation in the General Electric-Westinghouse case. There, adverse sanctions were threatened by the FCC to supplement the action of the Justice Department, because both agencies agreed on the nature of the legal violation the companies had committed.

An interesting example of the confusion that exists because of divided jurisdiction in the administrative process is provided by what will be called the El Paso Natural Gas Co. case (1956–62). The case involved the attempt of El Paso Natural Gas Co. to acquire the Pacific Northwest Pipe Line Corporation. The case was opened in 1956, when El Paso acquired a controlling stock interest in Pacific Northwest, and was ended in 1962, when the Supreme Court, which had been called in to settle the case in 1959, rendered its decision in *California v. Federal Power Commission.*[24] The issues were complex, but essentially the problem to be solved was whether the Federal Power Commission (FPC) had jurisdiction under the Natural Gas Act to make a final determination of the validity of the merger, or whether the Justice Department under the Clayton Act had jurisdiction. Many of the problems that arise as a result of overlapping jurisdictions stem from confusing statutory provisions, and this case was no exception. There were good reasons to support either the FPC or the Justice Department on the basis of the relevant statutes. Both had jurisdiction, and it fell to the Supreme Court to make a choice between them in order to resolve the controversy.

The relevant statutory provisions were section 7 of the Clayton Act and section 7 of the Natural Gas Act. The former provides that no company may acquire the *stock* of another if such an acquisition has the effect of substantially lessening competition and creating a monopoly. The Justice Department has the power to enforce the Clayton Act through the courts, along with the Federal Trade Commission and several other independent regulatory agencies (ICC, FCC, CAB, and the Federal Reserve Board), but excluding the Federal Power Commission. From the provisions of the Clayton Act it was clear that the Justice Department had jurisdiction over the El Paso case, because stock acquisition was involved. After El Paso acquired a controlling stock interest in Pacific Northwest, it decided that it wished to merge the *assets*

24. 369 U.S. 482 (1962).

of the two companies. Such a merger of assets had to be approved by the FPC under the terms of section 7 of the Natural Gas Act. Apparently, then, both the Justice Department and the FPC had jurisdiction. The former could legitimately attack the merger as a violation of the Clayton Act, whereas the latter had ultimately to approve the merger of the assets of the two companies, which it could prevent by refusing to issue a certificate of public convenience and necessity.

The sequence of events in the El Paso Natural Gas case indicates that El Paso, which was the direct party in interest, sought to use the Federal Power Commission as a lever against the Justice Department. The Justice Department initially filed suit in the United States District Court in Utah in 1957, seeking to restrain the merger of El Paso and Pacific Northwest through stock acquisition by the former, which it considered to be a violation of section 7 of the Clayton Act. Two weeks after the government action indicating hostility to El Paso's proposed merger, the company filed an application with the FPC for authorization to merge its assets with those of Pacific Northwest in addition to its stock. The company then immediately sought to have the antitrust action delayed, pending the outcome of its case before the FPC, which it had reason to expect would be favorable. El Paso had acquired a controlling interest in the stock of Pacific Northwest long before its application to the FPC for permission to merge further the assets of the two companies. It is probably not coincidental that its application to the FPC came directly after adverse Justice Department action. The company was attempting to use the divided jurisdiction of these agencies to place the FPC in opposition to the Justice Department.

After application was made to the FPC, infighting began to take place between the FPC and the Justice Department regarding which agency had the power to determine initially whether the merger was valid with respect to the jurisdictional area over which each had control, a merger of assets, and stock acquisition respectively. Any initial decision would substantially shape subsequent action. If the FPC determined that a merger of assets was valid, this would necessarily carry a great deal of weight in opposition to a subsequent anti-trust prosecution in the courts by the Justice Department, and if such a prosecution was carried out the FPC decision would provide substantial evidence for a court decision adverse to the Justice Department. Conversely, prior Justice Department action would prejudice the case before the FPC. The agency, then, which had primary jurisdiction over the case would control in a substantial manner the final decision on the validity of the merger. The FPC gained this initial advantage, and secured a decision from the District Court to which the Justice Department had taken its case to the effect that its decision would await the outcome of the Commission's proceedings.

The FPC approved the merger, and stated that it felt its decision should be immune from further consideration by the Justice Department. The Commission said it had taken section 7 of the Clayton Act into account in its determination of "public convenience and necessity," and found the public interest favored a merger of the two companies. The state of California appealed the FPC's decision to the United States Court of Appeals for the District of Columbia, which affirmed the decision of the Commission. California then appealed to the Supreme Court, which held in *California v. Federal Power Commission* that "orderly procedure" demanded that the Commission should await the decision of the District Court in the original anti-trust suit before rendering its own decision. In other words it decided in favor of initial Justice Department action in combination with the courts. Justice Douglas, for the majority, stated that

our function is to see that the policy entrusted to the courts is not frustrated by an administrative agency. Where the primary jurisdiction is in the agency, courts withhold action until the agency has acted. The converse should also be true, lest the anti-trust policy whose enforcement Congress in this situation has entrusted to the courts is in practical effect taken over by the Federal Power Commission.[25]

Justice Harlan, speaking for the minority, stated:

The holding does not turn on any facts or circumstances which may be said to be peculiar to this particular case. It is not limited to Federal Power Commission proceedings. Without adverting to any legal principle or statute to support its decision, the Court appears to lay down a pervasive rule, born solely of its own abstract notions of what "orderly procedure" requires, that seemingly will henceforth

25. *Ibid.*, p. 490.

govern every agency action involving matters with respect to which the anti-trust laws are applicable and anti-trust litigation is then pending in the courts.

I cannot subscribe to a decision which broadly works such havoc with the proper relationship between the administrative and judicial functions in matters of this kind. The decision . . . in effect transfers to the Anti-trust Division of the Department of Justice regulatory functions entrusted to administrative agencies. . . .[26]

Regardless of Harlan's warning that *California v. Federal Power Commission* would control all subsequent anti-trust proceedings involving divided jurisdiction, the vagueness of statutory standards coupled with agency pursuit of self-interest guaranteed that similar situations would arise in the future.

The criteria applied by the two agencies in their determinations regarding mergers differed. The Justice Department had to determine whether or not a merger would "lessen competition, or . . . tend to create a monopoly"; the Federal Power Commission had to decide whether the proposed merger conformed to the "public convenience and necessity." Although the two standards can easily be interpreted as one and the same thing, this is not likely to be the case where the Justice Department and an independent regulatory agency are concerned. Regulatory agencies tend to become promoters of the industry under their jurisdiction; hence, they are very likely to approve mergers that may improve the economic health of an industry and of particular firms. The Justice Department, on the other hand, has an institutionally oriented attitude opposed to mergers in general because they tend too much to a restraint of trade or monopoly. The regulatory agency tends to have a narrow and protective view; the Justice Department has a broad perspective which leads it to oppose mergers in one industry which would be at the expense of groups outside the industry.

The difference in attitude toward mergers is reinforced by the respective decision processes. The courts are the instruments of adjudication for the Justice Department, whereas a regulatory agency such as the Federal Power Commission has a relatively independent procedure for adjudication that is set forth in its

26. *Ibid.*, p. 491.

own regulations and in statutory provisions. Procedural patterns in adjudication give the regulatory agencies a great deal of power to shape decisions in terms of their constituencies, which always include as one of the most important components regulated industry groups. Although provision has been made for a certain degree of separation of judicial officers, or hearing examiners, within agencies from the agencies as a whole, they are actually subject to agency control in many respects, with the result that the courts are frequently far more independent in relation to powerful private corporations and groups subject to regulatory jurisdiction, than the respective dependent or independent regulatory agencies. The courts are strongly influenced by direct and substantial interests in adjudication, but not by a *particular* group of interests on a consistent basis.

Because agency attitudes and decision processes tend to favor industry interests, *judicial review* of administrative decisions is frequently initiated by groups that participate only as interested "outside" or "third" parties in administrative proceedings. In some instances they may not participate at all, but will nevertheless challenge an administrative decision because it affects them. For example, rate making decisions directly involve private corporations that wish to gain permission from an agency to charge certain rates to their customers. Their customers may be other corporations or simply the general consumer. The parties most directly concerned with rate making proceedings are usually the companies charging the rate, rather than those paying it. These companies usually spend the greatest amount of time and money in administrative hearings concerning rates, and other items that affect them directly, and favorable decisions are more likely than not obtained. The courts are used as independent appellate bodies by groups that are not able to control the agencies, which frequently results in appeal by third parties. The case of *California v. Federal Power Commission* illustrates this, in that a favorable agency decision for El Paso was appealed by the state of California, which had intervened in the Commission's proceedings because it had an indirect interest in the final decision. It represented the consumers of California, who presumably might have something to gain by preventing a merger that could result in a restraint of trade.

Administrative Law, the Constitution, and the Common Law

The Constitution poses several problems to the existence of administrative power both of a legislative and judicial nature. Strictly speaking, Congress is supposed to retain sole jurisdiction over legislation and not delegate this power to administrative agencies.[27] And, within the concept of the separation of powers, there is no provision for the exercise of judicial power outside of the regular court system. But judicial power was given to the agencies because it forms an essential part of effective *regulatory power*. Further, there were deficiencies in the courts which made them ineffective for the purpose of securing strong government regulation of industry. In any event the judicial power that now resides in the bureaucracy is not there to enable it to check the judiciary, which would have to be the reason in terms of constitutional theory.

The existence of judicial power in the hands of administrative agencies is not really incidental to the executive power as it is generally defined, and particularly not as it was defined in the Constitution. It is incidental to regulatory power, which is far broader than the executive function, and encompasses all three primary powers of government.

THE ROLE OF THE COURTS UNDER THE CONSTITUTION

Article III of the Constitution states that "the judicial power of the United States shall be vested in one Supreme Court, and in such inferior courts as the Congress may from time to time ordain and establish." The courts were to be independent of the other two branches of government because the nature of judicial power demands it. We have indicated that American constitutional theory requires that one branch should not exercise to a significant degree the powers of coordinate branches, and in particular that the executive should not have substantial legislative

27. For a discussion of the constitutional problems posed by the delegation of legislative powers, see Chapter 4, 155–205.

and judicial power. This theory was clarified in greater detail by Hamilton in *Federalist 78*.

First, Hamilton noted that in terms of organization "the complete independence of the courts of justice is peculiarly essential in a limited Constitution." This is important initially because the judiciary, possessing the power of *judicial review*, must act as a check upon the legislative body and upon its general power to make laws. The Constitution does not intend, according to Hamilton, that the legislators shall have the ability "to substitute their *will* to that of their constituents. It is far more rational to suppose, that the courts were designed to be an intermediate body between the people and the legislature, in order, among other things, to keep the latter within the limits assigned to their authority. The interpretation of the laws is the proper and peculiar province of the courts."

Further, Hamilton stated that judicial independence is necessary "to guard the Constitution and the rights of individuals from the effects of those ill humors, which the arts of designing men, or the influence of particular conjunctures, sometimes disseminate among the people themselves, and which, though they speedily give place to better information, and more deliberate reflection, have a tendency, in the meantime, to occasion dangerous innovations in the government, and serious oppressions of the minor party in the community." That is, the judges are supposed to protect the people from themselves, a job they could not perform properly if they were dependent upon the people directly, or indirectly, by being responsible to the legislature.

Finally, judicial independence exists to protect the rights of individuals generally in the adjudication of cases. Congress initially determines the jurisdiction of the courts and, hence, the type of cases that will come before the judiciary. But an independent judge can do a lot to shape the way in which the law is implemented. The judges determine the real nature of the law and the protections that will be afforded individuals, regardless of what Congress does.

The courts are competent to judge issues involving the Constitution and individual rights not only because their independence makes them less subject to political whims and passions, but also as a direct result of permanent tenure during good behavior, which will permit judicial specialization.

The right of the courts to exercise the power of judicial review was firmly established by Marshall in *Marbury v. Madison* (1803), in which he stated: "It is emphatically the province and duty of the judicial department to say what the law is. Those who apply the rule to particular cases, must of necessity expound and interpret that rule. If two laws conflict with each other, the courts must decide on the operation of each." [28]

THE CONSTITUTIONAL BASIS OF ADMINISTRATIVE LAW

The development of the bureaucracy has forced the courts to be extremely imaginative and flexible in the creation of doctrines that permit administrative agencies judicial power. This has been equally true with respect to administrative legislation as we will see in the next chapter. The constitutional question presented by bureaucratic exercise of judicial functions is how to reconcile them with the provision in Article III requiring that judicial power reside in the Supreme Court and inferior courts to be established by Congress.

The first justification for the location of judicial power in the hands of the bureaucracy is that the Constitution gives *Congress* the power to create the entire judicial system with the exception of the Supreme Court. Congress determines how many courts there will be, the number of judges, the jurisdiction of the courts, and so forth. The only thing it cannot touch is the Supreme Court and its *original jurisdiction;* Congress can change by law the appellate jurisdiction of the Supreme Court, as well as the number of judges on the Court. If it does not like something the Court is doing it can simply cut off jurisdiction from the type of case in which objectionable decisions are being rendered, provided the cases do not fall within the original jurisdiction of the Court. The latter includes only cases involving ambassadors, and disputes among states or in which the state is a party. This part of the Court's jurisdiction is extremely narrow. Virtually all of the important cases arise in the area of appellate jurisdiction; thus the potential power of Congress over the Supreme Court is very great indeed.

As far as the subordinate judicial system is concerned Congress

28. 1 Cranch 137, at 177 (1803).

determines everything. For this reason it has been possible from a constitutional viewpoint for Congress to place judicial power wherever it wishes. It has the power to set up administrative agencies and give them judicial power. It determines the kinds of appeals that may be taken to the courts from administrative decisions. It may say, as it has with respect to actions of the Veterans Administration, that administrative decisions shall be final and conclusive on all questions of law and fact. This virtually precludes judicial interference. Using this constitutional power Congress has delegated judicial power to the bureaucracy.

The courts have no desire to usurp the powers of coordinate branches of the government, and they have a deep respect for their role in the constitutional system. As a result, when Congress wishes to delegate particular powers to the administrative branch the courts will generally not raise objections. But while the judiciary has acquiesced in congressional delegation of judicial power to the bureaucracy, it has had to find constitutional justifications for permitting this apparent incursion on the courts' domain. One might say that the courts have had to find a way to rationalize in constitutional terms administrative power of a judicial nature. They have done this in a rather ingenious way. Essentially, they have stated that there are two kinds of judicial power: judicial power, stemming from Article III, and judicial power that does not stem from Article III, and is based on Article 1. The former is that which is normally considered appropriate for courts, and the latter involves power judicial in nature but not clearly provided for in Article III and not governed by its requirements. If Congress gives an administrative agency judicial power, it is not by definition Article III judicial power. Some would say it is not judicial power at all, and would label it "quasi-judicial" power. Again, this is a matter of definition. Adjudication by courts and agencies is very similar in form and effect. The major difference is that agencies are far more flexible in what they can do in exercising judicial power than the courts. The courts must adhere to the requirements of Article III, which means that they cannot exercise non-judicial functions, initiate cases, issue advisory opinions, nor accept matters for resolution that do not fit into the category of a "case and controversy." By making this distinction every problem concerning the proper location of judicial power becomes a matter of definition. The

Constitution says only that the powers that fall under the heading of Article III must reside in courts (that is, constitutional courts), and outside of the original jurisdiction of the Supreme Court Congress itself determines which powers are bestowed by Article III and which are not.

The courts, then, have found no constitutional objection to congressional placement of judicial power in the hands of administrative agencies. They have even aided the delegation of such power by inventing the necessary constitutional rationalizations. To some extent the courts must function in line with the political expectations of the community, which are more directly reflected in the other branches of the government. The reasons for establishing an administrative process with effective regulatory power, and hence effective judicial power, were compelling from the political and economic standpoint. The courts themselves had sabotaged numerous congressional attempts at regulation which used them as the judicial arms of regulatory systems. It would have been impossible politically, and questionable constitutionally, for the judiciary to declare unconstitutional congressional establishment of regulatory and other administrative agencies with judicial power. This fact does not in any way lessen the serious constitutional implications of the extraordinary power of the bureaucracy in the judicial realm. One of the principal ideas behind placing judicial power in a separate court system was to limit the other branches of government, and in particular the law-making power. When legislative and judicial power are combined in the same hands this important constitutional check is not present. While administrative agencies do separate their exercise of judicial and legislative functions to some degree under the terms of the Administrative Procedure Act, essentially the heads of the agencies have final decision-making authority in both the legislative and judicial spheres.[29]

ADMINISTRATIVE LAW AND THE COMMON LAW

The problems presented to the American constitutional system by the development of administrative law are not nearly as diffi-

29. For discussion of the provisions of the Administrative Procedure Act of 1946, see pp. 138–143.

cult to resolve as those that arise from the conflict between administrative law and the *common law*. The Anglo-American legal system is based upon common-law concepts and practices, and the Constitution can properly be termed a common-law constitution.[30] The term "common law" refers to legal principles and practices, made by judges, that have characterized the Anglo-American legal system. Of course these principles have changed from one period to another, but in the last few centuries some fairly consistent ideas have emerged that express the fundamental basis of the common-law system.

Rooted in common law is the principle that matters of a clearly judicial nature must be decided in courts that are properly organized and staffed with judges. This is because judges are knowledgeable not only in the substance of the law, as Hamilton pointed out, but in the process of reasoning from fact to conclusion. Courts by their very nature must be independent. Once the judiciary becomes dependent upon the executive or legislative branches it will cease to be part of a true common-law system.

Much of the philosophy of the common law was stated by Sir Edward Coke in the seventeenth century, in order to justify the position the courts of common law were taking against James I. This was a struggle on the part of the judiciary for supremacy in its own field. James wanted the courts to be subject to his direction as far as his royal prerogative was involved in particular cases, but Coke felt that only he, as Chief Justice, and those trained in the law could properly interpret the common law. Interference by the executive could not be tolerated. The common law, broadly conceived, encompassed the entire governmental system and allocated powers and rights to branches of the government and to private citizens. The common law, then, included the constitution and large areas of substantive law. By defining the common law in such broad terms Coke was really calling for a dominant judicial department that would be the ultimate arbiter of all

---

30. For excellent discussions of the common law basis of the Constitution see Edward S. Corwin, *The "Higher Law" Background of American Constitutional Law* (Ithaca: Cornell University Press, 1955); and J. A. C. Grant, *Our Common Law Constitution* (Boston: Boston University Press, 1960). For a broad and definitive analysis of American political thought in the 17th and 18th centuries see Clinton Rossiter, *Seedtime of the Republic* (New York: Harcourt, Brace, 1953).

constitutional and legal questions. The role of the courts in this ideal common-law system would have been far more significant than their intended role under the American Constitution. The judiciary was to be the most powerful branch of government, and was to have a far more positive role than that of merely acting as a check upon coordinate branches. In the American system the judiciary interprets a written constitution, but in a common-law system the courts apply general rules of reason, which may or may not derive from written documents, to prevent arbitrary action from any source, governmental or nongovernmental, in the community.

Consider the following two passages from Coke's writings. In rendering a decision in one famous case he pointed out that "it appears in our books, that in many cases, the common law will control acts of Parliament, and sometimes adjudge them to be utterly void: for when an act of Parliament is against common right and reason, or repugnant, or impossible to be performed, the common law will control it, and adjudge such act to be void." [31] The power of the judiciary was not only to extend to Parliament, but was to have general application. In speaking of the jurisdiction of the Court of Kings Bench he noted:

. . . this court hath not only jurisdiction to correct errors in judicial proceeding, but other errors and misdemeanors extrajudicial tending to the breach of the peace, or oppression of the subjects, or raising of faction, controversy, debate, or any other manner of misgovernment; so that no wrong or injury, either public or private, can be done, but that this shall be reformed or punished in one court or other by due course of law.[32]

This suggests that the power of the courts was to be pervasive. They were to make law as well as apply it.

The maintenance of a dominant judiciary acting on the basis of common-law principles came to be identified in much legal theory as equivalent to the supremacy of law. One of the basic premises of common-law theory was that the *executive* would tend to encroach more on the judicial field than the legislature,

31. *Dr. Bonham's Case*, 8 Co. 118a (1610), 77 English Reports 652.
32. 4 Institutes 71.

although in some instances collusion might exist between the legislature and the executive for this purpose. Coke's writings extolling the virtues of judicial supremacy were directed almost entirely against the King, who was understandably considered the gravest threat to the maintenance of an independent and powerful judicial branch. Throughout history it is the executive that has been considered by legal theorists to be the principal opponent to the maintenance of the common-law system. In the seventeenth century this idea was expressed by complete opposition to any kind of executive control of the judiciary; in the nineteenth century it was considered of crucial importance that "officials," i.e., those employed by the executive branch, be subject to common-law jurisdiction; in the twentieth century, the development of administrative law caused a variety of responses from common-law theorists. The fear of executive encroachment on the common-law system contrasts sharply with one of the basic premises of American constitutional thought, namely, that it is the legislative branch that will present the gravest threat to coordinate branches.

In the nineteenth century the best expression of common-law theory is to be found in Dicey's historic *Introduction to the Study of the Law of the Constitution* (1885),[33] which exerted a profound and prolonged effect upon British legal thought, and indirectly upon legal theory in the United States. It is not possible here to go deeply into the complexities of Dicey's thought, but the context of administrative law can not be understood without examining the essence of his famous treatise. Dicey was expressing what he felt was the true nature of the common-law system as it had evolved in Great Britain. Central to this system was the presence of the rule of law, which resulted from three characteristics of the common law.

First, "no man is punishable or can be lawfully made to suffer in body or goods [life, liberty, or property] except for a distinct breach of law established in the ordinary legal manner before the *ordinary courts of the land.* In this sense the rule of law is contrasted with every system of government based on the exercise by persons in authority of wide, arbitrary, or discretionary powers

33. A. V. Dicey, *Introduction to the Study of the Law of the Constitution* (London: Macmillan, 1885).

of constraint."[34] In this system the "ordinary courts" are the common-law courts, and the "ordinary legal manner" is equivalent to common-law procedure, which by that time had become precisely defined. Essentially, this procedure involved proper hearing and possible appeal before judgment could be rendered.

Second, the rule of law means "not only that . . . no man is above the law, but (what is a different thing) that . . . *every man, whatever be his rank or condition,* is subject to the ordinary law of the realm and amenable to the jurisdiction of the ordinary tribunals."[35] Here Dicey is referring to the fact that public officials are not immune from judicial scrutiny if they violate the common law.

Finally, Dicey points out that in the common law "the general principles of the constitution (as for example the right to personal liberty . . .) are with us the result of judicial decisions determining the rights of private persons in particular cases brought before the courts; whereas under many foreign constitutions the security (such as it is) given to the rights of individuals results, or appears to result, from the general principles of the constitution."[36] In brief, "our constitution . . . is a judge-made constitution, and it bears on its face all the features, good or bad, of judge-made law."[37]

Dicey echoes Coke in his elevation of the judiciary to the pinnacle of the constitutional system. Also, Dicey, like Coke, was more concerned with executive encroachment on the judiciary than with the possible expansion of the legislature in this direction. Coke was reacting against the King's attempts to control the judiciary for his own purposes, and Dicey was reacting against the French system of administrative law (*droit administratif*) and against the development of administrative law in Great Britain. At the beginning of the twentieth century he reluctantly admitted that there was increasing evidence that administrative agencies were beginning to assume judicial functions, and that because of this the rule of law as he defined it was being placed in jeopardy. Although Coke may have won his victory and es-

---

34. Dicey, *op cit. note* 9 (8th ed., 1915), pp. 183–184. Italics added.
35. *Ibid.,* p. 189.
36. *Ibid.,* p. 191.
37. *Ibid.,* p. 192.

tablished judicial supremacy in the common-law system, the doctrine of the rule of law at the time of Dicey was to face the more formidable obstacle of a combination of an expanding bureaucracy with judicial power. The battle was to be joined, but the bureaucracy was to win.

Ironically, Dicey's denial of the existence of administrative law in Great Britain impeded progress in establishing systematic judicial review of agency actions. After all, if administrative law and discretion do not exist, there is no need for judicial review. But as it soon became evident to Dicey and others that administrative adjudication was a reality, judicial review became recognized as an important check upon arbitrary and unauthorized administrative actions. While the courts in England cannot directly review legislative acts and declare them unconstitutional because of the doctrine of parliamentary supremacy that was firmly established after the Revolution of 1688, they can and do review actions of the executive to ensure that they are *intra vires* and in accordance with the law.[38]

AMERICAN CONSTITUTIONAL LAW AND
THE COMMON LAW CONTRASTED

Although the American Constitution is basically a common-law document, it does not elevate the judicial over the administrative branch to the extent that Coke, Dicey, and their adherents would have favored.[39] There have been many American common-law theorists, like Roscoe Pound, who lament the lessening power of the judiciary over the bureaucracy and feel that it has resulted

38. The relationship between the courts and administrative agencies in Great Britain is surveyed in S. A. De Smith, *Judicial Review of Administrative Action* (London and New York: Stevens and Sons Limited and Oceana Publications, 1959).

39. After the "Glorious Revolution" of 1688, parliamentary supremacy became a principle of the unwritten British Constitution, which precluded judicial review of parliamentary acts. But the 1688 revolution did not reduce judicial independence of the executive nor judicial supremacy over those aspects of public law not directly determined by Parliament. The Act of Settlement in 1700 solidified judicial independence of the executive and maintained judicial prerogatives to thwart arbitrary and unlawful executive action. The American tradition, of course, maintained the principle of judicial review of legislative acts, but it did not emphasize the role of the ordinary courts in controlling executive actions.

in a subversion of the common-law system.[40] However, the allocation of powers in our Constitution makes it very easy to bypass the judiciary in the allotment of judicial functions as has been noted previously. American constitutional theory does not place unusual power in the hands of the courts. It is true that Hamilton, who was more in favor of a strong judiciary than many at that time, had a fairly broad conception of judicial review and its importance to the maintenance of the constitutional system. But in *Federalist 78*, he was principally concerned with judicial control of legislative, not executive, actions. He recognized that at numerous points the judiciary could prevent the implementation of arbitrary action by Congress. At the same time he stressed that the judiciary would have to be checked, and judicial review was to be primarily for the purpose of keeping the actions of the other branches within well defined constitutional boundaries. It was not to enable the courts to substitute their will for that of the people, or for the specific provisions of the Constitution. The law was not to be judge-made, it was to emanate from the people as expressed in the Constitution. The courts were to be under the Constitution as much as any other branch.

THE NATURE OF COMMON-LAW PROCEDURE

Exactly *why* under the common law is it imperative that the judiciary monopolize judicial functions? Common-law theorists justify total court supervision of the judicial function on the grounds that the basic purpose of adjudication—protection of the rights of the *individual* through the *accurate determination of the facts* of the particular case—is best fulfilled by the personnel, structure, and procedure of the courts. Not only are judges expert in substantive law and independent, but common-law procedure, which the judiciary follows in many types of cases, is designed specifically to assure the protection of individual interests.

What are the fundamental attributes of common-law procedure? First, the party or parties charged with a particular offense,

40. Roscoe Pound, *The Spirit of the Common Law* (Boston: Marshall Jones Co., 1921).

or involved generally in a case and controversy, must be given sufficient notice of the nature of the proceeding in time to prepare their case. Like all areas of legal procedure this is a highly complex matter. It is not easy to define what constitutes proper notice in a given set of circumstances, although there are judicial rules that may be applied. Second, once notice has been served, the parties must ideally be given the opportunity to present their case in an open hearing before a judge (and sometimes a jury), who will render a decision on the basis of the record developed by the parties themselves. This part of the process is for the purpose of determining relevant facts ("adjudicative facts") concerning the parties. The hearing procedure therefore is structured to exclude irrelevant testimony, and to gain maximum information from the parties through cross-examination, and so forth. It is of the utmost significance that the information upon which the decision is to be made is to be gained from the parties through questioning by the parties. In other words the record is made entirely by the parties themselves on the basis of the information they possess, which means that the decision reflects the individual interests represented directly in the hearing. The judge applies the substantive law to the facts that are revealed by the parties and that are tested and found to be accurate through the procedures that are applied during the hearing. Finally, after the process has been exhausted, an opportunity for appeal should be present within legally prescribed limits. The entire case can not be re-heard except under highly unusual circumstances; however, particular points in question, for example, whether adequate evidence has been introduced to support conclusions reached, may be subject to review by a higher court.

The Transfer of Judicial Power to Administrative Agencies

To some extent administrative exercise of judicial power is accidental. It was not until the first decade of the twentieth century that administrative power was generally recognized to include judicial functions, and it was not until the New Deal that the American Bar Association and other legal groups began to emphasize that administrative agencies were exerting virtually a revolutionary effect upon our legal system.

How would our system of government work if the courts retained control over judicial functions? This can readily be illustrated by a few examples from history. In order to retain judicial supremacy in the common-law sense, and to a lesser degree in terms of the American constitutional system of separation of powers, the courts would have the responsibility of hearing in the first instance all cases and controversies under statutory and constitutional law. It would mean that administrative agencies would act as prosecuting arms of the government when they functioned in the judicial area. The final decision-making power would reside in the judiciary, and the agencies would have to plead their cases before the judges. Judicial procedure would be employed for all case disposition, with the resulting emphasis upon individual interests.

In the past the courts have exercised not only all judicial functions, but also what in modern terminology would be called administrative functions. For example, during the American colonial period and part of the nineteenth century the courts acted as rate-making bodies, setting tolls for public roads. They possessed various kinds of regulatory power, and in terms of the common law they were the correct repository of such power. In many instances the courts developed general rules through case by case determinations that became in effect legislation. In the absence of interest by legislative bodies it was only natural that the courts should step in to establish such rules. The courts thus resembled modern administrative agencies, possessing almost unchecked legislative and judicial power. For example, before statutory standards were created, there were all sorts of common-law rules governing how an employee could receive compensation for an injury resulting from his employment. The common law was substantive as well as procedural in nature, and in both respects it was shaped entirely by judicial action.

At the present, anti-trust litigation provides a good example of a field in which primary jurisdiction often resides in the courts. The Justice Department must rely entirely on the judiciary for enforcement. Many other agencies engaged in anti-trust enforcement have varying degrees of power independent of the courts, most notably the Federal Trade Commission; but even the FTC shares powers with the judiciary to some extent. The Justice Department acts as the primary prosecuting body, bringing many cases to the courts. It can not act independently to prevent restraints of trade because Congress has been unwilling to give it this power, ever since it passed the Sherman Act in 1890. Once again it is important to point out that the extent of judicial power over administrative agencies is determined by Congress, except as constitutional issues may be involved; in that case the courts will take jurisdiction regardless of congressional intent to the contrary.

Although agencies such as the Justice Department must rely upon judicial enforcement of their policies in particular cases, in relative terms the power of the judiciary to control administrative action by exercising primary jurisdiction in administrative law has virtually vanished. The Justice Department is the exception rather than the rule.

DEFICIENCIES IN THE JUDICIAL SYSTEM

The courts were unable to meet the demands that were made for the establishment of regulatory agencies; hence they were displaced in both the substantive and procedural areas. Their powers to determine substantive law were taken away in many regulatory fields as were their powers of implementation. In part, the courts failed to meet modern regulatory needs because of cumbersome *procedure*. More significant was the failure of common law to meet *substantive* requirements that arose primarily from an increase in democratic demands upon government.

THE COMMON LAW AS SUBSTANTIVE LAW

Picture for a moment government and society in the nineteenth century. *Laissez faire* was the operative ideal for much of the period, although the government acted as a promoter of business in many areas through tariffs, railroad subsidies, and so forth. But in general the sphere of legislative action was limited in comparison with what was to come in the twentieth century. The limitation of *statutory* law resulted directly in an increase in the scope of judge-made *common law*. Provided legislatures did not act the courts were frequently free to formulate all kinds of doctrines governing labor and business. The lack of legislative action meant that there was no particular conflict between the courts and Congress or state legislative bodies. Why was Congress relatively inactive? Because demands for action, particularly in regulatory fields, were rare until the last part of this period.

The legislation shaped by judicial action in the nineteenth century reflected a bias that stemmed from the position and procedure of the courts. They were largely independent; hence, they did not have to respond to pressure by the general public as did Congress and the President. This does not mean, of course, that judges do not accept the principles of constitutional democracy prevalent in the American community. But the courts were originally, and in general still are, purposely placed outside the direct democratic process. This fact made it possible and probable that judicial decisions would be somewhat out of touch with the more direct demands that were being placed upon Congress and the President from various groups in the community. Judicial procedure gave an advantage to groups and individuals more wealthy than the norm, for litigation is a time-consuming and expensive process. The judges themselves were rather conservative. They tended to be wealthy and somewhat detached from the people, in sharp contrast with the politicians, whose success depended then as now upon maintaining close contact with the needs and aspirations of the people. It is not entirely inaccurate to characterize the Supreme Court during the latter decades of the nineteenth century as the "property court," a term frequently used. The emphasis of this Court, as well as that of the judiciary generally, was upon the protection of private property, which was only natural, given the environment of judicial decision making. Even in the face of congressional opposition judicial protection of private property did not finally break down until the late 1930s, when the Supreme Court agreed that in some areas a more general public interest takes precedence over demands from wealthy private property interests.

When Congress and state legislative bodies began responding to demands for regulation in the late nineteenth century it was inevitable that the substantive standards developed would be in conflict with the common law; this, in fact, was one of the reasons for new legislation in the first place. The common law was considered inadequate to meet the complex problems arising from rapid industrial growth. At least it did not reflect the political demands of the time. The legal relationships established by the common law were not wanted by the newly powerful political groups; hence, an appeal was made to Congress and other legislative bodies to change the *substantive* legal rules that prevailed by substituting new standards for judicial legislation. The requirements of regulation were not met by the common-law judiciary in the substantive sense, nor in the procedural realm.

Those who have the power to implement the law through judicial determinations have in effect the power to control exactly what criteria will be used. Because the common-law courts were unwilling to change the substantive criteria of the law, the only way legislative bodies could assure the implementation of new and different standards was to create new agencies for enforcement; hence, the administrative agency became a common device to circumvent the courts and the substantive standards they insisted upon.

DEFICIENCIES IN JUDICIAL PROCEDURE

Apart from the problems presented by judicial insistence upon the maintenance of substantive policy standards that conflicted with those of legislative bodies at all governmental levels, judicial supremacy involved difficulties because of the nature of judicial *procedure*. In effect, this procedure is not suited to achieve the goals of effective and fair government regulation, in terms of the political demands that are placed upon government. In order to realize these goals, administrative procedure frequently emphasizes requirements of speed, lack of expense, and *expertise* in the area involved. Judicial procedure is somewhat inflexible in its emphasis upon notice and hearings as indispensable components of the decision making process, which may be entirely appropriate in some instances, but highly inappropriate in others. The record for decision in administrative law must contain more than the facts and opinions of the immediate and direct interests involved in a particular case. It is doubtful in many cases that judicial procedures, such as cross-examination, will bring out the necessary facts and their relation to broader policy considerations. Judicial procedure thus tends to shape the characteristics of substantive law, making it a reflection of direct and substantial interests. In administrative law the same result has been achieved in those agencies where primary emphasis has been placed upon the necessity of adhering to the judicial decision making model.

The element of time is always important to the realization of a just decision in a particular case and controversy. Under judicial procedure a case may stretch out over a long period, occasioning severe hardship for one or both parties involved. If administrative procedure imitates full-fledged court procedure several or more years may pass before a decision is made. On the other hand, if informal procedure is employed decisions can be made very rapidly.

The problem of time in the administrative process may be illustrated by reference to the Federal Power Commission. This independent regulatory agency has to pass on many classifications of rates charged to the consumer by natural gas companies. For the purpose of illustration a rate case can be considered as an instance of administrative adjudication. The FPC must determine in a particular case, with reference to a limited number of specified parties, the validity of the rates they wish to charge the public. Such validation involves, in effect, a controversy between private interests and the agency.

The FPC has attempted to dispose of rate cases and other related cases through a hearing process, which it feels is mandatory because of statutory requirements. The fact is, however, that it can not possibly dispose through hearings of all the cases relating to the natural gas industry over which it has jurisdiction. As a general rule, it permits a rate increase to go into effect upon application by a private company; after a hearing has been held on the validity of such an increase any reduction in the rate will be refundable to the consumers affected on a retroactive basis. At the present pace it will take the FPC ten or twenty years to determine whether or not present charges to consumers for natural gas are in fact valid; thus, in 1990 it may decide that a rate

charged in 1970 was not proper and require the company involved to refund the overcharge to the consumers affected, few
of whom will be around to receive their checks because they will
have moved, died, or will be otherwise unavailable. In areas in
which Commission authorization is required before companies
can engage in certain kinds of activity, delay may mean considerable hardship to the parties involved and may have a profound economic effect. For example, before many companies
will embark upon a program of expansion they may want to know
what rates they can charge for the particular service they will
give. If they want to construct new facilities, FPC delay would
affect a wide range of companies involved.

Although administrative delay may work to the disadvantage
of powerful economic interests, as when the FDA takes years
to allow a pharmaceutical company to market its products,
generally delay benefits economic interests because it defers
adverse regulatory action and, in many instances, even prevents
administrative decisions entirely. Powerful groups have always
been able to use the courts to gain their goals, although in the
last decade public-interest pressure groups in combination with
a judiciary often sympathetic to their goals have acted as a curb
on corporate power in some areas. Just as economic interests
dominated the judicial process through the skillful manipulation
of judicial procedure, they have been able to stall administrative action where the administrative process has become highly
judicialized. The combination of administrative agencies that
have adopted judicial procedures, with ultimate possibilities of
appeals to the courts, has given groups seeking to prevent administrative action a two-pronged avenue of approach. They
can first slow down administrative proceedings by filing numerous delaying notions (depositions, subpoena specifications, inter-
rogatory motions) with the administrative law judge who hears
the case in the first instance, and while administrative proceedings are pending they may file collateral attacks against the
proceedings in a federal court, although this latter course is
usually not fruitful because of the judicial doctrines of primary
jurisdiction and the exhaustion of administrative remedies that
require final agency action before judicial review. Should the
groups fail to get their way before the agencies, they then can

begin all over again by seeking judicial review of the agency decision, which causes further delay and may result in overturning the agency decision or having it remanded back for further consideration (which, of course, continues the suspension of final agency action).

An excellent example of how corporate interests in combination with administrative lawyers delay administrative proceedings is to be found in the long struggle of the Food and Drug Administration to establish standards for peanut butter, a struggle that began in July, 1959, and ended in March, 1971, with the publication of an FDA rule requiring a 95-per-cent peanut content for peanut butter.[41] Manufacturers had been including 20- to 25-percent hydrogenated oils (lard) in their peanut butter. The FDA, charged with protecting the purity of food products, proposed a rule in July, 1959, setting a 95-per-cent peanut-content requirement. The following sequence of events illustrates, as Joseph Goulden has pointed out, how skilled Washington lawyers manipulated the administrative and judicial processes to delay and ultimately to water down what the FDA originally wanted:

July 2, 1959. FDA Commissioner formally proposes, via publication in the Federal Register, a standard of identity for peanut butter calling for ninety-five percent peanut content. As required by law, he invites comments.

November 28, 1961. FDA, after two years of talks with industry, publishes order setting peanut level at ninety percent.

February 1, 1962. FDA decides industry objections warrant further study, and stays effective date of new standard. Industry proposes eighty-seven percent standard.

November 10, 1964. FDA publishes slightly revised standard, still at ninety percent level, and again invites comments.

July 8, 1965. After studying volumes of industry and consumer comment, FDA sticks with ninety percent.

Sept. 4, 1965. FDA receives formal request for public hearings from industry and sets one beginning October 18, 1965. Effective date of order stayed again.

November 1, 1965. After two postponements, public hearing begins, to run until March 15, 1966.

41. The peanut-butter controversy is brilliantly described in Joseph C. Goulden, *The Super-Lawyers* (New York: Weybright and Talley, 1971).

December 6, 1967. FDA publishes proposed findings of fact and standard (still at ninety percent) and invites comments.

July 24, 1968. FDA publishes final order, ninety percent standard.

November 7, 1968. Order stayed pending industry appeal to courts.

May 14, 1970. US Court of Appeals for Third Circuit affirms FDA order. Stay remains in effect pending further appeal.

December 14, 1970. US Supreme Court declines to review case.

March 3, 1971. FDA publishes notice making ninety percent standard effective in thirty days.[42]

Because delay of administrative proceedings more often than not benefits economic interests, proposals for reform of agency procedures to render the administrative process more effective have not succeeded. The trend has been in the direction of increasing judicialization of agency proceedings, which began immediately after the creation of the Interstate Commerce Commission in 1887, and which much later was reflected in the Administrative Procedure Act of 1946.[43] Another direction was taken by President Ford, who recommended de-regulation through a general lessening of the authority of regulatory agencies. By the mid-1970s the issue of delay because of over-judicialization was largely rhetorical. Both regulated groups and the larger number of administrative lawyers have a vested interest in a continuation of formal administrative adjudication, as do administrative law judges and lawyers employed by the bureaucracy. President Ford also found out that industry groups do not favor de-regulation of *their* industries, because it protects their economic interests. They certainly do not wish to enter the uncertain laissez-faire world of Adam Smith and the liberal economists. The main concerns of regulatory reformers in 1975 and 1976 were not the protective aspects of regulation, but the burdens imposed by agencies on business.

The duality of having both regulatory agencies and courts operating in the same areas through judicial procedures has led some observers to call for the placement of final regulatory authority either in the bureaucracy or in the courts. This would reduce the multiple possibilities of manipulation of judicial pro-

42. Ibid., pp. 186–187.

43. For a discussion of the Administrative Procedure Act of 1946 see below, pp. 138–143.

cedures by private interests. A former chief counsel of the Federal Trade Commission, in recommending the transfer of the Commission's adjudicative matters to federal district courts, stated that

It is manifest that the ability of any judicial entity to manage the issues before it justly and efficiently depends ultimately on its power to enforce its orders. The power of contempt, however infrequently used, is the cornerstone of effective judicial control. Yet the administrative law judges before whom commission cases are tried initially and the commission itself have no contempt (and therefore no enforcement) authority whatever. Accordingly, any order, whether procedural or substantive, of an administrative law judge or the Commission may be flatly disregarded (for valid or spurious reasons) by a respondent in a Commission proceeding. This action requires the extremely time-consuming and inefficient procedure of the Commission initiating enforcement proceedings (in effect a new law suit) in federal court.[44]

The lack of FTC enforcement power encourages collateral attacks in federal courts against Commission investigative and adjudicative actions during the proceedings, with respondents generally claiming violations of due process. Another contrary way of coping with the problem would be to increase the enforcement powers of the agencies in the adjudicative process. This, in effect, was done after the first decade of operation of the Interstate Commerce Commission proved that it could not operate effectively when it could not issue final orders without judicial approval. In the 1890s, powerful private interests effectively used the courts to prevent adverse ICC decisions. Certainly, it would not be possible to transfer all of the adjudicative activities of administrative agencies to the already overburdened federal district courts. However, such a transference would be interesting in the case of the FTC, especially since the courts (in particular, the District of Columbia District Court) have expertise in one of the most important areas regulated by the FTC, unfair methods of competition. The district courts already act as the adjudicative bodies for the Justice Department in the enforcement of the anti-trust laws. However, such an experiment

44. Peter A. White, "FTC: Wrong Agency for the Job of Adjudication," 61 *The American Bar Association Journal* 1242–1246 (1975).

should be undertaken very cautiously, especially since it might undermine the informal enforcement activities of the FTC that have proven so effective in carrying out agency policy. Private interests with the necessary time and money would have no incentive at all to settle informally their disputes with the FTC if assured of original court adjudication of their case.

An evaluation of proposals to extract the judicial functions from the agencies and place them in the hands of either regular courts or specialized administrative courts must take into account the *raison d'être* of the agencies in the first place. Constitutional courts (those created by Congress under the authority of Article III) cannot initiate action. And administrative courts would also not initiate cases, but would adjudicate cases brought to them by the agencies. The courts are umpires; they are passive. Administrative agencies, as agents of congressional policy, are not supposed to be umpires. They reflect group demands for positive action. They are active and initiate action in accordance with their policy goals.

Agency control over adjudication is necessary to insure that policy will be reflected in administrative orders resulting from adjudication. The courts have generally permitted the agencies to overturn the decisions of their own independent administrative law judges if they do so on the basis of policy considerations. For example, when the Federal Trade Commission ferrets out deceptive practices, either through its own investigations or through information gained from an outside source, it initiates action in the name of the FTC against the party involved. Its prosecuting arm is at the initial adjudicative stages separate from its adjudicative arm, which consists of administrative law judges independently appointed and not subject to direct Commission control. In the formal process, the administrative law judge will adjudicate the case in the first instance, hearing evidence presented by the investigative staff of the FTC. But after the administrative law judge renders his or her decision, the Commission may reverse it on policy grounds. The result is that the Commissioners of the FTC control the kinds of decisions rendered in most of the adjudicative cases it initiates. Many administrative agencies, like the FTC, initiate action to carry out what they consider to be the public interest. Their control of the judicial function means that they can complete the action they begin rather than make it possible for an outside court to veto their decisions. Their orders are subject to judicial review, but that review is limited in scope. Courts exercise judicial self-restraint when it comes to consideration of substantive agency policy. If the agency has followed the procedures outlined by Congress and adhered to its own procedural rules, and has supported its decision with sufficient evidence, the courts will not generally interfere.

JUDICIAL VS. ADMINISTRATIVE PERSONNEL

The exercise of judicial self-restraint in reviewing administrative decisions is based on the recognition by most judges that they are not as suited to making determinations that guide modern administration as are the agencies. The resources of the courts are in no way equal to those of the bureaucracy. And judges are more generalists than specialists, which puts them at a disadvantage in understanding the issues involved in administrative adjudication. Of course, this is not always the case, and judges on courts that consistently hear administrative appeals, particularly the Federal Court of Appeals in the District of Columbia, may have far more expertise than many individuals in handling agency adjudication. However, below the political appointees of the agencies who may also lack expertise, there is a relatively permanent staff, including administrative law judges, that deals with special areas of jurisdiction on a relatively consistent and permanent basis. From this, the staff develops expert knowledge that the average judge cannot duplicate. Although judges should be experts in applying facts to law, in administrative adjudication both the law and the facts may be highly complex, requiring specialization to exercise the judicial function properly.

Outside of the formal administrative process that is handled by administrative law judges with avenues of appeal to the heads of the agencies, the full staff of an administrative agency can be brought to bear upon an adjudicative matter. In addition to lawyers, agency staffs include economists, engineers, and other specialists, all of whom may be important in decision-making. It is in the informal area that the administrative agency can use more individuals in the decision-making process than courts. And, even in the formal area, the administrative law judge and many of the political appointees have been able to develop far more expertise than judges, who are generalists. Judges usually must hear cases in areas that encompass a very wide spectrum. They have to jump from divorce law to criminal law to estate law, and so on. Their task is imposing. Expecting ordinary judges to be able to deal competently with administrative cases is simply expecting too much. The scope of government regulation requires the exercise of judicial functions beyond the realm of the ordinary court system.

Administrative Law and Internal Agency Procedure

The scope and significance of administrative adjudication raise many problems concerning the way the judicial function should be exercised in the American system of government. The constitutional and common-law context within which judicial power is supposed to function has been noted. It is now necessary to consider some of the more important attempts that have been made to fit administrative adjudication into this framework.

The extensive delegation of judicial functions to administrative agencies was the direct result of the need to bypass both the substantive and procedural policies of the courts. Agencies were supposed to be flexible in both areas to meet regulatory requirements. At first, those groups within the American Bar Association that were later to become concerned with the growing power of the bureaucracy in the judicial area more or less ignored the development of the agencies. Some theorists, like Roscoe Pound, sounded an alarm in the early part of the twentieth century, stating that "executive justice" was beginning to replace "justice according to law," that is, the common law. Pound equated administrative procedure to Star Chamber proceedings, and noted that a vast change would have to take place in both the substantive and procedural aspects of the common law if the increasing power of the agencies was to be curbed. In 1914, in the *Columbia Law Review,* he wrote:

The experience of the past indicates that if we improve the output of judicial justice till the adjustment of human relations by our courts is brought into better accord with the moral sense of the public at large and is achieved without unreasonable, not to say prohibitive delay and expense, the onward march of executive justice will soon cease. But we [the legal profession] must be vigilant. Legislatures are pouring out an ever-increasing volume of laws. The old judicial machinery has been found inadequate to enforce them. They touch the most vital interests of the community, and it demands enforcement. Hence the executive is turned to. Summary administrative action becomes the fashion. An elective judiciary, sensitive to the public will, yields up its prerogatives, and the return to a government of man is achieved. If we are to be spared a season of oriental justice, if we are to preserve the common-law doctrine of supremacy of law, the profession and the courts must take up vigorously and fearlessly the problem of today—how to *administer* the law to meet the demands of the world that is.[45]

This expresses perfectly the contempt felt by conservative common-law theorists for administrative adjudication. To them, of course, the only solution was to transfer all judicial functions to the courts.

It soon became evident, however, that administrative agencies were to be a permanent fixture in the government. Men like Pound recognized by the time the New Deal had arrived that the old common-law dream of judicial supremacy could not be achieved. It was then obviously necessary, they felt, to do two things. First, make the agencies themselves as much like courts as possible when they exercise judicial functions. Second, expand judicial review as much as possible. At the beginning of the New Deal, in what was a delayed recognition that administrative law could not be abolished, the American Bar Association turned its attention to reforming the administrative process in accordance with these objectives.

The American Bar Association appointed its first committee on administrative law in 1933, and its first report echoed the concerns of men like Pound in its statement that:

45. Roscoe Pound, "Justice According to Law," 14 *Columbia Law Review* 1, at 21–22 (1914).

When . . . the administrative official exercises a quasi-judicial function, he may be expected to conform to the sort of procedure which has been found best adapted to the determination of the rights and obligations of the individual in his controversies with other individuals and with the government. Certain fundamental safeguards of notice, opportunity for hearing, and determination or review of issues of fact and of law by an independent tribunal (and eventually, on questions of law at least, by a court) are involved, and, indeed, are necessary if justice is to be done to the individual.[46]

The emphasis during this early period of legal concern with the administrative process was upon the *procedural* rather than the substantive aspects of administrative law. Of course many of the more conservative elements in the American Bar Association were basically opposed to the kind of governmental expansion that was taking place under the New Deal, and their answer was to try to place the agencies within a rigid set of controls. Other groups within the Bar Association, however, recognized the necessity of regulatory agencies but felt a genuine concern that the judicial procedures of the bureaucracy conform to those of the courts, with the courts exercising judicial review as a last resort.

The Association put on an intensive drive during the New Deal period to secure the passage of a general statute designed to mold the procedure of all agencies engaged in adjudication and rule making in the image of the courts. Such a general statute would contrast sharply with what had been the common practice of shaping the procedure of each agency in its enabling statute in terms of the particular job it was supposed to do. In 1940, Congress, in response to American Bar Association pressures, passed the Walter-Logan bill which was an extreme attempt to control administrative procedure, only to have it vetoed by President Roosevelt. The veto was not overridden. This Act essentially would have compelled administrative agencies to hold hearings similar to those held by courts in all cases of adjudication and rule making. It would have meant an extraordinary change in administrative practice and would have imposed an impossible burden upon the agencies. The Act did not take into account the vital role played by informal procedure in administrative adju-

46. "Report of the Special Committee on Administrative Law," 58 *American Bar Association Reports* 407, at 410 (1933).

dication, and its requirements for hearings in the legislative area of rule making did not conform to either constitutional or common-law theory. In addition, the Walter-Logan bill provided for judicial review of virtually all administrative decisions of a judicial nature; thus, it ignored the careful distinction the judiciary had been developing with respect to review of administrative decisions between points of law and points of fact. The former were completely reviewable, the latter only as they related to points of law.

World War II interrupted any serious consideration of a general statute to control administrative procedure, but in 1946 the American Bar Association finally achieved some of its objectives when the Administrative Procedure Act became law.[47] Originally the Act was designed to establish more uniform procedures among the agencies in both rule-making and adjudication. Formal administrative adjudication (where there is a statutory requirement for formal trial-type hearings before an administrative order takes effect) was required to follow procedures that were in many respects analogous to those of the regular courts. It provided for greater independence for those administrators, called "hearing examiners" or "trial examiners" in 1946 but now called "administrative law judges" by an order of the Civil Service Commission in 1972. These officials conduct initial administrative proceedings in adjudication and rule-making that involve formal hearings, which may be required by law or may be directed by the agency. The Act required that the agencies publicize their formal rules in the Federal Register. The APA also expanded the scope of judicial review. Amendments to the Act in 1966 and 1974, called the Freedom of Information Act, require agencies to disclose their records to "any person" making a request therefore, subject to a variety of exemptions. For example, the Freedom of Information Act does not apply to agency records that by executive order have been designated to be kept secret in the interest of national defense or foreign policy or that are related solely to internal personnel rules and practices of the agency. Trade secrets cannot be disclosed, nor can personnel and medical files of an individual, the disclosure of which

47. 60 Stat. 237 (1946), as amended by 80 Stat. 378 (1966), as amended by 81 Stat. 54 (1967) and 88 Stat. 1561 (1974), 5 U.S.C. §§551–559, 701–706, 1305, 3105, 3344, 6362, 7562.

would constitute "a clearly unwarranted invasion of personal privacy."[48] The move toward ending government secrecy was advanced with the passage of the "Government in the Sunshine Act" in 1976. This legislation toughened the Freedom of Information Act to make it more difficult for agencies to withhold information, and provided that the meetings of agencies headed by two or more persons appointed by the President and confirmed by the Senate would have to be open to the public, with certain stipulated exceptions.

Since the standards of the APA apply only to the formal administrative process (where formal hearings are required by law), they have limited applicability. Vast areas of administrative action are excluded from the purview of the Act. A major criticism of the APA is that it does not encompass informal administrative proceedings, thus making it an ineffective control over most administrative adjudication. In rule-making, the APA does require agencies to adhere to certain procedures even where there is no statutory requirement for hearing. Most agency rules must be published in the Federal Register in advance of their official promulgation, and interested parties must be given an opportunity to comment and petition for a change or revocation of the rules. These APA provisions governing rule-making, however, contain many exemptions, as is characteristic of other sections of the Act. This means that the agencies have a great deal of discretion in deciding whether or not to adhere strictly to APA guidelines.

What are the judicial standards that the Administrative Procedure Act makes applicable to hearings that are required by non-APA statutory provisions? Generally, in the area of formal administrative proceedings the APA requires procedures analogous in many respects to the judicial or common-law model, although never as strict as those decision processes. Thus, notice must be given of formal administrative proceedings; a separation of prosecuting and adjudicative functions within the same agency is to be maintained; certain rules of evidence are to prevail; a record of the proceedings is to be kept. The administrative law judge who presides at the hearing is to make the initial decision, which can be overruled by the agency on the basis of a different

48. 5 U.S.C. §552.

interpretation of policy or the introduction of new evidence; finally, appeal may, within limits, be taken to the courts.

The Administrative Procedure Act has clearly not fulfilled the expectations of its framers. In order to secure passage of the Act in the first place, many exemptions had to be written into it in response to strong pressures from the agencies in Congress. The numerous escape clauses of the APA lead to the exemption of large portions of the administrative process. The wording of the Act is often ambiguous, leading to the courts' responsibility of determining its scope and impact. The APA can be used either for judicial intervention in the affairs of the agencies or for judicial self-restraint. For example, although the Act contains provisions expanding judicial review of agency action, it also provides that agency action that is committed to agency discretion by law is not reviewable. But it is not so simple to determine exactly which actions lie within the legal discretion of the agencies, and it is very simple for the courts to find that agency action is discretionary if they do not choose to review the decisions of the agency. The APA has not been instrumental in increasing judicial control over the administrative process nor in molding agency procedures in the image of the courts. The ineffectiveness of the APA illustrates the limitation of statutes as mechanisms to change decision processes that have developed out of political and practical realities.

One major accomplishment of the APA that cannot be denied is the establishment, at least symbolically, of an independent class of administrative law judges. This has been done in conjunction with the separation of prosecuting and adjudicative functions within the agencies. Under the terms of the statute, administrative law judges are not subject to agency control either with respect to their job status or their conduct in relation to the cases they initially decide. When a lawyer takes a case to an administrative law judge, he enters a decision process outside of the agency's immediate sphere of control. The role of the administrative law judge is based on the judicial model of decision-making, which requires personal (as opposed to institutional) and independent judgment in the determination of individual rights and obligations. The problem in the implementation of this model in the administrative process is that the

APA permits the agencies to overrule their administrative law judges whenever they are so inclined. This may seem rather strange, and the question may legitimately be asked: Why bother to give administrative judges independence under such circumstances—that is, why make their decisions only initially independent? One reason may have been the expectation that many of the decisions of administrative judges would not be appealed to or taken by the agencies for review. If this had become the situation, *de facto* power would reside with the judges regardless of the ability of the agencies to review *de jure*. This has not, however, been the practice, and it is not uncommon for the agencies to overrule their own judges in cases involving important issues of public policy.

The very fact that administrative law judges are independent often creates conditions in which the agencies have to reverse or change their own judges' decisions. Lack of communication between the judges and the agencies and the inability of the agencies to control the actions of their judges cause the judges and the agencies to go in different directions on matters of policy. The testimony of Louis J. Hector, a former member of the Civil Aeronautics Board, before the Senate Subcommittee on Administrative Practice and Procedure of the Judiciary Committee in 1960 still bears eloquent witness to this dilemma:

> The hearing examiner who heard the *Seven States* case did not know what the [Civil Aeronautics] Board had in mind in terms of extent of service.
>
> The Board had in its own thinking come around to the conclusion that any town which had any reasonable chance of producing 5 passengers a day should have a chance to see if it could do so, and if it could then it should have an airline.
>
> The hearing examiner did not know this, because he is independent, and the Board could not talk to him.
>
> So he spent two years hearing evidence and turning out a 500-odd page opinion.
>
> It came up to the Board, and the Board's first reaction was, "This wasn't what we had in mind at all. We were thinking of a much more extensive route pattern." [49]

49. *Hearings pursuant to S. Res. 234 Before the Subcommittee on Administrative Practice and Procedure of the Senate Committee on the Judiciary*, 86th Cong., 2nd Sess., pp. 231–232 (1960).

Mr. Hector's remarks vividly illustrate the paradox of trying to establish administrative justice through a separation of policy making and adjudication within the agencies. If an agency is to implement policy, it must be able to control adjudication within its jurisdiction; policy considerations must always be part of the process of adjudication. It is actually impossible to separate the two areas without causing a power struggle between those who are presumably to be policy makers, and those who are to adjudicate individual cases. The historical struggle between the courts and the agencies illustrates the point.

The inherent differences between the administrative and judicial processes make it inappropriate to try to enforce a strict judicial decision-making model upon the agencies. Some of the most prominent scholars of administrative law, such as Professors Kenneth Culp Davis and Walter Gellhorn, have long recognized that informal administrative processes may be far more appropriate to the resolution of issues involved in both rule-making and adjudication than trial-type proceedings. Walter Gellhorn has stated that "some of this country's gravest administrative deficiencies stem from lawyer-induced over-reliance on courtroom methods to cope with problems for which they are unsuited."[50] Professor Davis flatly states that

The strongest need and the greatest promise for improving the quality of justice to individual parties in the entire legal and governmental system are in the areas where decisions necessarily depend more upon discretion than upon rules and principles and where formal hearings and judicial review are mostly irrelevant. We must try something that neither the legal philosophers down through the centuries nor our current study groups of the organized bar have tried—we must try to find ways to minimize discretionary injustice.[51]

Regardless of the sound views expressed in these warnings, the American Bar Association and, to a lesser extent, the Administrative Conference of the United States continue to recommend greater formalization of administrative procedures

50. "Administrative Procedure Reform: Hardy Perennial," 48 *American Bar Association Journal* 243–251.
51. Davis, *Discretionary Justice, op. cit.*, p. 216.

in both rule-making and adjudication.[52] The practicing bar continues to recommend elimination of most of the exemptions to the APA, greater judicialization of rule-making proceedings, expanded judicial review of agency actions, and a stricter separation of policy-making and adjudicative functions within the agencies. Proposals for administrative courts, which have a long history, are continually cropping up. Senator Robert Taft (R., Ohio), for example, introduced a bill in 1975 to revive the old 1955 Hoover Commission proposals to create administrative courts.[53]

Although proposals for greater judicialization of the administrative process are continually pouring out of various study groups associated with the bar, there has not been a single change made in the Administrative Procedure Act in this direction since it was originally passed in 1946. This reflects a general recognition of the exigencies of the administrative process in Congress as well as the power of the agencies to prevent general legislation that would further restrict their procedural flexibility. But the agencies continue to be restricted by their enabling statutes, and the tradition of requiring hearings (although not necessarily trial-type hearings) before administrative orders can be made has been continued in statutes governing the more recently created agencies such as the Department of Transportation, the Environmental Protection Agency, the Consumer Product Safety Commission, and the Nuclear Regulatory Commission. Statutory hearings need not be of the full-trial type (oral testimony with cross-examination) unless expressly required by the enabling statute because the APA, although it does impose certain judicial standards to be followed by the agencies, does not go so far as to mandate the right of cross-examination in administrative proceedings.

52. The Administrative Conference, established in 1966, is composed of private citizens and government officials concerned with administrative law. It is almost exclusively dominated by members of the practicing bar, which is strongly reflected in its recommendations for greater judicialization of administrative proceedings.

53. Congressional Record, 94th Cong., 1st Sess., September 4, 1975, Vol. 121, p. S15240.

The Nature of Judicial Review

Aside from attempting to mold internal administrative procedure to conform to the judicial model, the American Bar Association, the Administrative Conference, practicing private attorneys in administrative law, and most legal scholars have supported the removal of obstacles to judicial review of administrative orders and, to a lesser extent, of administrative rules.[54] But practical necessities dictate limited judicial review. Clearly, the courts cannot exercise broad review powers over all administrative decisions, even in the formal adjudicative realm. The courts cannot, and should not, review administrative matters that are non-judicial in character. Parties seeking judicial review must have standing, which requires a case and controversy affecting their interests, or their rights under statutory, constitutional, or common law. These requirements alone eliminate most administrative decisions from the purview of the courts. And even where the conditions of judicial review are met, the courts are reluctant, when considering a case on the merits, to delve too deeply into issues that they feel are more properly resolved by the agencies. In deference to the expertise of the agencies and their policy responsibilities, the courts have tended to limit review to legal questions concerning such matters as *ultra vires* action and whether or not proper procedures have been followed to protect the rights of private parties.

The right to judicial review of agency actions stems from both statutory and constitutional law, although more from the former than the latter. The statutes governing agency procedure contain provisions which either explicitly grant judicial review to parties aggrieved by agency action, preclude review completely, or simply fail to mention the subject. Where explicit provisions exist for review the courts designated by the statute must act as initial appellate bodies. Where there is preclusion of judicial review, the courts will receive a case only if they feel there is a *constitutional* right involved, which would be an

---

54. For a discussion of judicial review of administrative rule-making see pp. 78–79, *supra*.

extraordinary situation in terms of prevailing judicial practice.[55] Where statutes say nothing about judicial review, the presumption is in favor of reviewability. This has particularly been the case since the passage of the Administrative Procedure Act in 1946, since it contains a general, although qualified, clause which states that "any person suffering legal wrong because of any agency action, or adversely affected or aggrieved by such action within the meaning of any relevant statute, shall be entitled to judicial review thereof."[56] Justice Harlan, speaking for a majority of the Supreme Court in *Abbott Laboratories v. Gardner* in 1967, noted:

a survey of our cases shows that judicial review of a final agency action by an aggrieved person will not be cut off unless there is persuasive reason to believe that such was the purpose of Congress. . . . Early cases in which this type of judicial review was entertained . . . have been reinforced by the enactment of the Administrative Procedure Act. . . . The legislative material elucidating that seminal Act manifests a Congressional intention that it cover a broad spectrum of administrative actions, and this Court has echoed that theme by noting that the Administrative Procedure Act's "generous review provision" must be given a "hospitable" interpretation. *Shaughnessey v. Pedreiro*, 349 U.S. 48, 51 . . . . again in *Rusk v. Cort* [369 U.S. 367] at 379–380, the Court held that only upon a showing of "clear and convincing evidence" of a contrary legislative intent should the courts restrict access to judicial review.[57]

Since the Abbott case involved judicial review of administrative rules at the pre-enforcement state, before an actual case and controversy in the true judicial sense existed, a presumption of reviewability was somewhat unusual. The willingness of the

55. Such an extraordinary case is *Wolff v. Selective Service Local Board No. 16*, 372 F.2d 817 (2nd Cir. 1967). In this case, the Court of Appeals held that although the Selective Service Act made pre-induction classifications by local boards final, judicial review of pre-induction classifications made *ultra vires* the Selective Service Act were subject to judicial review. The Wolff case involved punitive reclassification of students from II-s (deferred) to I-A (immediately available for induction) because they had demonstrated against the Vietnam war at the offices of a Selective Service local board in Ann Arbor, Michigan.

56. 5 U.S.C.A., § 702, APA, § 10a.

57. *Abbot Laboratories v. Gardner*, 387 U.S. 136, at 137 (1967). For further discussion of the Abbott case see pp. 78–79, *supra*.

Supreme Court to allow judicial review of administrative rules that had not yet been enforced, in the absence of any specific statutory provision for such review, fortifies a strong presumption of reviewability.

Private parties can challenge agency action in the courts even though their specific legal rights may not be involved. Where the specific statutes that control agencies provide for judicial review to persons aggrieved or adversely affected by the agencies' decisions, the courts have adopted liberal rules granting standing to persons who challenge agency action as *private attorneys general* to vindicate the *public interest* rather than their specific legal rights. As early as 1940, in the case of *Federal Communications Commission v. Sanders Radio Station,* the Supreme Court held that although the Sanders Radio Station had no legal right to protection against economic competition, it nevertheless could challenge the granting of a license to a rival station in the same area because it was a proper party to represent the public interest.[58] The FCC is mandated by a statute to carry out the public interest, convenience, and necessity in the granting of broadcast licenses. Sanders Radio Station would have been financially affected if the FCC had allowed a competitor to operate in its territory. This gave to Sanders Radio Station a personal interest in the case and would give it the incentive to act as an effective private attorney general. The private attorney general's role is to point out agency errors of law and see to it that they are remedied either by the agency or in the courts.

In 1942, in *Scripps-Howard Radio, Inc. v. FCC,* the Supreme Court reaffirmed its policy of granting standing to parties acting as private attorneys general where the statute governing the agency allowed aggrieved or adversely affected parties to appeal.[59] In *Sierra Club v. Morton* (1972) the Supreme Court pointed out that the Sanders and Scripps-Howard cases "established a dual proposition: the fact of economic injury is what gives a person standing to seek judicial review under the statute, but once review is properly invoked, that person may argue the

58. 309 U.S. 470 (1940).
59. 316 U.S. 4 (1942).

public interest in support of his claim that the agency has failed to comply with its statutory mandate."[60]

Following the lead of the Supreme Court in the Sanders and Scripps-Howard cases, the United States Court of Appeals for the second circuit held in *Associated Industries of New York State, Inc. v. Ickes* (1943) that *consumers* of coal were "aggrieved persons" under the judicial review provisions of the Bituminous Coal Act of 1937.[61] Traditionally, only producers of coal would have the requisite substantive legal interest at stake to obtain judicial review. The court argued, however, that consumers were financially affected and that even though this was not a "substantive" legal right they are authorized to speak as private attorneys general. The Associated Industries case implied that in the absence of a specific statutory provision for judicial review for aggrieved persons, consumers would not have had standing under constitutional, statutory, or common law.[62] In the Associated Industries case, the Court continued to emphasize injury to economic interests as being the touchstone for granting standing to private attorneys general.

In response to civil rights and environmental activism, the 1960s witnessed an expansion of standing by the courts. In 1966, the District of Columbia Court of Appeals ruled that the Federal Communications Commission had to give standing to representatives of the listening audience that challenged the renewal of a Mississippi television license.[63] These "consumers," however, differed from those that had been given standing in such cases as Associated Industries, for they would not be economically affected by the FCC's action in granting or denying the application for a television license. Nevertheless, the court held that the listening audience did constitute consumers whose interests had to be taken into account in the FCC's deliberations.

60. 405 U.S. 727, at 737 (1972).

61. 134 F.2d 694 (2nd Cir. 1943). The Bituminous Coal Act provided that "any person aggrieved by an order issued by the Commission in a proceeding to which such person is a party" could seek judicial review in an appropriate Court of Appeals.

62. This conclusion was supported by the Supreme Court in *Joint Anti-Fascist Refugee Committee v. McGrath*, 341 U.S. 123 (1951).

63. *Office of Communication of United Church of Christ v. FCC*, 359 F.2d 994 (D.C. Cir. 1966).

The court did not hold that *all* representatives of the listening audience who had claimed an interest in the proceeding had to be given standing. But, the court held, "the Commission must allow standing to one or more of them as responsible representatives to assert and prove the claims they have urged in their petition."[64] Therefore, the Commission was required to give standing to at least one legitimate representative of the public interest.

By requiring the FCC to allow participation by private attorneys general in its proceedings, the court was rejecting the position of the Commission that it could effectively represent the public interest when acting by itself. This had been the original contention of the FCC in its denial of the petitions for intervention by the representatives of the listening public. The expansion of permissible intervenors in Commission proceedings, each of whom would have standing to challenge the FCC's action in court, had its effect. Although on remand to the Commission the challenged license was renewed, the newly legitimate intervenors challenged the action in court and succeeded in getting a reversal. A new licensee was selected that gave substantial representation to the interests of blacks in the listening area. The court's decision resulted in station licensees paying far more attention to the interests of minority groups and women, both in terms of hiring practices and in programming. Insufficient accommodation of these interests could lead to a court challenge of a license renewal.

The courts have expanded standing for environmental as well as minority interests. In *Scenic Hudson Preservation Conference v. FPC.* (1966), the Court of Appeals granted standing for judicial review to the Scenic Hudson Preservation Conference, which represented a number of non-profit conservationist organizations, in several towns that had special interests affected by the Federal Power Commission's grant of a license to Consolidated Edison Corporation to construct a hydroelectric power plant at Storm King Mountain in Cornwall, New York. The interests of the appellants, who had been parties to the proceeding before the FPC, were not exclusively economic. The FPC had

64. *Ibid.*, p. 1006.

claimed that the appellants did not have standing for judicial review because they did not make any claim of personal economic injury as a result of the Commission's decision. The court's opinion stated:

In order to insure that the Federal Power Commission will adequately protect the public interest in the aesthetic, conservational, and recreational aspects of power development, those who by their activities and conduct have exhibited a special interest in such areas, must be held to be included in the class of "aggrieved" parties under Section 313 (b) [Section 313 (b) of the Federal Power Act provides that "any party to a proceeding under this chapter aggrieved by an order issued by the Commission in such proceeding may obtain a review of such order."] We hold that the Federal Power Act gives petitioners a legal right to protect their special interest.[65]

Although the court stated that the Scenic Hudson Preservation Conference did have sufficient economic interests to allow standing because several of the conservation groups within the Conference owned seventeen miles of trails, some of which would be eliminated by the construction of a reservoir necessary for the project, the main emphasis in the case was on the special non-economic interests of the petitioners in the "aesthetic conservational and recreational aspects of power development" that provided the basis for standing. By granting standing to conservationist groups whether or not they had economic interests that would be affected by agency actions, the courts opened the door to widespread challenges of formal administrative decisions affecting the environment. Consolidated Edison did finally secure a license from the FPC, but persistent court challenges by environmental groups delayed the project so that it was still not completed a decade after the first challenge in the Scenic Hudson case in 1966.

The Scenic Hudson case was interpreted by both environmental groups and many appellate courts to grant standing to groups wishing to challenge administrative action where those groups had demonstrated a special interest in the subject mat-

---

65. *Scenic Hudson Preservation Conference v. FPC,* 354, F.2d 608, at 616 (2nd Cir. 1965), cert. denied 384 U.S. 941 (1966).

ter.[66] However, the Supreme Court in 1972, in *Sierra Club v. Morton*, put a stop to such a liberal interpretation of the requirements for standing to challenge administrative actions.[67] The Sierra Club, a long-established conservationist organization with a keen interest in environmental problems, filed a suit in June 1969, in the Federal District Court for the Northern District of California seeking a declaratory judgment and injunction to prevent the Forest Service within the Interior Department from approving a recreational development of Walt Disney Enterprises in the Mineral King Valley, adjacent to the Sequoia National Park in California. The final Disney plan had been approved by the Forest Service in January, 1969. The Sierra Club sued under the judicial review provisions of the Administrative Procedure Act, claiming "a special interest in the conservation and sound maintenance of the National Parks, Game Refuges, and Forests of the country."[68] The District Court granted the preliminary injunction, but this was reversed by the Court of Appeals on the basis that the Sierra Club's complaint contained no allegation that its members "would be affected by the actions of [the respondents] other than the fact that the actions are personally displeasing or distasteful to them."[69] The Supreme Court sustained the Court of Appeals, noting that:

the party seeking review must have himself suffered an injury.

. . . [A] mere "interest in a problem," no matter how long-standing the interest and no matter how qualified the organization is in evaluating the problem, is not sufficient by itself to render the organization "adversely affected" or "aggrieved" within the meaning of the APA.[70]

Those who seek judicial review under the Sierra Club case doctrine must have a direct stake in the outcome of the proceedings. The Court made it clear that organizations and individuals should not be able to "vindicate their own value

66. See, for example, *Citizens' Committee for the Hudson Valley v. Volpe*, 425 F.2d 97 (2nd Cir. 1970).

67. *Sierra Club v. Morton*, 405 U.S. 727 (1972).

68. *Ibid.*, p. 727.

69. 433 F.2d 24, at 33 (9th Cir. 1970).

70. *Sierra Club v. Morton*, 405 U.S. 727, at 740 (1972).

preferences through the judicial process."[71]

The Sierra case did not significantly tighten the requirements for standing. This was evident when, in 1973, the Supreme Court confronted the case of *United States v. Students Challenging Regulatory Agency Procedures.*[72] The Students Challenging Regulatory Agency Procedures (SCRAP) was a group of George Washington University Law students which, under the guidance of an imaginative professor, was putting its classroom knowledge of administrative law into practice by attempting to challenge what it considered to be undesirable actions of various regulatory agencies. The group had challenged a decision of the Interstate Commerce Commission in 1972 that permitted the nation's railroads to impose a freight surcharge of 2.5 per cent on almost all freight rates for a seven-month period pending action by the Commission on carrier petitions for permanent increases in freight charges. SCRAP's complaint alleged that the ICC orders would affect the environment by discouraging the shipment of recyclable goods, which would now be more expensive to transport. The students alleged that the ICC action would reduce the use of recyclable goods, which would have the effect of causing more refuse to be discarded in national parks in the Washington area, which they used. Moreover, the reduction in the use of recyclable products would require increased use of raw materials that would result in destruction of timber and unnecessary extraction of raw materials, all of which would have a profound impact on the environment and directly and indirectly on the members of SCRAP. The group alleged that before the ICC could take such action, it must issue an environmental-impact statement under the terms of the

71. *Ibid.*, p. 741. The dissenters in the Sierra Club case were Justices Douglas, Brennan, and Blackmun. Justice Douglas wrote the most interesting dissent, claiming, in effect, that persons who understand the values represented by trees and other natural objects should be able to represent them in court. He noted "contemporary public concern for protecting nature's ecological equilibrium should lead to the conferral of standing upon environmental objects to sue for their own preservation. See Stone, "Should Trees have Standing? Toward Legal Rights for Natural Objects," 45 S. Cal. L. Rev. 450 (1952). This suit would therefore be more properly labeled as Mineral King v. Morton."

72. 412 U.S. 669 (1973).

National Environmental Policy Act of 1969.[73]

The student members of SCRAP had learned their lesson from the Sierra case and were very careful to allege that the challenged administrative action caused them personal harm. The Supreme Court upheld their right to standing, stating that they were adversely affected and aggrieved within the meaning of section 10 of the Administrative Procedure Act, which they had cited to obtain review. The students resided in the Washington area, and claimed that they used the National Parks there. The ICC's action might result in more refuse in those parks and in the depletion of some raw material resources and timber in the Washington area; this very possibly might harm the members of SCRAP. On this basis, standing to challenge the agencies' action must be granted. The SCRAP case reaffirmed the principle that economic harm does not have to be demonstrated to challenge administrative decisions. Moreover, the court's decision liberally interpreted section 10 of the Administrative Procedure Act to grant standing to those adversely affected and aggrieved by agency action. At the time the court adopted a liberal view of standing, it was careful to exercise judicial self-restraint on the procedural basis that the courts lacked jurisdiction to enjoin preliminary ICC action on rates.

The case of *United States v. SCRAP* illustrates that liberalizing the requirements for standing does not necessarily result in greater judicial control of administrative action. Once allowing standing, the courts may nevertheless be reluctant to overrule an administrative decision on the merits. Judicial claims of lack of jurisdiction or inexpertise in administrative matters are typical modes of judicial self-restraint. Moreover, the courts over the years have adopted a number of doctrines to limit access to judicial review of administrative actions. Many of these are absolutely necessary if the courts are not to be overburdened and administrative agencies are to be permitted to act effectively within the boundaries of their delegated authority. For example, the courts have adopted the doctrine of exhaustion of administrative remedies, which requires in almost all cases that a

73. 42 U.S.C., § 4332 (2) (c). SCRAP alleged that its members "suffered economic, recreational and aesthetic harm directly as a result of the adverse environmental impact of the railroad freight structure" (412 U.S. 669, at 679 [1973]).

final agency action must be taken before judicial review can be obtained. This eliminates inappropriate and unnecessary judicial meddling in the affairs of the agencies at the preliminary stages of proceedings. Unless important procedural issues are involved that may affect the outcome of the proceedings, preliminary administrative actions are hypothetical in terms of their ultimate impact on private parties. Early judicial review may be entirely unnecessary.

While a judicial doctrine that requires a case to be "ripe" for judicial review before court intervention is both reasonable and practical, some judicial barriers to review seem overly protective of the bureaucracy. This is true, for example, of the doctrine of sovereign immunity, which holds that the sovereign cannot be sued without its consent. An ancient principle of Anglo-American jurisprudence is that "the sovereign can do no wrong." The government must be permitted to take those actions necessary to sustain itself, and unless it allows itself to be sued, such actions cannot be challenged. These untouchable areas involve government protection of its property, control over the public treasury, and the maintenance of effective public administration. Private actions impeding the government in these areas cannot be sustained under the doctrine of sovereign immunity without governmental consent unless it can be shown that the government or its agents have acted unconstitutionally or beyond their statutory authority. The doctrine of sovereign immunity has protected agents of the government from private suits for damages because of improper acts.[74] And, it has prevented suits against the government for ejectment from lands claimed to be public and suits alleging improper and illegal distribution of public assets.[75]

74. See *Gregoire v. Biddle*, 177 F.2d 579 (2nd Cir. 1949), cert. denied 339 U.S. 949 (1950); *Bivens v. Six Unknown Named Agents of the Federal Bureau of Narcotics*, 403 U.S. 388 (1971). The Bivens case reflected a change in the doctrine of sovereign immunity because it did not grant immunity to narcotics agents involved in an early-morning raid without a warrant upon a private apartment. But the court did allow the agents to defend themselves successfully simply by alleging that they acted in good faith and with a reasonable belief in the validity and necessity of the arrest and search.

75. See respectively *Malone v. Bowdoin*, 369 U.S. 643 (1962); *Larson v. Domestic and Foreign Commerce Corporation*, 337 U.S. 682 (1949).

Judicial review of administrative action remains limited. The extraordinary volume and scope of administrative decisions simply cannot be subject to judicial scrutiny. Judicial review is usually confined to the formal orders of administrative agencies, which not only exclude the vast informal administrative process but also most administrative rule-making from court challenges. Perhaps the greatest limitation of all on judicial review is the time and expense involved, which limits access to the courts for the most part to organized groups. While consumer- and public-interest-oriented groups have helped to represent the broader public in administrative proceedings and in the courts, judicial review is inaccessible to the average individual. The courts have not, and probably cannot, provide an effective check upon the growing power of the bureaucracy.

CHAPTER 4   The Bureaucracy and Congress

ARTICLE I, section 1 of the Constitution states that "all legislative powers herein granted shall be vested in a Congress of the United States, which shall consist of a Senate and House of Representatives." Section 8 enumerates congressional powers and provides that Congress shall have all powers "necessary and proper" to implement them. These provisions are used to justify the establishment of administrative agencies, which become in effect instruments of congressional policy. Congress, however, is supposed to control the agencies it creates, for the Constitution clearly indicates that primary legislative power is to reside in the Senate and the House of Representatives. In Chapter 2 the outlines of congressional-administrative interaction were suggested; particular emphasis was placed on the reasons behind the decisions of Congress to create agencies and delegate substantial authority to them. The purpose of this chapter is to consider congressional-administrative interaction in more precise detail. Four areas of political concern will be assessed. First, the constitutional problem of delegation of legislative power to administrative agencies directly or through the President; second, the role of the bureaucracy in the exercise of functions that were to reside in the legislature; third, the way in which the bureaucracy directly influences Congress in the legislative process through lobbying and propaganda; fourth, the implications of the legislative activities of administrative agencies in terms of the American constitutional system.

The Delegation of Legislative Power

In Chapter 3 the nature of judicial review of administrative decisions was discussed, and it was pointed out that for the most part the courts have retreated from exercising meaningful review through the adoption of doctrines that permit wide administrative discretion. In no area is this more apparent than in the delegation of legislative power by Congress. The general nature of most congressional bills that govern the implementation of regulatory and other programs by administrative agencies has been noted. The question posed here is exactly how broad can such congressional delegation be and still conform to constitutional standards? In analyzing this question it is necessary to turn to judicial interpretation of the Constitution regarding the delegation of power.

THE CONSTITUTIONAL PROBLEM

The nature of the constitutional problem can be explained briefly. First, primary legislative power is supposed to reside in Congress under Article I. What constitutes "primary" legislative power in a particular policy area requires interpretation of the Constitution, and therefore becomes the responsibility of the judiciary. Congress can not by itself determine the kinds of delegations it may make because the over-all determination involves constitutional criteria; since *Marbury v. Madison* (1803) this has been considered the province of the courts. If Congress does not set limits to the legislative power it delegates to the agencies or the President, the courts may declare such statutes unconstitutional and thus null and void. The only notable cases in which this was done occurred during the New Deal period. Since the beginning of World War II every instance of congressional delegation of legislative power to the President or the administrative branch has been upheld.

The central position of the judiciary in formulating standards for the delegation of legislative powers means that decisions can only be made if a case and controversy exists.[1] Any discussion of legal and constitutional doctrine centers upon specific instances of administrative adjudication or rule-making that subsequently reach the courts. The private party wishing to challenge a particular congressional delegation must first be involved in a reviewable case before the agency to which the delegation has

1. *Muskrat v. United States*, 219 U.S. 346 (1911); *United Public Workers v. Mitchell*, 330 U.S. 75 (1947).

been made. The judiciary will not render advisory opinions on the validity of general administrative policy decisions. When such policy is implemented in a specific case affecting the rights and obligations of private or governmental parties the situation ceases to be advisory. Upon appeal the case may be reviewed by the judiciary.

As a result of the case and controversy requirement for judicial action, the question of delegation of legislative power is narrowed in two directions. First, although legislation is implemented through adjudication and rule-making, many instances of administrative action in these areas are not subject to judicial review. What may be a case and controversy in the general sense may not conform to judicial criteria. Other problems, such as time, expense, and administrative sanctions may prevent review. The difficulty of obtaining review means that the validity of congressional delegations is not automatically raised in the courts. Second, the courts will usually not review *substantive* policy issues except as they relate to questions of legal and constitutional *procedure*. Thus, problems concerning the delegation of legislative power do not involve as a general rule what policies Congress has adopted, but whether or not the policies have been stated clearly enough so that the agencies implementing them and the courts upon review can ascertain congressional intent, and whether the *procedures* Congress has authorized the agencies to employ conform to constitutional standards.[2] Insofar as Congress is concerned, the essential problem of delegation of powers involves the need for congressional retention of control over policy formulation. Primary concern must be focused upon the delegation of legislative power rather than judicial power, except as the latter forms an integral part of the regulatory function.

Theoretically the courts require in the delegation of legislative power that the intent of Congress be stated clearly enough so that *ultra vires* action can be prohibited. That is, if an agency exercising delegated power attempts to act beyond the power conferred upon it by statute the courts must be able to prevent it. The statute in question must, therefore, indicate what Congress

2. See, for example, *Kent v. Dulles,* 357 U.S. 116 (1958).

wants the agency to do in clear terms so that upon review of a particular administrative action the courts may be able to say either: "This is permitted by Congress"; or "This action is outside the scope of authority granted by Congress." In this way primary legislative power theoretically remains in Congress. If a constitutional question is involved, the courts can determine *ultra vires* action regardless of statutory language. If a statute is unclear as to the procedural policy to be followed by an agency, and if the agency adopts a procedure which the courts subsequently find to be unconstitutional, the courts will not hold the statute unconstitutional but only the particular agency action. In such a situation the courts will tend to say upon review that they must interpret the intent of Congress to include constitutional procedure where statutory language is vague, otherwise the statute itself is unconstitutional by definition.[3]

Prior to the New Deal period various congressional delegations of power were unsuccessfully attacked as unconstitutional, particularly questions relating to tariffs. It was the practice of Congress to delegate the power to raise or lower tariffs on certain commodities to the President, and in some instances to administrative officials, provided certain conditions existed. For example, the Tariff Act of 1890 gave the President the power to suspend the free introduction of "sugar, molasses, coffee, tea and hides" into the United States if he found that countries producing and exporting these commodities were levying "reciprocally unequal and unreasonable" duties on agricultural or other products from the United States. After such a presidential suspension of free trade in these commodities, certain duties specified by Congress were to go into effect automatically. In 1892 the Supreme Court upheld this delegation of power in stating that "legislative power was exercised when Congress declared that the suspension should take effect upon a named contingency. What the President was required to do was simply in execution of the act of Congress. *It was not the making of law.* He was the mere agent of the lawmaking department to ascertain and declare the event upon which its expressed will was to take effect."[4] This was, in fact, a rather narrow delegation in view of what was to come.

3. *Ibid.*
4. *Field v. Clark*, 143 U.S. 649, at 693 (1892). Italics added.

The Tariff Act of 1922 gave the President far broader discretion than previous legislation to adjust tariffs whenever he found differences in production costs between the United States and competing foreign countries. Needless to say the Act did in fact give him law making power; however the Supreme Court, recognizing the need for such presidential power, found that this was not an unconstitutional delegation.[5] Since the New Deal, Congress has virtually abdicated its legislative power in the tariff field and given the President and the Tariff Commission the primary responsibility in the establishment of tariffs. The passage of the Trade Expansion Act of 1962 represented a major increase in presidential discretion in this area, not only in relation to Congress but also with respect to the Tariff Commission. Thus for a long period of time Congress has not chosen to exercise effective law making power in the tariff field, although by means of cumbersome procedure it has a veto power. The tariff field is typical of many, and illustrates the complete change that has taken place since the framing of the Constitution between the President and the administrative branch on the one hand, and Congress on the other. The former in combination initiate most legislation, while the latter may veto. A congressional veto, however, is far more difficult to achieve than a presidential veto, for Congess can not for the most part act as a cohesive unit.

UNCONSTITUTIONAL DELEGATIONS OF POWER

The only cases in which the Supreme Court held congressional statutes unconstitutional on the basis of undue delegation of legislative power occurred during the New Deal. The fact that the Court was openly hostile to President Roosevelt's political goals has caused some observers to feel that the Court often acted from political bias when it ruled much of the New Deal legislation unconstitutional. This point of view is supported by the extraordinary delegations that occurred after the 1937 attempt by Roosevelt to "pack" the court.

The New Deal legislation which delegated too much legislative power was the famous, and perhaps notorious, National Industrial

5. *J. W. Hampton, Jr. & Co. v. United States*, 276 U.S. 394 (1928).

Recovery Act of 1933. Section I contained a congressional "declaration of policy," couched in vague terminology, that declared
a national emergency to exist and stated that it was the policy
of Congress to increase the flow and amount of interstate and
foreign commerce through various devices, including greater
cooperation among groups within particular industries. The Act
then went on to delegate the power to implement its vague policy
standards to the President and subordinate agencies or officials
designated by him. Section III gave him virtually complete discretion to establish codes of fair competition within industries if
he felt them to be warranted by prevailing economic conditions.
There was really no check upon his power in this respect, for
the policy directives of Congress were worded so that they could
be interpreted almost in any way. The Act was designed to benefit business interests by allowing them to eliminate wasteful
competitive practices and cutthroat competition and, in the
petroleum industry, by restricting over-production. Businessmen were not unanimous in support of the Act, however, and
some firms sought relief in the courts from presidential and
agency action that had been taken under the Act's authority.
In 1935, the Supreme Court struck down a section of the Act for
unconstitutional delegation of legislative power in *Panama Refining Co. v. Ryan;*[6] later that year, in the historic case of
Schechter Poultry Corp. v. United States, it declared the entire
Act unconstitutional on the same basis.[7] In the latter decision the
Court examined the provisions of the Act in detail and unanimously found that

. . . Section 3 of the Recovery Act is without precedent. It supplies
no standards for any trade, industry or activity. It does not undertake
to prescribe rules of conduct to be applied to particular states of fact
determined by appropriate administrative procedure. Instead of prescribing rules of conduct, it authorizes the making of codes to prescribe them. For that legislative undertaking, section 3 sets up no
standards, aside from the statement of the general aims of rehabilita-
tion, correction and expansion described in section one. In view of the
scope of that broad declaration, and of the nature of the few restrictions that are imposed, the discretion of the President in approving

6. 293 U.S. 388 (1935).
7. 295 U.S. 495 (1935).

or prescribing codes, and thus enacting laws for the government of trade and industry throughout the country, is virtually unfettered. We think that the code-making authority thus conferred is an unconstitutional delegation of power. . . .[8]

The scope of this Act was too much even for those on the Court sympathetic to the purposes of the New Deal and willing to allow flexible congressional delegations.

In what respect does the delegation of legislative power in the National Industrial Recovery Act of 1933 differ from previous and subsequent delegations, all of which have been held constitutional? In some respects the delegation held unconstitutional in *Schechter* was actually broader and more unlimited than that found in most subsequent and previous congressional statutes. This idea is best supported by the concurring opinion of Justice Cardozo in the *Schechter* case. He had previously disagreed with the majority of the Court in the *Panama* case; he found in the section of the Recovery Act in question adequate standards expressed by Congress to support the delegation of power that had been made to the President.[9] He supported the idea of flexible criteria as adequate to justify the delegation of legislative power; however, with respect to Section III of the Recovery Act and the powers it conferred he noted:

. . . Here . . . is an attempted delegation not confined to any single act nor to any class or group of acts identified or described by reference to a standard. Here in effect is a roving commission to inquire into evils and upon discovery correct them.

I have said that there is no standard, definite or even approximate, to which legislation must conform. Let me make my meaning more precise. If codes of fair competition are codes eliminating "unfair" methods of competition ascertained upon inquiry to prevail in one industry or another, there is no unlawful delegation of legislative functions when the President is directed to inquire into such practices and denounce them when discovered. For many years a like power has been committed to the Federal Trade Commission with the approval of this court in a long series of decisions . . . . Delegation in such circumstances is born of the necessities of the occasion. The industries of the country are too many and diverse to make it

8. *Ibid.*, pp. 541–542.
9. 293 U.S. 388, at 434–435 (1935).

possible for Congress, in respect of matters such as these, to legislate directly with adequate appreciation of varying conditions. . . .

But there is another conception of codes of fair competition . . . [by which] a code is not to be restricted to the elimination of business practices that would be characterized by general acceptance as oppressive or unfair. It is to include whatever ordinances may be desirable or helpful for the well-being or prosperity of the industry affected. In that view, the function of its adoption is not merely negative, but positive; the planning of improvements as well as the extirpation of abuses. What is fair, as thus conceived, is not something to be contrasted with what is unfair or fraudulent or tricky. The extension becomes as wide as the field of industrial regulation. If that conception shall prevail, anything that Congress may do within the limits of the commerce clause for the betterment of business may be done by the President upon the recommendation of a trade association [or through independent presidential action] by calling it a code. This is delegation running riot. No such plenitude of power is susceptible of transfer. The statute, however, aims at nothing less, as one can learn both from its terms and from the administrative practice under it. . . .[10]

To Cardozo the Recovery Act meant a virtual abdication of congressional power in the economic sphere.

THE SCOPE OF DELEGATED POWER SINCE THE NEW DEAL

Since the New Deal extraordinary delegations have taken place, particularly during the World War II era; however, relative to the kind of delegation that Congress attempted in the Recovery Act of 1933, these later delegations have been limited in several respects. In general, the scope of administrative power is curtailed in congressional delegation. Standards of delegation are often vague and result in a great deal of administrative discretion, but usually the area of discretion has boundaries, which is the first limiting factor. Agencies cannot rove about from one field to another and prescribe legislation wherever it is considered to be necessary. For example, the Interstate Commerce Commission is limited to the rail, trucking, and certain aspects of the shipping industries; the Federal Communications Commission is limited to the radio, television, telegraph and telephone industries. Most

10. 295 U.S. 495, at 551–553 (1935).

other regulatory and nonregulatory agencies have reasonably definite jurisdictions.

An additional restraint results from the fact that it is quite common for the agencies themselves to prescribe standards that are self-limiting. If an agency takes action that violates its own standards a court upon review quite likely will invalidate the action and remand the case to the agency. In this respect the courts have taken the position that it is not always necessary for Congress to set forth in detail standards to guide administrative agencies in exercising delegated power, but that it is important for such standards to emanate from some source—usually the agencies themselves.[11] The theory behind this requirement is that as long as criteria exist governing agency activity the bureaucracy will be limited. The problem is, however, that Congress is not the primary source of limitation; thus, the theory that Congress must retain primary legislative power has been substantially altered in practice with the growth of bureaucracy. To a considerable extent the delegation of power doctrine requiring a clear statement of legislative intent has shifted to require simply that administrative action be limited in some way through the establishment of standards which may or may not be congressional in origin.

A virtual abdication of congressional power to the President and the administrative branch was brought about by World War II. Extraordinary delegations were made and upheld by the courts, and it was during this period that the substitution of administrative for congressional standards was allowed. For example, the Emergency Price Control Act of 1942 authorized a Price Administrator, who was to be head of the Office of Price Administration (OPA), to fix prices for commodities, rents, and services which "in his judgment will be generally fair and equitable and will effectuate the purposes of this Act." The purposes of the Act were "to stabilize prices and to prevent speculative, unwarranted, and abnormal increases in prices and rents. . . ." The Administrator was "so far as practicable" to consult with representatives of the industries and to "give due consideration

11. See Henry J. Friendly, *The Federal Administrative Agencies* (Cambridge: Harvard University Press, 1962) for a detailed consideration of the importance of administrative standards.

to the prices prevailing between October 1 and October 15, 1941." In 1944 the Supreme Court upheld this delegation of power in *Yakus v. United States* with the statement that

it is for Congress to say whether the data on the basis of which prices are to be fixed are to be confined within a narrow or a broad range. In either case the only concern of courts is to ascertain whether the will of Congress has been obeyed. This depends not upon the breadth of the definition of the facts or conditions which the administrative officer is to find but upon the determination whether the definition sufficiently *marks the field* within which the Administrator is to act so that it may be known whether he has kept within it in compliance with the legislative will.[12]

Further,

the standards prescribed by the present Act, *with the aid of* the 'statement of considerations' required to be made by the Administrator, are sufficiently definite and precise to enable Congress, the courts and the public to ascertain whether the Administrator, in fixing the designated prices, has conformed to those standards.[13]

Justice Roberts dissented in *Yakus,* objecting to what he considered an unconstitutional delegation of legislative power. Roberts stated that in his opinion *Yakus* clearly overruled *Schechter,* and that in fact there was little difference in the extent of delegation that took place under the statutes involved in these cases. Although an argument can be made for this point of view, it is probably more correct to say that relative to the Recovery Act, the Emergency Price Control Act of 1942 represented a narrower delegation of congressional power. In the Recovery Act the ability of the President, or an administrator designated by him, to effect "codes of fair competition" encompassed virtually any action that could be taken. It authorized price setting and general control of labor relations and business practices. The Emergency Price Control Act was limited to price setting; hence the field of administrative jurisdiction as well as the specific powers that could be exercised by the OPA were designated. Within this field the OPA possessed what amounted to virtually total discretion, but in this respect it is similar to many administrative agencies.

12. *Yakus v. United States,* 321 U.S. 414, 425 (1944). Italics added.
13. *Ibid.,* p. 426. Italics added.

In addition to the Emergency Price Control Act of 1942, other World War II statutes were challenged as being unconstitutional delegations of legislative power, but in every instance they were upheld in the Supreme Court.[14] Similarly, most of the delegations of power made by Congress to the various regulatory agencies have been challenged and upheld consistently by the judiciary.[15] Where does this leave us today? Does it mean that any transference of power from Congress to the bureaucracy will not meet constitutional or legal obstacles? In general terms, this conclusion is accurate. The necessity of broad administrative discretion in the legislative area is recognized. There is simply no other way to conduct the business of government given its present scope and complexity. Although many congressmen consider the agencies to be "agents of Congress" when they exercise legislative functions, the vagueness of statutory terminology, the leniency and limitations of the courts in controlling standards of delegation, and the political difficulties Congress faces in attempting to control the agencies once they have been given legislative and other powers, all indicate administrative domination of the legislative sphere.

In addition to the regulatory statutes, delegation from Congress to non-regulatory agencies is equally broad; a typical example may be found in the legislation governing the Defense Department. Congress has authorized the Secretary of the Army to:

. . . procure materials and facilities necessary to maintain and support the Army, its military organizations, and their installations and supporting and auxiliary elements, including:

(1) guided missiles;
(2) modern standard items of equipment;
(3) equipment to replace obsolete or unserviceable equipment;
(4) necessary spare equipment, materials, and parts; and
(5) such reserve of supplies as is needed to enable the Army to perform its mission.[16]

14. For an example of virtually uncontrolled delegation of legislative power during the war see *Lichter v. United States*, 334 U.S. 742 (1948).

15. For examples see *ICC v. Brimson*, 154 U.S. 447 (1894); *New York Central Securities Corp. v. United States*, 287 U.S. 12 (1932); *Federal Radio Commission v. General Electric*, 281 U.S. 464 (1930).

16. 10 U.S.C. 4531. 70A Stat. 253 (1956).

The Secretary of the Air Force is directed to purchase necessary aircraft or airframe tons to maintain superiority in the air; this essentially constitutes congressional intent as it is stated in the relevant statutes. The Secretary of the Navy has equally broad discretion; all three Secretaries are now subordinate to the Secretary of Defense. The same kind of congressional delegation is common outside the realm of defense policy; it would be called extraordinary except for the fact that it has become the rule rather than the exception.

Although the Schechter rule of non-delegability of legislative authority has not prevailed, its ghost still haunts the courts and is occasionally brought to life in the arguments of private plaintiffs seeking redress from government action and in dissenting opinions. For example, in *Arizona v. California* (1963), the issue was raised regarding the permissible extent of the authority of the Secretary of the Interior in allocating the waters of the Colorado River among seven western states under the terms of the Boulder Canyon Project Act of 1928.[17] The Act did contain vague guidelines that the Secretary was to follow in allocating the waters, and limited the amount of water that he could allocate each year. However, these standards alone did not meaningfully limit the Secretary's authority. Under the Act, the Secretary was authorized to construct a dam in order to create a storage reservoir. In allocating waters from the dam, he was to follow an order of legislative priorities

first, for river regulation, improvement of navigation, and flood control; second, for irrigation and domestic uses and satisfaction of present perfected rights [to use the waters of the Colorado River] . . . ; and third, for power.[18]

The majority of the Court found that these standards, in conjunction with other guidelines and limits stated in the Act, were sufficient to justify giving power to the Secretary of the Interior over the Colorado River waters: "We are satisfied that the Secretary's power must be construed to permit him, within the boundaries set down in the Act, to allocate and distribute the waters of the main stream of the Colorado River."[19]

17. 373 U.S. 546 (1963).
18. 45 Stat. 1057, § 6 (1928).
19. 373 U.S. 546, at 590 (1963).

Justice Harlan, joined by Justices Douglas and Stewart, dissented vigorously from this part of the majority's opinion. Justice Harlan granted that the "present perfected rights" standard did guarantee California a certain share of the Colorado River waters, and the Act did provide a ceiling for water that could be allocated to California. Beyond these limits, Justice Harlan found no adequate guidelines in the statute to justify granting the Secretary of the Interior such broad authority to allocate the Colorado River waters:

But what of that wide area between these two outer limits? Here, when we look for the standards defining the Secretary's authority, we find nothing. Under the court's construction of the Act, in other words, Congress has made a gift to the Secretary of almost one million five hundred thousand acre feet of water a year, to allocate virtually as he pleases in the event of any shortage preventing the fulfillment of all of his delivery commitments.
    The delegation of such unrestrained authority to an executive official raises, to say the least, the gravest constitutional doubts. See . . . *Schechter Poultry Corp. v. United States*, . . . *Panama Ref. Co. v. Ryan*, . . . *Youngstown Sheet and Tube Co., v. Sawyer*. . . . The principle that authority granted by the legislature must be limited by adequate standards serves two primary functions vital to preserving the separation of powers required by the Constitution. *First*, it ensures that the fundamental policy decisions in our society will be made not by an appointed official but by the body immediately responsible to the people. *Second*, it prevents judicial review from becoming merely an exercise-at-large by providing the courts with some measure against which to judge the official action that has been challenged."[20]

The Schechter rule remained in the minority in *Zemel v. Rusk*, decided by the Supreme Court in 1965.[21] The Department of State had denied a citizen's request to have his passport validated to travel to Cuba as a tourist. The citizen then instituted a suit against the Secretary of State and the Attorney General, seeking a judgment that he was entitled under the Constitution and the laws of the country to travel to Cuba and, *inter alia*, that the 1926 Passport Act unconstitutionally delegated legislative authority to the President and the Secretary of State. The Act provided that "the Secretary of State may grant and issue

20. *Ibid.*, pp. 625–626.
21. 381 U.S. 1 (1965).

passports, and cause passports to be granted, issued, and verified in foreign countries . . . under such rules as the President shall designate and prescribe."[22] Chief Justice Earl Warren wrote the opinion for the Court's majority of six, and in regard to the issue of delegation of legislative authority he noted the broad nature of the delegation but dismissed the argument that it was unconstitutional on the basis that the executive must have more discretionary authority in foreign than in domestic affairs.[23] Justice Black strongly dissented on this point, stating:

quite obviously, the government does not exaggerate in saying that this act "does not provide any specific standards for the Secretary" and "delegates to the President and Secretary a general discretionary power over passports"—a power so broad, in fact, as to be marked by no bounds except an unlimited discretion. It is plain therefore that Congress had not itself passed a law regulating passports; it has merely referred the matter to the Secretary of State and the President in words that say in effect, "We delegate to you our constitutional power to make such laws regulating passports as you see fit." . . . For Congress to attempt to delegate such an undefined law-making power to the Secretary, the President or both, makes applicable to this 1926 Act what Mr. Justice Cardozo said about the National Industrial Recovery Act: "This is delegation running riot. No such plentitude of power is susceptible of transfer." . . . *Schechter Poultry Corp. v. United States,* . . . *Panama Refining Co. v. Ryan.* . . .

Our Constitution has ordained that laws restricting the liberty of our people can be enacted by the Congress and by the Congress only. I do not think our Constitution intended that this vital legislative function could be farmed out in large blocs to any governmental official, whoever he might be, or to any governmental department and/or bureau, whatever administrative expertise it might be thought to have.[24]

Justice Black clearly implied that he would limit the Schechter rule to laws affecting civil liberties and civil rights, and would not apply it broadly to the economic realm as the New Deal Court had done.

In 1967, the Schechter rule was again resurrected by Justice

22. 44 Stat. 887, 22 U.S.C. § 211a (1958 ed.).

23. The key case cited by Warren for precedent was *United States v. Curtiss Wright Corp.,* 299 U.S. 304 (1936).

24. 381 U.S. 1, at 21–22 (1965).

Brennan in a concurring opinion in *United States v. Robel*. The case concerned a section of the Subversive Activities Control Act of 1950, which provided that a member of a group that the Board had designated to be a "Communist action organization" could not engage in any employment in any defense facility. While the majority of the Court held that this section of the Act was an unconstitutional abridgement of the First Amendment right of association, Justice Brennan held that the unconstitutionality came from congressional vagueness in delegating authority to the executive. Recognizing the necessity for broad delegation, Justice Brennan nevertheless held that in this case, fundamental liberties were at stake, requiring stringent congressional control of administrative action. He noted that "the numerous deficiencies connected with vague legislative directives . . . are far more serious when liberty and the exercise of fundamental rights are at stake."[25] The implication was explicit that the Schechter rule should apply primarily where civil liberties and civil rights are at stake. Justice Brennan noted that "Congress *ordinarily* may delegate power under broad standards. . . . No other general rule would be feasible or desirable. Delegation of power under general directives is an inevitable consequence of our complex society, with its myriad, ever-changing, highly technical problems."[26] The area of civil liberties and civil rights, however, is not ordinary.

Another surfacing of a Schechter plea occurred before a three-judge District Court in the District of Columbia in 1971.[27] The Economic Stabilization Act of 1970 was challenged as an unconstitutional delegation of legislative authority because of lack of guiding standards for the executive. The Act authorized the President to issue orders and regulations that he deemed "appropriate to stabilize prices, rents, wages, and salaries at levels not less than those prevailing on May 25, 1970. Such orders and regulations may provide for the making of such adjustments as may be necessary to prevent gross inequities." In August, 1971,

25. 389 U.S. 258, at 275 (1967).
26. *Ibid.*, p. 274.
27. *Amalgamated Meat Cutters and Butcher Workmen v. Connally*, 337 F. Supp. 737 (D.D.C. 1971).

the President issued an Executive Order stabilizing prices, rents, wages, and salaries for a ninety-day period at levels that were not to exceed those prevailing during the thirty-day period ending August 14, 1971. The Cost of Living Council was created to administer the stabilization program. Challenged as a grant of "unbridled legislative power" to the President, the Act was sustained, with the three-judge Court choosing to use the Yakus precedent rather than the now more radical Schechter decision. The Court noted in particular the Act's requirement for administrative standards to be developed if wage and price controls were to be continued by the President. Such administrative standards, the Court held, were an adequate substitute for the lack of explicit congressional guidelines. The Court found that the Act, considered in light of historical precedents, supported the ninety-day freeze. Any subsequent administrative action would be limited by judicial review that would take into account explicit administrative standards and the general guidelines of the statute.

It is possible to conclude that there are no constitutional or legal restrictions that have impeded in any substantial way the trend toward greater delegation. This situation has not, of course, resulted from administrative usurpation, but from congressional desire. It is a necessary attribute of the modern democratic state.

The Bureaucracy and Legislation

Normally, the legislative process is thought of in terms of Congress and congressional committees, the President, and political parties. The bureaucracy is always considered a factor in legislative formulation, but more often than not it is felt to be appropriately placed in the background. This is because the idea of a neutral civil service under the control of both the President and Congress is generally accepted. The fact, already suggested, that the administrative branch is neither neutral nor controlled in any substantial way can now be elaborated.

ADMINISTRATIVE RULE MAKING

Administrative agencies were in many instances created both to formulate legislation through rule making and to recommend legislative proposals to Congress. Rule making involves filling in the details of congressional enactments, which administrative agencies are generally empowered to do on their own initiative. The actual volume of rule making, which governs the day-to-day activities of groups subject to government regulation, far exceeds the business of Congress and constitutes in many areas the life-blood of the legislative process. The resurgence of Congress following Watergate, which caused it to flex its muscles not only toward the Presidency but also toward the bureaucracy, led to numerous proposals in 1976 to establish a legislative veto either by a single House of Congress or by concurrent resolution of administrative rules. The legislative-veto provision has been used in many legislative enactments in the past, but has been largely ineffective because of the lack of congressional incentives to become involved in the day-to-day activities of the bureaucracy. The extraordinary interest of the 94th Congress (1975–1976) in controlling administrative rule-making reflected a recognition that the bureaucracy had indeed become a dominant force in the legislative process.

A few examples should serve to indicate the importance of rule making by the bureaucracy. The Federal Trade Commission Act of 1914 states (§ 5) that "unfair methods of competition in commerce, and unfair or deceptive acts or practices in commerce, are hereby declared unlawful." Further, the Act provides that the "Commission is hereby empowered and directed to prevent persons, partnerships, or corporations . . . from using unfair methods of competition in commerce and unfair or deceptive acts or practices in commerce." What is an "unfair" method of competition? Congress does not say in the Federal Trade Commission Act, nor do other acts shed much light on the subject. The Clayton Act, for example, contains more detailed provisions but the wording is such that the Federal Trade Commission, charged with the administration of this Act along with other agencies, still possesses virtually complete discretion in formulating rules under it. The last chapter pointed out the ways agencies differ in their interpretation of the anti-trust laws (the *El Paso Natural Gas* case), a situation which follows from the failure of Congress to lay down specific rules in most regulatory fields.

Although the Clayton Act was to be a more precise indication of congressional policy in the anti-trust field than the Sherman

Act or the Federal Trade Commission Act, it was couched in language that was anything but clear, a passage from Section 2 will illustrate:

. . . [I]t shall be unlawful for any person engaged in commerce, in the course of such commerce, either directly or indirectly, to discriminate in price between different purchasers of commodities of like grade and quality, where either or any of the purchases involved in such discrimination are in commerce, where such commodities are sold for use, consumption, or resale within the United States or any Territory thereof or the District of Columbia or any insular possession or other place under the jurisdiction of the United States, and where the effect of such discrimination may be substantially to lessen competition or tend to create a monopoly in any line of commerce, or to injure, destroy, or prevent competition with any person who either grants or knowingly receives the benefit of such discrimination, or with customers of either of them: *Provided,* that nothing herein contained shall prevent differentials which make only due allowance for differences in the cost of manufacture, sale, or delivery resulting from the differing methods or quantities in which such commodities are to such purchasers sold or delivered: *Provided however,* that the Federal Trade Commission may, after due investigation and hearing to all interested parties, fix and establish quantity limits, and revise the same as it finds necessary, as to particular commodities or classes of commodities, where it finds that available purchasers in greater quantities are so few as to render differentials on account thereof unjustly discriminatory or promotive of monopoly in any line of commerce; and the foregoing shall then not be construed to permit differentials based on differences in quantities greater than those so fixed and established. . . .

This statute is not cited to confuse but to illuminate. It may look fairly precise on the surface; however, more careful observation reveals that the entire effect of this section depends upon *administrative interpretation* of imprecise and vague terminology. After initial agency interpretation of such words as "discriminate," "competition," and "monopoly" the meaning of anti-trust policy is shaped, subject of course to final judicial approval. Thus, if one seeks to determine the nature of anti-trust policy in the United States, greater attention has to be given to administrative and judicial policy directives and decisions than to congressional enactments. [28]

28. For further discussion of administrative rule-making see *supra,* pp. 76–154.

A major reason for the power of the bureaucracy in policy formulation is the frequent lack of congressional incentives to adhere to the Schechter rule and establish explicit standards for administrative action. This is particularly true in the regulatory realm, an area involving political conflict that legislators often wish to avoid. Congress is always willing to deal *rhetorically* with problems requiring regulation and with the area of regulatory reform, but real decisions on the part of the legislature will undoubtedly raise the ire of powerful pressure groups on one side or the other that are affected by government regulation. This is particularly true today with the existence of numerous public-interest groups, especially those concerned with consumer and environmental issues, which are constantly pressuring Congress for regulatory legislation that is strongly opposed by industry associations. And government regulation affects far more than private industry and consumer groups, particularly in this day of regulation of such environmental concerns as air and water pollution. State and local governments are profoundly involved in and affected by the regulatory process in such areas. The EPA, for example, regulates state and local governments in air- and water-pollution. In both of these key policy areas, Congress has delegated broad authority to the EPA to set standards for air and water indicating permissible levels of pollutants. The Agency now becomes the center of political controversy, Congress having removed itself to the background. The net effect of this is that whatever is done is up to the EPA and not up to the legislature. And the EPA, like all administrative agencies, is highly sensitive to political inputs, for if they are ignored the Agency will be under attack.

The same political sensitivities that often lead to the failure of Congress to take concrete action to meet pressing public problems exist in the bureaucracy as well. That is why most regulatory agencies have failed to take action independent from the wishes of the most powerful groups within their constituencies. Although public-interest pressure groups have attempted to counter the power of the regulated industries, the latter still tend to prevail on essential matters before the agencies.

More often than not, administrative agencies are authorized, but not required, to formulate rules governing the parties within their jurisdiction. It is for this reason that agencies often can legally choose to formulate policy on a case-by-case basis rather than through general rule-making. But what happens when Congress specifically mandates agencies to formulate standards? An instructive example is the Safe Drinking Water Act, passed by Congress at the end of 1974 in response to startling revelations of cancer-causing agents in the drinking-water supplies of New Orleans. The bill had been pending since 1972, but it took imminent danger to the public safety to spur congressional action. The Act *required* the EPA within 180 days of enactment to issue interim standards to safeguard public drinking-water supplies and provided that the standards would become final within eighteen months of their issuance. The standards were to govern permissible levels of chemicals and bacteriological contaminants in water supplies and to establish criteria for taste, appearance, and odor of drinking water. The states were to have the initial enforcement power, but if they failed to act the EPA could bring civil suits to force conformity with its policies. Congress, in characteristic fashion, was transferring the burden of solving an important problem to an administrative agency—the EPA. But placing responsibility on the shoulders of administrators does not guarantee action, even in the fact of explicit legislative mandates for administrative policy-making. The agency must deal with the same complex factors that confront Congress and often cause it to delay—problems of conflicting political pressure and lack of expertise to deal with new policy areas.

Almost two years after the passage of the Safe Drinking Water Act, the EPA had failed to carry out its responsibilities to establish standards governing permissible levels of water contaminants except in the cases of lead and mercury, which were entirely non-controversial. In other areas, the EPA has refused even to issue standards governing contaminants that have been linked directly to cancer. Why? Because such standards are controversial with the communities that must pay for purification of water, and because of lack of expert knowledge concerning the effects of most contaminants found in the nation's water supplies. Standards that would reveal a city's water supply to be dangerous would inevitably bring the ire of city officials down upon the EPA. A major problem posed by the retreat of Congress from the policy-making area and the broad delegation of authority to administrative agencies is not always arbitrary and oppressive administrative action, but sometimes, as in the case of the EPA and its responsibilities to regulate drinking water, failure of the agencies to act effectively and responsibly.

It is not just in the regulatory realm that administrative agencies determine much of the public policy that is finally implemented. A major difference between regulatory and non-regulatory agencies is that the latter carry out their programs through expenditures of federal funds directly or through grant-in-aid programs to the states. Agencies in such Departments as Health, Education, and Welfare, Defense, Agriculture, Interior, Housing and Urban Development, and Transportation carry out vast programs through the management of public funds. Congress has attempted to tighten its control over the budgetary process in recent years; however, a large amount of discretion necessarily remains in the hands of these massive governmental Departments. They determine the conditions for the disbursement of funds and thereby shape the programs and policies for which they are responsible. Their policy implementation, then, is not through regulatory rule-making, but through administrative rules governing expenditures. In order to control administrative action in this area, Congress needs effective budgetary controls. The passage of the Budget and Impoundment Control Act of 1974 was a step in this direction, for it created machinery through the Congressional Budget Committees in each body to establish budgetary priorities so that matters would not get out of hand, and established the Congressional Budget Office to assist both the Budget Committees and other committees involved in budgetary matters.

The end of the 94th Congress in 1976 saw Congress debating "sunset" legislation, initially introduced by Senator Edmund Muskie (D., Maine), Chairman of the Senate Budget Committee and of the Senate Subcommittee on Intergovernmental Relations of the Government Operations Committee. "Sunset" legislation was held to be the new panacea of Congress to control the bureaucracy, for it required after a specified period of time not to exceed five years that every budget authorization be reviewed *de novo*, and, in the process, zero-base budgeting procedures would be used under which agencies would have to justify their programs and activities. Both the Budget and Impoundment Control Act of 1974 and the "sunset" legislation proposals of 1976 reflected a resurgent Congress that hoped to deal in more than a rhetorical fashion with the problems of bureaucratic domination. But the problem of congressional control of the bureaucracy is not one of legal authority or even congressional machinery, for Congress has always had adequate authority and procedures to control the bureaucracy. Any authorization committee could, on its own initiative, require *de novo* review of administrative programs at any time after authorizations have lapsed. The problem is one of congressional *incentives*, and it seemed clear that these would not be likely to change except in a rhetorical fashion to deal with vague constituent uneasiness about the growth of government.

Reasons for Administrative Domination in the Legislative Process

What leads to the power to formulate public policy in a developed governmental system generally?

CONSTITUTIONAL AND LEGAL AUTHORITY

First, to make public policy or legislate, which are both the same thing generically, a governmental group, whether in the legislative, executive (administrative), or judicial branch, must possess constitutional and legal authority. Statutory authority to legislate is given in very broad terms by Congress to the President and the bureaucracy; thus, there is no lack of legal authority in the administrative branch. The conclusion that may be reached is that at the present time Congress and the bureaucracy possess roughly equal constitutional and legal authority to legislate. Congress can theoretically take this authority away from the administrative agencies, though it would never do so because of the very reasons that have necessitated the rise of administrative policy formulation in the first place. To renounce the role of the bureaucracy in legislation would be essentially the same thing as abolishing the administrative branch almost completely, which is neither practically nor politically possible.

ORGANIZATIONAL PATTERNS AND POLITICAL SUPPORT

Second, the ability to formulate policy depends upon organizational patterns and the attainment of *political support,* and here are the most important clues to explain administrative power over legislation. Congress operates through the committee system, and the chairmen of committees are focal points in the decision process. But the committees cannot by themselves generate enough support to pass legislation except in rare instances, although they can delay the consideration of particular bills. There is really no group within Congress that controls the decision process, since the party system is weak at the national level. Thus Congress can not act as a unit through a party majority in either house, and patterns of political support for any congressionally sponsored policy are changeable and diffuse.

Proposed congressional bills must first gain support within the appropriate committees in both houses. Then they must be reported on and passed by the entire body, which is split into two separate groups that are frequently in conflict, the House and Senate. In order for a bill to pass there must be outside political support favoring it. Where will such support materialize? Constituents acting as individuals are not as important as organized group support of congressional decision making; hence, a balance of interest group support must generally be attained before Congress can act. This fact, in addition to the battle for political survival that most congressmen must engage in, results in a network of relationships that are established among particular congressmen and congressional committees, and outside groups and key individuals in the elites of these groups. One of the best sources of political support is to be found in the administrative agencies concerned with the desired legislation, for these agencies constitute the key interest groups in the majority of cases.

The bureaucracy, like Congress, must also obtain political support before embarking upon new legislative programs, but in many instances it either already possesses such support from clientele groups or has the tools to achieve it without much trouble. Administrative policies often have virtually automatic political support which will in turn have significant impact upon Congress, for the groups that support the bureaucracy are more frequently than not very powerful economically and politically.

If an administrative agency wants to embark upon a new policy that is not immediately popular politically, it will have to employ various devices to secure political backing. But even then it is in a better position than the groups within Congress that may also want to innovate, because administrative agencies have greater power, and each possesses by itself greater ability to act as a unit than Congress, which must act through congressional committees and individual congressmen. If the Defense Department wants to cut back on the RS-70 or B-1 bomber program, a vital program (and originally a new departure in defense policy), an administrative directive is issued to this effect, and unless overwhelming political opposition is encountered the order is carried out. The Defense Department controls the expenditure of vast sums of money and hence groups within the armaments industry are in particular instances more or less at the mercy of Defense officials. As a whole the Department must maintain general political support, but this is not difficult. Although some industry groups may be unhappy about the curtailment of programs directly affecting them, there are always others that benefit. On balance the Defense Department has automatic political support for virtually anything it wants to do, provided the total defense budget remains roughly the same or increases. Through a vigorous Secretary of Defense it possesses the ability to act rapidly and with firmness in the formulation of policy, whereas Congress, because of its diffuse internal power structure, can not act in the same way even if it possesses the information to make complex policy decisions, which is not always the case.

THE CASE OF THE SUPERSONIC BOMBER PROGRAM

The relative power positions of Congress, the bureaucracy, and the President in an important area of public policy are well illustrated by the long battle that has taken place over whether or not to fund a supersonic bomber strike force. There is little doubt that in this struggle, which has lasted from the early 1960s to the late 1970s, the Defense Department, especially when acting in conjunction with the President, has dominated. The resurgent post-Watergate Congress has not been any more effective in controlling the power of DOD than the relatively weaker pre-Watergate Congresses.

In the early 1960s, the issue was whether or not to expand or to cut back on the supersonic bomber (first called the B-70, and later the RS-70). At the outset, the issue was whether or not to cut back on the RS-70 in the 1963-fiscal-year budget. Powerful Congressmen—in particular, Carl Vinson of Georgia, then Chairman of the House Armed Services Committee—the Defense Department, and the President became involved. The case centered upon an executive-legislative struggle to control a military budget item that provided funds for the development of the RS-70. One of the most important powers Congress can exert to control the administrative branch is thought by many to be the power of appropriation of money. In the past this control over the purse was feared and was an important reason why Madison and Hamilton in *The Federalist* and others at the time felt Congress would dominate the coordinate branches of government. After all, without money the bureaucracy, the President, and the judicial branch would be powerless. For this reason the Constitution states that both the President and the Supreme Court Justices shall at least receive compensation for their services which shall not be reduced during their continuance in office. But appropriations are vital to far more areas than salaries. In these areas Congress can do anything it wishes; thus, it theoretically can easily bring co-ordinate branches into line through the threat of removal of a portion or all of their appropriations.

Although this argument sounds reasonable, the fact is that the scope and complexity of modern government has resulted in the transference of the bulk of the budgetary power to the President and the administrative branch. This state of affairs continues even after the Budget and Impoundment Control Act of 1974. Congressional procedures in budgeting are more centralized and co-ordinated, but the principal budget for the government is formulated for the most part by the powerful Office of Management and Budget in conjunction with the President and administrative agencies. Only after it is cleared by the executive is it submitted to Congress for approval. The real process of negotiation occurs between the administrative agencies and the Presidential bureaucracy (OMB) rather than between the agencies and Congress. After it is approved by the executive, it is submitted to the legislature. In spite of attempts in recent years to change the budgeting process, either to the adoption of a form of program budgeting or through zero-base budgeting, the budgetary process remains essentially incremental at both executive and legislative levels.[29] Congress makes few significant changes in the executive budget, usually cutting back, if at all, only in areas where there is no strong political opposition to reductions. And reduction of agencies' budgets are not made just by Congress. The administrations of Nixon and Ford saw vigorous presidential initiatives in the direction of budget cutting, only to find Congress on the other side of the fence, often restoring funds cut out of the executive budget by OMB.

Whether Congress restores or reduces executive budgetary requests, the fact remains that only a handful of Congressmen have the time or energy to read the budget, which is extraordinarily bulky. The congressional budgetary process is highly specialized, with the Appropriations Committees of the House and the Senate dominating, the Budget Committees of both Houses acting as timid overlords. Even small appropriation bills run to several hundred pages, whereas the total budget is equivalent to thousands of pages. The skill and effort that the administrative branch puts into the formulation of a budget are generally respected in congressional quarters, where there is neither the staff nor the time for adequate review. In 1962 a defense appropriation of close to fifty billion dollars was passed in the House of Representatives unanimously in a matter of a few minutes. Congresses of the 1970s spend only a few days debating defense appropriations. Even the Armed Services Committees and Defense Appropriations Subcommittees are largely adjuncts of the Defense Department.

The case of the RS-70, although involving a relatively small amount of money, illustrates the way in which the executive

29. Proposals for "sunset" legislation contain provisions requiring zero-base budgeting before the authorization committees of Congress. It is somewhat doubtful, given the failure of the PPBS budget procedure in the late 1960s that was strongly backed by the President and the then-Bureau of the Budget, that requirements for zero-base budgeting will fundamentally alter the tendency of both administrators and legislators to fall back on an incremental approach.

dominated Congress in the era before Watergate. The executive was on the side of *cutting* the budget, while key congressional forces that for years had developed close relations with the military were in favor of expansion of funds for the supersonic bomber. In formulating the military budget for the fiscal year ending June 30, 1963, Secretary of Defense Robert Mc-Namara and his advisers in conjunction with the President proposed that funds for the development of a supersonic bomber, called the RS-70 ("reconnaissance strike"), be drastically cut and that the plans for production of the bomber on a mass scale be dropped entirely. This was in line with a shift in defense policy toward greater reliance upon missiles for both offensive and defensive purposes. McNamara had nothing against manned bombers as such, but he felt that a changing technology was rendering them obsolete. As is always the case when important issues of defense policy are concerned, powerful individuals and groups both within Congress and the Defense Department itself opposed his decision. The Secretary of Defense always has to contend with his own service chiefs, as well as with key congressmen. In this respect the process of policy formulation is highly political, and the domination of certain policy spheres by the bureaucracy does not in any way eliminate the political factor. Agencies are more frequently than not in conflict with each other, and in the case of large agencies or departments intra-agency political conflict is as acute in many instances as inter-agency conflict.

The decision to reduce manned bombers and the RS-70 in particular met the immediate opposition of Carl Vinson, who had represented Georgia in the House of Representatives since 1914. Vinson was a legend on Capitol Hill, and was reputed to be a powerful influence on the military, not only because he was the chairman of the House Armed Services Committee, but because of his long acquaintance with the military field, which had resulted in a certain degree of inside knowledge as well as close ties with key military figures. He was chairman of the Naval Affairs Committee from 1931 to 1947, and in 1962 had been chairman of the Armed Services Committee for all but two years since 1949. Regardless of the legend, the fact was that the Armed Services Committees in both the House and the Senate had not been particularly important in military policy formulation in post-war years,

and with the exception of the areas of manpower and construction, the legislation emanating from these committees gave
complete discretion to the military bureaucracy, for the terminology used was typically imprecise and could be interpreted in a
variety of ways. Insofar as the RS-70 was concerned, Congressman
Vinson was not the only figure opposed to the elimination of the
program in 1962. The Air Force, theoretically within the Defense
Department and subject to the Secretary's control, also favored
a manned bomber buildup, and Air Force Chief of Staff General
Curtis LeMay expressed vocal opposition to McNamara's proposals. In addition to Air Force opposition, various congressmen
and private groups led by North American Aviation, Inc., which
would be adversely affected by the cancellation of military contracts in connection with the program, opposed any cutback.

The general plan of McNamara was initially to allocate 171
million dollars to North American Aviation, Inc., and its subcon-
tractors, to build three test models of the RS-70. This figure was
subsequently raised to 223 million dollars. The proponents of the
program, spearheaded by Vinson and LeMay, wanted a minimum
of 491 million dollars spent the first year, and ultimately 5 to 10
billion dollars. The House of Representatives supported the Defense Department in its final defense appropriation bill, largely
because George Mahon (D., Texas), chairman of the powerful
Appropriations Subcommittee on Defense, was in favor of this
course of action. Vinson and others were unable to overcome
the combination of a powerful administrative agency with a
powerful congressional committee.

The Senate, on the other hand, did not go along with the Defense Department, and appropriated the 491 million dollars that
had been requested for the RS-70. The net result of a divided Congress on this issue was that the Defense Department triumphed
by threatening, with the support of the President, to refuse to
spend money that Congress appropriated against its wishes.
Before the Budget and Impoundment Control Act of 1974,
Presidents from Thomas Jefferson to Richard Nixon used their
constitutional authority to see that the laws were faithfully
executed as well as the Anti-Deficiency Act and specific legislative and appropriations statutes to impound funds appropriated
by Congress. The Anti-Deficiency Act granted broad discre-

tionary authority to the President to apportion funds in an effective, economical way.[30] Some statutes—for example, the 1973 Agriculture-Environmental and Consumer Protection Appropriation Act—required the establishment of reserve funds pending the determination of need by the administrative agencies involved. The 1974 Labor-HEW Appropriations Act authorized the Departments of Labor and HEW to withhold specified amounts or percentages of appropriated funds.[31]

The early 1960s dispute over the supersonic bomber was worked out politically between the Secretary of Defense and key members of Congress. The Senate-House conference committee on the RS-70 finally authorized the expenditure of 362 million dollars, but McNamara had a tacit agreement with the House conferees that he would not spend the entire appropriation. Thus the House conferees, who supported the Defense Department, agreed to go through the motions of authorizing additional expenditure so that quick agreement could be reached with the Senate. At the same time they recognized that final power resided with the Secretary of Defense, who would use their informal support to implement the program he desired in the first place.

Secretary of Defense Robert McNamara's victory in cutting back funds for the supersonic bomber illustrates the advantage of a relatively cohesive bureaucratic force impacting upon a generally fragmented Congress. The general fragmentation of the policy process works to the disadvantage of Congress and groups within Congress relative to the bureaucracy, particularly if the President supports an administrative agency. Many of the constitutional powers of Congress are meaningless in view of the general lack of congressional unity. The fact that there is no

30. 31 U.S.C. 665; 16 Stat. 251 (1870) as amended. See also Louis Fisher, *Presidential Spending Power* (Princeton, N.J.: Princeton University Press, 1975).

31. See Public Law 92-399 (1973); Public Law 93-192 (1974). Precedents had clearly been established in the Defense area for the impoundment of funds, beginning with the largest impoundment in history up to that date by President Harry S. Truman in 1951. In the early stages of the struggle over the supersonic bomber, Congress was fully aware that it could authorize expenditures and appropriate money but that it could do little to force the President or DOD to spend the money. Congress could have *mandated* expenditures, but this would have been without precedent in a defense-policy field.

consistent and cohesive majority rule in the legislature gives particular agencies far more power than would otherwise be the case. In some instances if there is a balance of power among opposing agencies Congress may swing the decision one way or the other. More often than not, however, the balance is held by the President, who can always act with greater dispatch than Congress. The President acts as a source of political strength in such cases, which, when combined with that of the agencies, often cannot be effectively challenged by Congress.

In 1963, the President and Secretary of Defense Robert Mc-Namara were acting together to prevent the appropriation of large amounts of money for the development of a supersonic bomber. They were able to prevent the Air Force and its allies in Congress and the armaments industry from achieving their goals. But the President and the Secretary of Defense, no matter how powerful they may be when acting in combination at any given time, remain only temporal forces on the long-term policy-making scene. Relative to the President and the Secretary of Defense, the military bureaucracy and senior Congressmen or members of Congress from safe districts on their way to establishing seniority have far more permanency.

After the Air Force and its congressional allies were stopped by Secretary of Defense McNamara and President Kennedy in their quest for large appropriations for the development of a supersonic bomber, they continued to press their case during the administrations of Lyndon Johnson, Richard Nixon, and Gerald Ford. By 1976, the Air Force had succeeded in obtaining the necessary funds for the development of supersonic-bomber prototypes, and began pressing vigorously for appropriations for full-scale production even before the prototypes had been fully tested. The post-Watergate 94th Congress (1975–1976), however, was more hesitant than the pre-Watergate Congresses in bending to the will of a united executive. Nevertheless, it was not able to overcome the combined pressure from the President, the Secretary of Defense, and the military on the supersonic-bomber issue. Funds for the production of the supersonic bomber (now called the B-1) were voted by an overwhelming majority in the House, temporarily deferred in the Senate, and, in conference, the administration finally achieved its inevitable victory. The staying power and expertise of the bureaucracy won out on the supersonic-bomber issue, and the bomber is now scheduled for production.

INFORMATION AND POLICY MAKING

A final important factor should be noted as a determinant of policy making power: legislation today, in regulatory and non-regulatory fields alike, requires specialized information on the part of policy makers before it can be conceptualized, drafted, and implemented. Policy areas are for the most part highly technical with respect to legal, economic, and political factors. While expert knowledge does not require a Ph.D. in mathematics, engineering or other scientific subjects, nor in the social sciences, it does, on the other hand, demand an intimate acquaintance with the issues that arise in the particular policy areas that are the concern of modern government. It is knowledge that can only be acquired from specialization and experience.

Several problems arise regarding the relationship between information and the policy process. First, because there are numerous areas of specialization it is necessary to have a broad division of labor in government. Second, *within* particular policy fields there are a variety of areas of specialized competence that must be applied before the total picture can be understood. This further expands the division of labor required. Congress attempts to meet this situation through its committee system, which essentially results in dividing the legislative sphere into numerous units that are then assigned to permanent standing committees. Temporary policy problems are met through the creation of *ad hoc* or select committees, which hopefully are disbanded when there is no longer a need for them. For example, the Senate Select Committee on Intelligence Activities was created at the beginning of 1975, and after extensive investigations completed its report in April, 1976. As a result of the Select Committee's recommendations, the Senate established a permanent Select Committee on Intelligence to oversee the operations of the CIA and other intelligence agencies.

Even before Watergate and its attendant recognition of the need to restore some balance of power between the President and Congress, the legislature had attempted to strengthen its internal procedures to cope with the growing dominance of the bureaucracy. In 1946, Congress passed the Legislative Reorganization Act, which its optimistic sponsors hoped would put Congress back in the running against the overriding power of the bureaucracy in the policy-making process. That Act expanded the Legislative Reference Service (now the Congressional Research Service) as a separate branch of the Library of Congress to supply information to legislators and their staffs. It increased personal and committee staffs to provide Congress with greater expertise. The permissible scope of private bills was reduced in order to allow legislators to concentrate more on public bills. In this regard, the Federal Tort Claims Act of 1946 allowed the government to be sued directly in certain areas where governmental agents had committed torts against private parties. In such cases, members of Congress were not permitted to introduce private bills to pay compensation, and, in addition, under the 1946 Legislative Reorganization Act they could no longer introduce private legislation to pay pension claims, construct bridges, or correct military records. In all of these areas, a great deal of congressional time had been spent in the past. The 1946 Act finally attempted to streamline the committee system by reducing the number of committees and the number of committee assignments for members of Congress and, at the same time, emphasized the need for committee oversight of administrative agencies.

The streamlining of the congressional committee structure and the expansion of staff under the Legislative Reorganization Act of 1946 failed to achieve the goals of the sponsors of the legislation. Congress became more rather than less cumbersome, and its ever-growing staff failed to counterbalance the inevitable advantages of bureaucratic expertise in legislation and the broader policy-making process. Renewed congressional concerns over bureaucratic domination were reflected in the Legislative Reorganization Act of 1970, which strengthened congressional procedures in information-gathering in the fiscal and budgetary areas, expanded committee staffs, and strengthened the Congressional Research Service. However, the primary purpose of the Act was not to restore Congress to an equal footing with the bureaucracy, but to democratize and make more open the internal procedures of the legislature by making them less secret.

Another congressional attempt to increase its expertise and access to information came in 1972 with the creation of the Office of Technology Assessment. Under its mandate, OTA has extraordinary potential to develop expertise since it can sequester any experts that it wishes from the bureaucracy to work on congressional legislation that has technological implications (which, broadly defined, would include most legislation). OTA, however, has not fulfilled the promise of its sponsors and has largely resorted to contracting private firms and individuals for technological studies. The position of OTA within Congress remains primarily academic. What little expertise it has been able to garner has not approached in scope and impact that of the powerful agencies of the executive branch.

The 93rd and 94th Congresses (1973–1974; 1975–1976) continued efforts to strengthen the legislature vis-a-vis the executive. In the fall of 1973, the House Select Committee on Committees, chaired by Richard Bolling (D., Missouri), held extensive hearings on committee organization in the House with a view toward improving efficiency and establishing greater access to decision-making within the House. A year later, on October 8, 1974, the House adopted a greatly watered-down version of the recommendations of the Bolling Committee. That Committee had recommended major realignments of committee jurisdictions and limitation on the number of major committees on which a member could serve to one. The vested interests of the House, particularly the senior members, rose in opposition to this plan and voted instead for the substitute plan issued by a Democratic Caucus Committee, chaired by Julia Butler Hansen (D., Washington). The Hansen Plan changed some committee jurisdictions and altered certain House procedures, but left the internal power structure of the House largely intact. The Hansen Plan tripled the professional staffs of permanent committees, and granted the minority party control of one third of the staff of each committee. Under the Hansen Plan, each substantive committee was to maintain continuous oversight of administrative activity within its jurisdiction; and to aid legislative oversight, the Plan granted all standing committees subpoena authority without the necessity for approval through House resolutions, and created a legislative classification office to clarify committee jurisdiction for particular federal programs. The Plan did not limit the number of major committees on which a member could serve, as the original Bolling Committee had.

The Senate as well as the House has, in recent years, paid a great deal of attention (often more rhetorical than real) to increasing internal efficiency, expanding its staff expertise, and strengthening legislative oversight of administrative activity. The Senate was careful to make public during the 94th Congress its creation of an outside commission of prominent citizens to investigate internal Senate organization and procedures with a view toward providing more efficient operation. Senate insiders well knew that the "Culver Commission," as the group was informally named (after one of its chief sponsors, Democratic Senator John C. Culver of Iowa), would not find anything radically wrong, and would certainly not make recommendations that would in any way disturb the intricate internal power balances of the institution.

While the Senate continued to press for additional staff, Stephen Isaacs in a series of articles in the *Washington Post* in 1975 revealed the well-known fact on the Hill that professional committee staff members are often attached to the personal staffs of Senators on the committees. Senators Henry Jackson (D., Washington) and Edward Kennedy (D., Massachusetts) were particularly cited for their successful acquisition of a large number of committee staff for their personal use. The size of staff under a Senator's control is a symbol of power, and those who are successful in acquiring expert staff may become more effective legislators, and more capable of acting independently of the bureaucracy. However, the internal politics of the House and the Senate tends to defeat a unified and consistent congressional approach to formulating legislation. More importantly, the substance of legislation becomes less important than the form and the desire of members to pass legislation per se to advance their status within Congress.

Just as the internal incentives for power and status tend to decrease the ability of Congress to establish independent expertise to control the bureaucracy, the external *electoral* congressional incentives also detract from congressional effectiveness in this area. Members of Congress always have to face the real or imagined possibility of losing their jobs. At given intervals the resources of Congress are not geared to effective policy-making or counterbalancing the bureaucracy, but rather to gaining re-election. Even in relatively safe districts, Representatives and Senators expend a great deal of their congressional staff resources on securing re-election. The electoral instability that affects Congressmen also causes insecurity among staff, and congressional turnover results in staff turnover or shifts of staff from one committee to another. The often-frenetic activity surrounding election campaigns detracts from the ability of Congress to maintain serious and sustained contact with specialized policy areas. By contrast, administrators who are not political appointees are able to maintain continuous contact with fields under their jurisdiction.

Although Congress has made strenuous efforts to fulfill its constitutional responsibilities, neither its committees nor its staff aids are any match for the administrative branch with respect to knowledge and information in particular areas of legislation. Much of the staff employed by Congress comes directly from the administrative branch, in which initial competence was acquired in an atmosphere where the points of view of the agencies predominated. Sometimes these viewpoints carry over to congressional staff members. Beyond its own staff, Congress must rely upon information that comes directly from the agencies concerned in particular policy fields. Needless to say, the kinds of information that reach congressional committees and congressmen often determine their attitudes toward policy questions. To a considerable extent when the administrative branch can control the channels of information to Congress it can control the policies supported by that body.

Though administrators and administrative agencies also have constituents, they do not have to enter the electoral process, and therefore can react to their constituents in a manner quite different from elected officials. The agencies have more power over their constituents than any individual congressman, and they are not subject to the capricious whims of typical voters. Their political support tends to be more consistent and permanent because the agencies have greater durability and more immediate power over constituents than most members of Congress. Thus, although the bureaucracy must maintain political consent for its actions, it possesses more techniques and time to achieve it than members of Congress.

The electoral process not only results in congressmen spending much of their time campaigning, but profoundly affects the kinds of issues and therefore the types of information with which they must be familiar. Political consent is achieved by congressmen through a proper emphasis upon personal and local issues that, for the most part, are not particularly relevant to national policy. Administrative agencies, on the other hand, achieve consent through the adoption of *policies* that will win the approval of powerful groups within their constituency.

With respect to increasing the importance of policy issues in political campaigns, this is not in line with the results of recent research into the characteristics of electoral behavior. The voter often is not interested in complex policy matters, and it is no insult to the electorate to say that many areas of policy should not be subject to electoral choice. All of the electorate should not have to debate the merits of one missile as opposed to another in defense policy; nor safety measures in the control of aircraft; nor whether the interest rate should be high or low; nor the level of tariffs, and so forth. Of course matters such as these are always subject to discussion in the electorate; however, the idea that the entire electorate should take an interest in all issues of public policy is obsolete in the modern democratic state. Congress, as one group representing the public, does not have to formulate public policy in every instance in order to conform to a constitutional and democratic system of government.

The answer that may be given to the problem of inadequate congressional information in policy fields is to increase staff aids and in addition to put campaigning on the basis of policy issues rather than personalities. There is really no way, however, to accomplish either of these objectives. The staff aids to Congress could not possibly be increased enough to counterbalance the bureaucracy. Even if congressional staff were strengthened at the present time, this would not transform Congress into a dominant and effective legislative body again. An overwhelming number of key staff positions in Congress are filled by lawyers, whose expertise is crucial to the drafting of legislation but who do not always possess the substantive knowledge necessary to deal adequately with complex areas of public policy. A major problem of developing congressional expertise is the necessary divorce between congressional staffs and the operational end of agency activities. This separation cuts Congress off from a rich source of knowledge directly relevant to the development of public policy.

The politicization of congressional staff applies not only to the personal and committee staffs of members, but also to those separate staff agencies of Congress that have been created to supply expertise in particular areas: the Congressional Budget Office and the General Accounting Office. The Congressional Budget Office (CBO), created by the Budget and Impoundment Control Act of 1974, is supposed to act in an impartial and objective manner in supplying expertise to Congress. In fact, it operates within a highly charged political milieu which prevents it from taking strong positions in opposition to the bills of Senators and Representatives. The relationship between the CBO and members of Congress, particularly the more powerful and active ones, is much the same as the relationship between the members of the presidential bureaucracy and a strong and opinionated President. Both the congressional and presidential staff must operate with a great deal of finesse and tread very lightly in expressing opinions that differ from those for whom they work.

The General Accounting Office is another important branch of Congress, set up to provide the legislature with information and, more particularly, to control administrative operations through auditing procedures. The GAO takes an adversary position to executive agencies, descending upon them with hordes of auditors to see whether or not the letter of the law has been followed. Upon the discovery of "misappropriation" of funds by the executive, statements are issued to the press and Congress is fully informed. Both the CBO and GAO have the theoretical potential to delve into all aspects of policy development and implementation. However, each takes a narrow view of its role, the CBO concentrating on the budgetary implications of policy, and the GAO tending to adhere strictly to auditing matters. Moreover, the GAO usually acts after the fact in providing information to Congress, which limits its usefulness to legislators. Although members can call upon the GAO to provide assistance in drafting legislation, conducting investigations, and doing research on legislative and policy problems, the narrow auditing orientation of the GAO limits its effectiveness as a congressional staff arm. Moreover, the GAO is more like the regular bureaucracy than other agencies of Congress. Created in 1921 under the Budget and Accounting Act, the GAO has developed a great deal of independence of the institution it is supposed to serve. In many instances, members of Congress feel a greater rapport with particular administrative agencies under their jurisdiction than with such legislative arms as the CBO and the GAO.

The Congressional Research Service within the Library of Congress, and the Office of Technology Assessment are additional staff arms that Congress has created to supply it with information. While the CRS does have a number of highly trained professionals on its staff, it is still very small and incapable of meeting the vast resources of the bureaucracy in its capabilities of supplying expertise to Congress. Like the other staff arms of Congress, the CRS must remain neutral over contrasting legislative proposals, recognizing always that there is both a majority and a minority party in the institution that it must serve. The necessary political neutrality of the CRS and the other staff arms of Congress put them at a disadvantage when confronting administrative agencies that can marshal all their expertise behind a particular policy position, thus combining political maneuvering with expertise to reach their goals. The director of the CRS finds it far easier to support "non-partisan" legislation that, in theory at least, strengthens Congress as a whole vis-à-vis the executive, such as the Budget and Impoundment Control Act of 1974 and the "sunset" legislation introduced in 1976, rather than the more particularistic goals of individual members. The CRS provides more expert service to Congress than the Office of Technology Assessment, which has not yet developed the necessary internal staff to begin to counterbalance the technological expertise of the administrative agencies.

A major reason for the failure of Congress to develop competent internal expertise, particularly through independent staff offices such as the CBO and the Office of Technology Assessment, is that these staff arms tend to be identified, like the staffs of individual committees, with powerful Senators and Representatives whose influence was instrumental in setting them up. The Office of Technology Assessment, for example, is strongly identified with Senator Edward Kennedy, who was instrumental in establishing it. Therefore, it was not considered a neutral agency by many members of Congress—at least not during the years immediately following its establishment.

The Congressional Budget Office also is not considered totally neutral within the congressional context since powerful members such as Senator Muskie, Chairman of the Senate Budget Committee, have more access to the CBO than the ordinary member. Senator Muskie's influence was important in establishing the CBO, and his position as Chairman of the Budget Committee continues his potentially greater access over that agency. In the House, Congressman Richard Bolling (D., Missouri) was a strong force in creating the CBO, and to many House members CBO is closely identified with the politics of Bolling or with the Chairman of the House Budget Committee, Brock Adams (D., Washington). There is a keen recognition on the part of powerful chairmen of committees that their jurisdiction may be lessened by effective operations of the budget committees in conjunction with the CBO. This fact of the internal political life of Congress reduces the potential of the CBO as an effective staff agency for Congress as a whole. As long as Congress is divided into feudal states, the members of the individual fiefdoms, which include not only the committees, but often agencies acting in conjunction with them, will trust only their own patriotic staff. Even the old-line staff agencies of Congress, the GAO and the CRS, which are not identified with the political ambitions of any individual members, may be viewed with a certain amount of distrust because they are outside of the boundaries of the congressional fiefdoms. Thus, it is not simply the greater expertise of the bureaucracy that tends to dominate the congressional process, but the fact that administrative agencies may be more closely aligned with congressional committees than Congress's own staff arms.

Administrative Lobbying
and Propaganda

The ability of administrative agencies to marshal support in favor of particular programs is often severely tested, and as a result the agencies have frequently created public relations departments on a permanent basis to engineer consent for their legislative proposals. It has been estimated that the executive branch spends close to half a billion dollars a year on public relations and public information programs.[32] Not all of this expenditure is for political purposes, for there are a number of legitimate public information programs that administrative agencies must undertake. But whatever the percentage may be for non-political purposes, it is obvious that agencies are expending huge amounts of funds, time, and effort on indirect and direct lobbying activities. Administrative personnel engaged in public relations are not so open about their activities as their counterparts in private advertising and public relations firms, for the myth that the bureaucracy is "neutral" must be maintained if possible. However, through what might be called undercover devices, the bureaucracy engages in extensive lobbying and propaganda activities.

The agencies are faced with the problem of engineering consent in Congress, and in those groups under their jurisdiction which are directly affected by their decisions. If these latter groups are powerful the administrative agencies that gain their approval for particular policies will also have automatic congressional support in those quarters to which the groups have access. The entire Congress will not be affected, but key committees dealing in the same areas as the agencies are likely to be persuaded one way or the other if powerful agency clientele groups apply pressure. In some policy fields Congress must act affirmatively to effect the legislative proposals of the bureaucracy. In others, administrative agencies can take action independently; however, in these cases they always face the possibility of adverse congressional and clientele group reaction. Congressional

32. J. William Fulbright, *The Pentagon Propaganda Machine* (New York: Vintage Books, 1971), p. 17.

investigations are always unpleasant and they may affect the balance of political support unfavorably if they turn up administrative irregularities.

Administrative agencies function to a considerable extent as freewheeling interest groups, and in their use of propaganda activities they are no exception. They not only seek to apply pressure at critical points in the political process, but also strive to maintain a favorable image of themselves before the public generally and before specific groups which they consider important in the battle for political survival. The armed forces, for example, employ numerous devices, from the recruiting poster to the full-length motion picture, to convey their importance to the public. Particular services, sometimes in conjunction with their clientele groups, attempt to persuade the public, congressmen, and the President of their worth relative to coordinate Services. The Pentagon offers help to contractors and scientists wishing to support programs the military favors. This aid may be in the form of research assistance for writing articles, help in publishing articles, and any technical aid necessary to help a defense contractor advertise the need for particular weapons systems. The Defense Department (DOD) has openly admitted to the Senate Appropriations Committee that it spends over forty million dollars a year for public-relations activities, and employs over four thousand people in a public-relations capacity,[33] and defense contractors undertake on their own to support through propaganda the Services for which they supply weapons. Rockwell International Corporation, prime contractor for the B-1, engaged in extensive lobbying and public-relations activities to support the B-1 bomber. In effect, Rockwell International was supporting an important policy of the Air Force and aiding the military in achieving its objectives in Congress. Defense contractors are often willing to boost any Service that uses their products, although of course good relations are maintained with all Services, for they too are actual or potential customers. Such activity supplements that of the Services and is designed to influence policy makers in the bureaucracy as well as in outside departments and groups. In other words, the bureaucracy lobbies itself in cases where the significant decision making power

33. *Ibid.*, pp. 25–27.

resides in the administrative branch.

Congress has always been concerned with administrative lobby-ing and propaganda in much the same way that it has given at-tention to similar activities in private groups. The Federal Regu-lation of Lobbying Act of 1946 requires the registration of groups and individuals attempting to influence legislation before Con-gress, but it applies only to private groups and not to adminis-trative agencies. When the Government Operations Committee of the Senate drafted and reported a major new lobbying bill in the 94th Congress that tightened registration and reporting requirements for those lobbying the Congress, it explicitly ex-cluded lobbying by the executive branch. This reflected the fact that lobbying by administrative agencies is technically illegal according to the law and a willingness on the part of members of Congress to overlook what are, in fact, executive lobbying activities by calling them something else, such as "liai-son," or "public information." Private corporations attempting to influence Congress in the same ways that administrative agen-cies do are highly suspect, and their more intensive lobbying efforts are subject to strong criticism, although they cannot, of course, be prohibited. If General Motors Corporation, for ex-ample, tried to lobby Congress in the same manner as the Defense Department, heated objections would be raised. Imag-ine the President of General Motors personally stalking the halls of Congress to buttonhole key members, with the aid of a staff of several hundred. The Defense Department maintains a full-time staff of two hundred and ninety-four persons (by its own ad-mission), costing over six million dollars a year, employed in full-time lobbying activities which the Pentagon calls con-gressional "liaison." The assignments the Defense Department gives to its professional lobbyists include setting up military briefings for members of Congress, acting as tour director on congressional trips overseas, and arranging field trips for legis-lators.[34] A few legislators are concerned about the scope of execu-tive-branch lobbying of Congress. Senator Patrick Leahy (D., Vermont) is one of this group, and has flatly stated with reference to the Pentagon that "I want to be able to identify who is doing

34. See Richard J. Levine, "Capitol Hill Soldier," *The Wall Street Journal*, January 21, 1976, p. 1.

the lobbying and how much it is costing."[35] As one Army general puts it, "I believe the key to successful legislation is knowledge, and that means educating the congressmen. So I make a special effort to keep the Hill offices informed about Army programs."[36] While executive-branch lobbying has its critics on the Hill, it is accepted by the large majority of Congressmen and staff. After all, behind the rhetorical barbs that Congress and the executive agencies fling at each other is a general recognition that they are in the same exclusive club of government leaders and policy-makers.

Many private groups maintain substantial lobbying staffs in Washington, but they do not have quite the same access and privileges as administrative agencies. They cannot conduct congressmen on expense-free tours of Europe, provide free medical care, and make the life of congressmen more enjoyable in a number of other respects. Administrative agencies do this and for the most part questions are not raised. When private groups attempt similar activity, charges of "bribery" or worse are likely to be leveled.

Congress has attempted to deal with the public relations activities of the administrative branch by legally prohibiting the expenditure of public funds for "publicity" or the hiring of "publicity experts," unless expressly authorized.[37] Congress condones some administrative publicity that is required to carry out vital programs. It does not, however, sanction the general use of public relations men by the bureaucracy, and from time to time particular congressmen unleash attacks upon administrative agencies that have used propaganda to support programs they oppose. Officials may be called before congressional committees to answer charges that they have used illegal public relations techniques, or the matter may be referred to the Justice Department for "proper" action. However, rarely, if ever, are severe steps taken to curb propaganda by the bureaucracy, because there is no focal point of political power in the American system capable of taking such action and making it stick. For example, on occasion the President instructs agencies to support his programs in Congress, but this

35. *Ibid.*
36. *Ibid.*
37. 18 U.S.C. 1913. 62 Stat. 792 (1948).

leads to congressional charges of "muzzling" and encouragement of administrative independence. If Congress, through individual members, charges officials with engaging in questionable propaganda in favor of important presidential programs, it means that the agencies involved receive support from the President and, with regard to legal charges, from the Justice Department.

An interesting illustration of administrative lobbying occurred in 1962, when Sargent Shriver, director of the Peace Corps and brother-in-law of President Kennedy, sent letters on official government stationery to all members of Congress in an effort to bolster the agency's request for a substantial increase in appropriations. While this was only a mild form of lobbying, Representative Lipscomb, a Republican from California, charged that public funds were being used to influence Congress, and that this constituted a legal violation. In 1948 Congress passed a bill which said in part:

No part of the money appropriated by any enactment of Congress shall, in the absence of express authorization by Congress, be used directly or indirectly to pay for any personal service, advertisement, telegram, telephone, letter, printed or written matter, or other device, intended or designed to influence in any manner a member of Congress, to favor or oppose, by vote or otherwise, any legislation or appropriation by Congress, whether before or after the introduction of any bill or resolution proposing such legislation or appropriation.[38]

This statute has the usual ambiguous "escape clause" which provides that it does not bar communications between the bureaucracy and Congress through "proper official channels" concerning legislation or appropriations that administrators "deem necessary for the efficient conduct of the public business." Congressman Lipscomb, basing his decision on this statute, requested Attorney General Robert Kennedy to determine whether or not Shriver had broken the law. The reply from the Justice Department was that the law does not apply to the heads of agencies. The reasoning given for this was that the President has the responsibility to recommend legislative proposals to Congress, which necessitates delegation to agency heads who, as subordinates to the President,

38. 62 Stat. 792 (1948).

have constitutional immunity from congressional action designed to restrict them in their relations with Congress.

The Federal Energy Agency, created on a temporary basis in 1973, came under strong attack for its public-relations activities when it was being reviewed by Congress for continuation in 1976. In just a few short years, the FEA had built up a public-relations staff of one hundred and twenty persons who were not only supplying public information but also attempting to build grass-roots support for policies favored by the President, including gas deregulation. As in the case of the Pentagon and other executive lobbying, the question was raised as to the borderline between legal and excessive public advocacy and political activity. After criticism from both the House and the Senate, the Energy Administrator, Frank G. Zarb, agreed informally with the House Subcommittee on Energy and Power of the Interstate and Foreign Commerce Committee to cut his public-affairs staff to sixty-three persons, a third of whom would be involved in answering Freedom of Information Act requests and distributing agency publications.

Regardless of statutory restrictions, administrative agencies continue to lobby Congress, and will undoubtedly continue to do so in the future. Congress may prevent the hiring of "publicity experts," but this does not prevent the agencies from employing such people under the cloak of a different title. Congressional appropriations are usually not itemized specifically, and the bureaucracy has a great deal of leeway in determining how it will spend public funds. And, regardless of particular congressional outbursts against administrative propaganda and attempts to influence legislation, the bureaucratic strength in the legislative field really stems from congressional dependence upon the information and political support that the agencies possess. Congress wants the bureaucracy to play an important role in the legislative process, and indications to the contrary are sporadic and insignificant.

What are the implications of the extensive use of propaganda and public relations techniques by the bureaucracy? Some observers may feel this development has grave results and may lead to the destruction of the democratic process. If the agencies can engineer consent for their programs will it not be impossible to control them within the framework of our democratic system? The problem of administrative propaganda and lobbying, however, is minor compared to the broader role the bureaucracy plays in the political system. The agencies do not gain the power they have solely through propaganda or lobbying. As far as Congress is concerned, its deficiencies in such areas as information, organization, political support, and so forth, are far more responsible for its delegation of legislative power to the bureaucracy than the public relations activities of the agencies. Although some have painted a dark picture of a society controlled by "Madison Avenue" and public relations men, it is quite obvious that congressmen are far from being so gullible. It is one thing to sell toothpaste, and quite another to sell a political program. The agencies are dealing with experienced politicians in Congress, and with experts who are also politically astute in the numerous private interest groups. It takes far more than propaganda to persuade those who have definite political interests at stake. This is not to dismiss the importance of administrative propaganda and lobbying, but only to put it into proper perspective.

Conclusion

The American constitutional system is predicated on the belief that legislation should be formulated in a democratic and representative atmosphere. With respect to the representative function, the structure and personnel of the bureaucracy conform to many basic constitutional requirements. The administrative branch is highly representative, and it may even be argued that it is more representative than Congress. In many respects the only difference between the legislature and the bureaucracy is that the former is elected. This fact, however, does not necessarily increase the representative character of Congress. This raises the very difficult question of what constitutes adequate representation? What does the term "representation" mean? Essentially, it means that those who represent groups or individuals will act in terms of their interests as the groups or individuals themselves conceive them. Direct accountability through the electoral process is one way that may aid in bringing this about, but it is not the only way. It is quite possible for an elected official to be unrepresentative. Eventually he may be thrown out at the polls for acting in such a manner. The manipulation of party nomination procedures, the existence of one-party states, public apathy, and other factors may aid in making it possible for a congressman to be unrepresentative in relation to his constituency. And what is more important, the seniority rule still prevails in Congress, and the chairmen of powerful committees are more representative of the particular sets of interests most directly affected by committee decisions, called the "policy constituency" of the committee, than of the broader public that is also affected by their policy decisions. But Congress can become an important instigator of change, particularly when public unrest is rampant, as in the late 1960s and the Watergate era. On such occasions, Congress has risen above vested economic interests and has been far more innovative and responsive than the executive. For example, Congress has acted to safeguard some environmental interests, passing broad-ranging legislation requiring control over air, water, and noise pollution. It has attempted to curtail excessive government secrecy through the passage of the Freedom of Information Act in 1966 and subsequent amendments that strengthened it. It refused during the Nixon era to acquiesce in presidential impoundment, eventually passing the Budget and Impoundment Control Act. It has limited the ability of the President to make war without consulting Congress in the War Powers Act of 1973. It has curbed Agriculture Department and presidential attempts to limit the Food Stamp program. It has angrily investigated H.E.W. mismanagement and inefficient distribution of benefits funds, particularly supplementary-income benefits to disabled persons. Congress has also attempted, although not succeeded, in reforming regulatory agencies that have become overly responsive to industry interests. In all of these areas, Congress has been more responsive to the public pulse than the bureaucracy.

Powerful pressure groups of all kinds will frequently be better represented in the bureaucracy than in Congress. It is quite possible they will be a more important part of an administrative constituency than of a congressional constituency. Many observers have noted instances in which agencies become the "captives" of the groups they regulate. Of course there are cases in which private groups dominate congressional constituencies, but these are less common. The congressman is dealing with individual voters who are subject to the influence of a variety of groups to which they belong or with which they identify for other reasons. Moreover, congressmen have less permanency of tenure than administrators and administrative agencies, and concentrate upon policy issues less than the bureaucracy. These characteristics of Congress tend to turn the primary attention of private groups to the administrative branch to secure effective representation. These groups are likely to develop a valuable rapport over a long period of time with the agencies that regulate them, which produces a continuity of representation that is very difficult to achieve in Congress. In addition, pressure groups also find a greater knowledge and understanding of the policy viewpoints they wish to see implemented. This is particularly true when policy fields require expert knowledge in order to comprehend the nature of the problems involved.

The group representation that the framers of the Constitution were concerned about originally was that of the states. Today, because of the proliferation and importance of private pressure groups, the representation of their interests in the formulation of governmental policy is an important element in our constitutional system. The increasing nationalization of interest groups reduces the meaningfulness of state representation. Given the greater access of these groups to the bureaucracy, constitutional representation of groups today is perhaps better achieved through the administrative process than in Congress. This is why such public-interest pressure groups as Common Cause and the various Nader organizations have sought to effect change through Congress and the courts rather than by going directly to administrative agencies. In the regulatory field in particular, Ralph Nader feels that it is necessary in many cases simply to abolish the agencies before policies favoring special interests can be changed. The nature of representation in bureaucracy certainly supports John C. Calhoun and the group theorist's view of the proper function of government; but the easy access of pressure groups to administrative agencies, combined with the fact that these agencies often have final power to determine policy, would make many of the framers of the Constitution, particularly James Madison, who strongly opposed factious control of the governmental process, turn over in their graves.[39]

The constitutional system emphasizes the importance of continuity and information. James Madison and Alexander Hamilton, in *The Federalist*, felt the subjects of legislation could be divided roughly into those requiring information about the local needs of constituents and those demanding a broader knowledge of the national interest. Foreign policy, for example, falls into the latter category. Today, with the tremendous expansion in the volume and complexity of legislation there is little doubt that the bureaucracy often fulfills the needs for continuity and information better than Congress. The important innovative role of Congress should not be overlooked, and it must be recognized that it is the electoral input—or, as a minimum, the perception of members of Congress as to the needs of individual constituents—that usually leads to important policy changes. After innovation there must be implementation, and the role of the bureaucracy becomes paramount. In the implementation process, the needs of groups especially affected by policy decisions largely determine the kinds of demands that are made upon the agencies. Once legislation is passed, the legislative constituency shifts from Congress to the bureaucracy and to particular committees of Congress. At this point, the legislative constituencies properly understood no longer conform precisely to the electoral constituencies of Congressmen. In addition to a change in the nature of the constituents from whom information must be obtained in the modern legislative process, the subject matter of legislation itself is more complex. In these respects although administrative policy formulation is out of line with the legislative machinery of the Constitution, it conforms in spirit to the basic theory behind the constitutional system.

Finally, Madison and Hamilton noted the importance of locating responsibility for results in the legislative process in a group

39. John C. Calhoun's development of group theory is contained in his classic *Disquisition on Government* (New York: D. Appleton and Co., 1853). Madison's views are contained in Paper No. 10 of *The Federalist*, discussed *supra*, pp. 29-31.

that actually possesses the ability to maintain contact with appropriate policy fields from the inception of legislation to its conclusion. Here too, administrative agencies are better equipped than Congress to provide continuity to policy development. Moreover, although they are not directly accountable to the people through the electoral process, they are indirectly accountable.

The fact that Congress is more prone to veto than to initiate legislation does not necessarily detract from the vital role it plays in the political system. The bureaucracy has been established by Congress to do a job that it clearly can not do by itself, and although the administrative branch has become dominant in the legislative sphere Congress still performs important governmental functions. Major legislative changes must be approved in Congress, which frustrates the wishes of administrative agencies more frequently than they would like. Congress may also focus public attention on matters of importance through its investigations, and in this way help the electorate to become better informed. And, it remains an important representative of state and local as well as individual interests. Congress also is a training and testing ground for the Presidency, as is witnessed by the fact that from Truman to Ford all Presidents, with the exception of Dwight Eisenhower, had a congressional career before occupying the White House. Presidents such as Lyndon Johnson and Gerald Ford took a very definite congressional perspective into the White House. And in the case of President Johnson it remained throughout his administration; he attempted to run his Presidency much as he had run the majority leadership in the Senate.

Whether or not an apprenticeship in Congress helps a President to deal with the bureaucracy is impossible to determine; it is bound, however, to make the Presidents far more aware of the political nature of the bureaucracy and its close connections with Congress. For in the final analysis, the bureaucracy is a creature of Congress. It serves the internal purposes of various key Senators and Representatives—the chairmen of appropriations committees and subcommittees, and the chairmen of substantive committees that have jurisdiction over the agencies. While Congressmen rhetorically attack "bureaucracies" in general, particularly in election years, they quietly protect their favorite administrative agencies. They are, after all, in the same exclusive Washington club some would call a ruling elite. And the President is often considered to be the common enemy.

CHAPTER 5   The Presidency and the Bureaucracy

THE PRESIDENT is the man who gets things done in Washington, or so the myth goes. He is Commander in Chief, and the leader in virtually every area of government. Critics abroad and at home tend to place the blame on the President for anything they think is wrong with the United States. President Eisenhower, for example, was subjected to a great deal of foreign criticism for inaction in foreign policy just as he was criticized by many at home for failure to implement effective programs in such areas as civil rights. Richard Neustadt reports a pertinent comment of President Truman before he left the White House in 1952 as he thought of Eisenhower as President: "He'll sit here . . . and he'll say, 'Do this! Do that!' *And nothing will happen.* Poor Ike—it won't be a bit like the Army. He'll find it very frustrating." [1] Even if the President has not been a General, he is bound to be frustrated at many points, and one of the principal sources of frustration is always the bureaucracy. Presidential candidate Jimmy Carter promised to reform the bureaucracy once in office, but Presidents have inevitably been frustrated because of their lack of real power over administrative agencies.

The purpose of this chapter is to indicate the nature of the relationship that exists between the President and the administrative branch. The discussion will involve, first, the constitutional and political position of the Presidency in the government generally, and the relationship of this position to the functions exercised by the administrative branch; second, the instruments and difficulties of presidential control; third, the implications of the relationship that exists between the agencies and the President.

1. Richard E. Neustadt, *Presidential Power* (New York: John Wiley & Sons, Inc., 1960), p. 9.

The President, the Constitution, and the Bureaucracy

Very frequently the beginning student of government tends to lump the Presidency and the bureaucracy together under the heading of "The Executive." It should be clear that this cannot be done. Under the Constitution the President is the executive, but this does not necessarily give him the power to control the bureaucracy. Lack of such control is often the case even when Congress makes specific provision for presidential supervision. When Congress removes all or part of an agency's operations from presidential jurisdiction, as it has done with over one hundred agencies, the President's influence is weakened even further.

In a discussion with one of his top administrators, Franklin D. Roosevelt is reported to have said:

> . . . When I woke up this morning, the first thing I saw was a headline in the New York Times to the effect that our Navy was going to spend two billion dollars on a shipbuilding program. Here I am, the Commander in Chief of the Navy having to read about that for the first time in the press. Do you know what I said to that?
> No, Mr. President.
> I said: 'Jesus *Chr*-rist!'

Roosevelt reportedly continued:

> The Treasury . . . is so large and far-flung and ingrained in its practices that I find it is almost impossible to get the action and results I want—even with Henry [Morgenthau] there. But the Treasury is not to be compared with the State Department. You should go through the experience of trying to get any changes in the thinking, policy, and action of the career diplomats and then you'd know what a real problem was. But the Treasury and the State Department put together are nothing as compared with the Na-a-vy.[2]

Variations on this story have been repeated in the administration of every President since Washington, both weak and strong, and in periods of crisis as well as of calm.

The constitutional powers the President possesses are not suf-

2. Marriner S. Eccles, *Beckoning Frontiers,* ed. by Sidney Hyman (New York: Alfred A. Knopf, 1951), p. 336.

ficient to control the bureaucracy. Constitutional ambiguity has produced congressional interference in the affairs of administrative agencies at numerous points. Even in areas in which there is a relatively clear constitutional mandate for presidential control—as Commander in Chief of the armed forces, for example —there is no automatic guarantee of presidential domination.

The constitutional system has fragmented the bureaucracy and made it virtually impossible for any one person or group to exercise meaningful control on a continuous basis. Article II of the Constitution may seem to provide for strong presidential control over the administrative branch, but the separation of powers system generally negates much of this control. Regardless of the intentions of the framers of the Constitution, the government they created did not enable the President to exercise controlling power over the bureaucracy.

On the other hand, the nature and evolution of the Presidency supports the notion that the President has important responsibilities which necessitate a high degree of presidential domination over the activities of administrative agencies. Several factors concerning the basis and evolution of the office should be emphasized in this respect. First, the Constitution, regardless of the separation of powers, makes the Presidency the focal point of leadership in our political system. This is particularly true in foreign affairs, for the framers recognized that effective diplomacy had to be conducted with dispatch from an office which possessed the ability to act with unity. But unity in the executive, as Hamilton pointed out in *Federalist 70*, is desirable for all governmental actions even though it may be of unusual importance in foreign affairs. Clearly, if such unity is to be achieved, it is necessary to make the bureaucracy accountable to the President for many aspects of its operation, and this was recommended in *Federalist 72*.

In the second place, the Constitution gives the President important responsibilities toward legislation that have become more important with the growth of the institution of the Presidency and the wane of Congress as an effective legislative body. One could argue that the legislative activities of the administrative branch should be conducted under presidential direction; that is if leadership is to be provided in the governmental system as a whole it must come from the President. Such leadership is of obvious importance in the formulation of public policy that affects not only the nation but the world.

Finally, perhaps the most important consideration of those supporting presidential control of the bureaucracy is that the Presidency today is the focal point of democracy in America. The serious abuses of the powers of the "imperial Presidency" manifested during the administrations of Presidents Lyndon B. Johnson and Richard M. Nixon were, fortunately, aberrations in our history. While the Presidency has perhaps been viewed too sanguinely by many observers in the past, and while all Presidents have been highly partisan, none but Nixon has carried the high powers of the office to the extreme of violating both the spirit and letter of the law. But given the possibility of abuse of the imperial powers of the Presidency, the bureaucracy is an important check on the office.[3] The fact remains, however, that while the imperial Presidency may be subject to abuse, its powers also are frequently necessary for effective and democratic government. And the Presidency remains potentially the most democratic of all governmental institutions in the world. When the people elect a President by popular landslide, they have a right to expect him to bring about governmental change, and this requires control over the bureaucracy. It is for this reason that as bureaucracy has become a dominant force since the era of Franklin D. Roosevelt, Presidents have made major efforts to strengthen White House controls over the administrative branch. If the President cannot influence the bureaucracy, he can, in effect, do very little to change public policy.

The presidency has great potential in our political system for the development of a combination of responsibility and accountability, which James Madison and Alexander Hamilton thought would be an important characteristic of the legislature even more than the President. Putting aside for the moment the major problems of abuse of the power of executive privilege, if there is a need for "decision, activity, secrecy, and dispatch" in gov-

3. See Peter Woll and Rochelle Jones, "Bureaucratic Defense in Depth," *The Nation*, September 17, 1973, pp. 229–232.

ernment, to use the words of Alexander Hamilton in *Federalist 70*, with a dependence on the people, the Presidency can provide it in many fields. Certainly, until the administration of Lyndon B. Johnson, many aspects of constitutional theory and political development supported a strong Presidency, including the necessity of control over the bureaucracy. Once concern with abuses of power that occurred during the Nixon years has subsided, the Presidency will again become the dominant force in the federal government.

Problems of Presidential Control

Constitutional, legal, and political factors shape the kind of power the President possesses over particular administrative agencies. The President stands at the center of an extraordinarily complex and diverse system of government, and he, as all politicians and agencies, must strive to maintain a balance of political support in his favor. The numerous checks that each branch of the government has with respect to coordinate branches means that the President cannot simply order something to be done and expect it to happen. The President's order may be heeded, but not until the individual to whom the order has been given feels it is in his interest to obey: this is, of course, the essence of real authority in contrast to constitutional and legal authority. Nevertheless, it is because the Constitution fragmented the political system in the first place that the President is in such straits. Authority is never given to the President without some constitutional check in another branch of the government. And more general constitutional provisions, such as the Tenth Amendment which supports federalism, make it impossible for the President to develop a cohesive political majority.

In the discussion of Congress and the bureaucracy in the last chapter it was noted that several factors are involved in determining the power of a governmental branch or agency to legislate: (1) constitutional and legal authority; (2) political support; (3) organizational cohesiveness or unity; (4) information. On balance the bureaucracy's superiority in these areas gives it an advantage over Congress in the legislative process. The very same factors relate to the ability of the President to control the bureaucracy not only in the legislative process but with regard to all administrative functions. The ability to control, as opposed to the ability to formulate and implement legislation, also goes somewhat beyond these considerations and involves such powers as appointing and removing those over whom control is to be exercised. But the ability to appoint or remove administrative officials depends to a very large extent upon political support regardless of where the legal authority to take such action resides. Thus, in terms of the above categories, although the appointive and removal power falls initially under constitutional and legal authority, it involves political support to an equal degree. An assessment of presidential power over the administrative branch can be made by analyzing each of these categories in turn. The fact that they are interrelated should always be kept in mind.

CONSTITUTIONAL AND LEGAL AUTHORITY

Administrative agencies are created and structured by Congress. With the exceptions of the Environmental Protection Agency and the Department of Health, Education, and Welfare, authority given by Congress to the President, there are no other important permanent agencies now existing that have not been directly established by statutory authority. And, both the EPA and HEW operate within the framework of a number of specific legislative enactments, even though the agencies per se were not created by Congress. During periods of national emergency, Congress may grant the President extraordinary authority to conduct the affairs of the nation, and for this purpose it may authorize him to assume complete control over the bureaucracy. Such legal authorization does not mean the President becomes a dictator, but it means that more than at any other time his principal limitation will have to come from stubborn administrators. During war, the Supreme Court and Congress retreat from the field of battle for which the Constitution so carefully provided, and the democratic process survives in the ever-present ordered conflict among administrative agencies.

World War II provides an important illustration of virtually total legal domination by the President over the administrative branch. It is instructive to observe the way in which Congress transferred to the President the legal authority to shape and control the bureaucracy during this brief period. In 1941 the First War Powers Act was passed which provided in part:

That for the national security and defense, for the successful prose-cution of the war, for the support and maintenance of the Army and Navy, for the better utilization of resources and industries, and for the more effective exercise and more efficient administration by the President of his powers as Commander in Chief of the Army and Navy, the President is hereby authorized to make such redistribution of functions among executive agencies as he may deem necessary, including any functions, duties, and powers hitherto by law conferred upon any executive department, commission, bureau, agency, govern-mental corporation, office, or officer, in such manner as his judgment shall deem best fitted to carry out the purposes of this title [Act], and to this end is authorized to make such regulations and to issue such orders as he may deem necessary. . . . *Provided* . . . That the au-thority by this title granted shall be exercised only in matters relating to the conduct of the present war. . . .[4]

The Act further provided that Congress was to retain control over appropriations to the administrative branch, and that at the end of the war presidential reorganizations and redistributions of functions were to be null and void. It was on the basis of this statute that President Roosevelt established the Office of War Mobilization (OWM), a "super-agency" with virtually unlimited *authority* and, under the direction of James F. Byrnes, an un-usually powerful agency within carefully drawn limits.

Conflict among administrative agencies was so intense during World War II that at times the bureaucratic strife was referred to as the "battle of Washington." OWM had to contend with in-trenched bureaucratic interests, and it was principally through skillful political maneuvering that it was able to achieve relative success in its attempt to coordinate the war effort. The nature of its authority was relevant primarily because Byrnes, as its chief, was considered to be an Assistant President. As Herman Somers has pointed out in his excellent account of OWM, "the ability of an over-all policy agency to implement the powers granted it, either by Congress or an executive order, depends chiefly on the status it wins within the government. The condi-

4. 55 Stat. 838 (1941).

tions of the President's order gave OWM a more elevated position than it would have enjoyed under the proposed legislation." [5] OWM was not an operating agency, but was engaged entirely in policy formulation and coordination. Lacking clientele groups, it had to rely mostly upon the President for political support. During a war period this type of arrangement may work fairly well, but even in such critical times old-line administrative agencies are unwilling to give up what they think are their prerogatives.

The experience of OWM vividly illustrates that a policy co-ordinating agency with all the legal authority of the President behind it, without significant congressional opposition, and with no judicial interference, cannot necessarily exercise effective control over the bureaucracy as a whole. Somers notes that "there is no doubt that Byrnes' steadfast devotion to the principles that OWM must not administer anything, must not interfere with normal operations of existing agencies, and must protect their prestige and status, was a pillar of strength for the new agency." [6] Byrnes was careful not to step beyond the bounds of his real power, regardless of his sweeping legal authority. Those who feel that the President should be "Chief Administrator" in fact should not forget the experience of OWM, nor the more general problems Roosevelt faced as he tried to exert his constitutional prerogatives as Commander in Chief and Chief Executive during a war period, when presidential authority is greater than at any other time.

Although the President may be given virtually unlimited legal authority over the administrative branch during wartime, in normal periods his authority is curtailed. In this respect he cannot invoke constitutional prerogatives with any degree of forcefulness or urgency. Of course the Constitution says he shall be vested with "executive power," and "may require the opinion in writing, of the principal officer in each of the executive departments, upon any subject relating to the duties of their respective offices." He is also to "take care that the laws be faithfully executed," and he is Commander in Chief of the armed forces. But these powers

5. Herman M. Somers, *Presidential Agency* (Cambridge: Harvard University Press, 1950), p. 50.

6. *Ibid.*, p. 60.

are mere words unless the President can persuade the bureaucracy to act in accordance with his point of view. If he cannot do this during wartime when he usually has acquiescence of Congress and the judiciary, how can he hope to achieve control over the sprawling administrative agencies during time of peace? Congress in particular becomes his adversary in normal times, and gives legal authority to administrative agencies that fortifies them against presidential intrusion into their affairs. Congress also becomes a basis of political support for agencies that wish to defy the President.

The way in which the bureaucracy inevitably controls Presidents was demonstrated during the administration of Richard Nixon, when he attempted to marshal all of the constitutional and legal authority of the office as well as its political power to control the executive branch. He even went so far as to try to make the Executive Office of the President (EOP) more dependent on the White House by abolishing the Bureau of the Budget under his reorganization power (which Congress allowed to lapse in 1974 because of presidential abuses) and recreating the same agency by executive order and calling it the Office of Management and Budget.[7] President Nixon wanted to centralize control of the bureaucracy in the White House not just for administrative efficiency, but also, more importantly, for political control. Using constitutional prerogatives and statutory authority, he attempted wide-ranging impoundment of funds appropriated by Congress for programs that he did not feel should be funded at the levels the legislature wished. He sought significant reorganizations of the bureaucracy under his reorganization authority, and, in major cases, he recommended that departments be reorganized and consolidated through the enactment of new congressional legislation. President Nixon was not embarking upon a new course in seeking to dominate the bureaucracy, but was simply attempting to extend by the scope of his actions the power of the imperial Presidency to its outer limits. But President Nixon found, as had Presidents before and after him, that the bureaucracy is a formidable force not easily reorganized or subject to control through such devices as

7. See Reorganization Plan No. 2 of 1970, discussed below, pp. 232 ff.

impoundment. When stirred up, the bureaucracy will attack, sometimes in force. With the exception of the creation of the Office of Management and Budget to replace the old Bureau of the Budget, and the establishment of the Domestic Council within the Executive Office of the President, none of President Nixon's reorganization plans succeeded in passing Congress. Congress proved itself to be a strong ally of the bureaucracy. Congress often supports the independence of administrative agencies from White House control by preventing administrative reorganization, and by continuing statutory limits upon presidential authority.

STATUTORY CHECKS ON PRESIDENTIAL POWER

The primary legal checks upon presidential power over the bureaucracy come from statutes, which determine basic organizational patterns. Statutes may limit the President's control over particular spheres of activity by assigning sole responsibility for action to an administrative agency or officer. In such situations the President loses directive power over important policy areas unless, once again, he can somehow persuade an agency to follow him. In this way much of the activity of the independent regulatory commissions is legally removed from presidential supervision; even members of his own Cabinet possess authority to act in various fields without consulting him. Moreover, Congress frequently gives independent authority to subordinate bureaus within executive departments. With such legal authority as a starting point, a stubborn official can defy the wishes of the President again and again. Unless the President wants to make an issue of such defiance and, as a last resort, ask the official to resign, there is little he can do. Many other considerations enter the picture, such as the political support of the President as opposed to that of the defiant agency or official, the President's relations with Congress and the status of his proposals in that body, congressional support of the agency, whether the administrator in question is covered by the merit system, and so forth. Although legal authority is not enough by itself to support administrative defiance of presidential wishes, there is no doubt that clear-cut legal authority for agency independence helps the bureaucracy to ignore presidential demands.

The Merit System · One of the most important legal limitations upon both the appointive and removal powers of the President is the merit system. The extension of the merit system during the twentieth century has resulted not only from congressional enactments, but also from executive orders. In fact, the greatest expansions of coverage have come from the President, who has of course congressional authorization to "blanket" the civil service, that is, bring it under the protection of the merit system. Under the terms of the Ramspeck Act of 1940 the President can extend this protection to virtually all of the federal bureaucracy. Regularized procedures have been established for the recruitment of personnel as well as strict rules for dismissal. Congress has further complicated the system through the creation of veterans' preferences, which aid that group regardless of talent, both with respect to recruitment and reductions in force. Some observers feel these laws have seriously reduced the effectiveness of the merit system and hampered the various presidential attempts that have been made to improve federal personnel administration.

There seems to be a paradox in the fact that the merit system, which has been expanded principally through the actions of various Presidents, is one of the greatest limitations upon presidential ability to control the bureaucracy. But it must be remembered that new agencies usually tend to be advocates of the President under whom they have been created. This follows from the necessity of administrative agencies to maintain a balance of political support in their favor. When they are first established it is usually imperative that they turn to the President for this purpose, for he is the most logical and available source of immediate support. It is not until later that they develop independent interests which may lead them into opposition with the President, who by then will most likely be a different person and possibly of a different party than the man who was in office when the agency was first established. It takes time to create effective liaison with clientele groups, and in some instances such groups will not be immediately identifiable to the newly formed agency. Frequently groups that are at first opposed to the agency will later become an important source of clientele support, as was the case with the railroads and the Interstate Commerce Commission. Perhaps an even more striking example is the Tennessee Valley

Authority, which now has the strong support of groups that were at first not uniformly enthusiastic. During the Eisenhower period these groups rallied around the TVA to prevent presidential diminution of its sphere of activity, and today no serious presidential candidate is going to attack the TVA (as Senator Barry Goldwater inadvertently did in the presidential campaign of 1964) without arousing a storm of protest.

In the twentieth century the greatest increment in the bureaucracy came during the New Deal, and all the new agencies of that period were rooted in the philosophy of the "Roosevelt Revolution," as Professor Mario Einaudi has termed this era.[8] Roosevelt may have had a "honeymoon" with Congress for only the first hundred days, but his honeymoon with the bureaucracy lasted for a considerably longer period. It was only natural that many of the men and women going into the federal service in the thirties were initially or became pro-Roosevelt, but at first they were generally not under the protection of the merit system. By placing these new civil servants under the merit system Roosevelt was taking the very course of action necessary to protect the New Deal and at the same time reward dedicated career public servants. Similarly, President Truman brought a considerable portion of the bureaucracy under the protection of the merit system before he faced the uncertainty of the 1948 election. Extending the merit system guarded the interests of the New Deal-Fair Deal public servants. A major frustration of both Presidents Nixon and Ford with the bureaucracy was the fact that it is largely oriented toward the policies of the Democratic party. The merit system was protecting civil servants whose views were diametrically opposed to those of the Republican White House.

The Roosevelt and Truman actions suggest that a great deal of what might be called "merit system politics" can be exercised by the President. On the other hand, political interests opposed to the President are logical in their desire to have the bureaucracy put under the protection of civil service, for this prevents the President from improper political manipulation of the administrative branch while he is in office. His interests may best be served

8. Mario Einaudi, *The Roosevelt Revolution* (New York: Harcourt, Brace & World, Inc., 1959).

by extending the merit system only when he faces the possibility of being defeated at the polls. Thus timing becomes important. But it is inevitable politically that the merit system will continue to be extended as far as possible, and at the present time it covers well over ninety per cent of the bureaucracy.

Until the presidential election of 1976, Democratic presidential nominees since the New Deal have supported for the most part the maintenance of the administrative branch and even the expansion of the bureaucracy to meet pressing public problems. Until Democratic presidential candidate Jimmy Carter promised to make major reforms of the bureaucracy although not necessarily through the elimination of agencies, "down with big government" and "abolish big bureaucracy" have been the rallying cries of the Republicans. The past experiences of Republican Presidents in failing to make significant changes in the bureaucracy suggest that no Democratic President, even with a large majority in Congress, will be able significantly to alter vested bureaucratic interests. This is because both pressure groups under the jurisdiction of administrative agencies and powerful committee chairmen in Congress find it in their interests to maintain the patterns of bureaucratic organization to advance their own power. The merit and the civil service system means that the only way public employees can be reduced is through the elimination of bureaucratic functions, an unlikely event requiring the co-operation of the White House and Capitol Hill.

The frustrations of President Eisenhower in 1952 and President Nixon in 1968 with the bureaucracy illustrate the way in which the merit system helps to limit the ability of the President to bring about personnel changes in the administrative branch. Before and after President Eisenhower's election in 1952, he promised to review the activities of the administrative branch and to reduce what he hinted were large numbers of unproductive and, in the spirit of the times, disloyal civil servants.[9] Although during the preceding administrations the

9. For an excellent account of the change in administration that took place in 1952 see Herman Miles Somers, "The Federal Bureaucracy and the Change of Administration," 48 *American Political Science Review* 131–151 (1954).

views and actions of the agencies frequently had not been in accordance with the wishes of Presidents Roosevelt and Truman on numerous occasions, the bureaucracy was generally imbued with the idea that it should be active in the regulation of the economic life of the country and positive in making legislative recommendations to Congress and the President. Both Roosevelt and Truman preferred a bureaucracy that seized the initiative, even if this meant a certain amount of opposition to presidential desires from time to time, over a bureaucracy that was unresponsive and passive.

In general the criteria upon which the agencies were operating in 1952 were somewhat out of line with the Republican Party's officially stated position favoring the withdrawal of government from many areas in which it had participated actively during the Democratic period. President Eisenhower, who agreed basically with the Republican philosophy, faced the problem of attempting to initiate new policies through a bureaucracy that was hostile to much of what he wanted to do. The only way he could do this, or so he felt, was to make many personnel changes, but the merit system presented a formidable obstacle. Another tack might have been to try to win the bureaucracy to his point of view, or at least act in a way which would not result in bureaucratic hostility. But for the most part this course of action was not taken, and the President set out to reduce the number of civil servants generally and in particular to concentrate upon discovering and firing disloyal and corrupt administrators. The atmosphere in the bureaucracy during the first years of Eisenhower's administration was one of suspicion and distrust. But very few changes were actually made among the permanent career officials and the bureaucracy was able to maintain its independence within the merit system. The fact that this system protected many policy-making officials raised questions in the minds of some, who felt the country had voted for a change and should have seen it implemented.

After his election in 1968, President Nixon confronted many of the same problems that frustrated President Eisenhower in dealing with the bureaucracy. President Nixon was a more actively conservative President than Eisenhower, and therefore felt more acutely the need to dismantle government programs that had been the trademark of the "liberals." Unlike Eisenhower, however, Nixon had not been elected by a landslide but by the narrowest of margins. A minority President, he did not have a popular mandate to change the government, and he was to find that Congress, dominated by Democrats, would play its traditional game of using the bureaucracy as a weapon against presidential intrusions upon its power. Any abolition of governmental functions—the only way the President could reduce personnel covered by civil service—required the approval of Congress, which was not forthcoming. Ironically, during the Nixon administration there was unprecedented growth in the *presidential* bureaucracy (the Executive Office of the President), while no significant reductions were made in federal personnel in regular administrative agencies. The President found it difficult even to reduce personnel in agencies within his own Executive Office, as is witnessed by the long and bitter struggle to abolish the Office of Economic Opportunity (OEO), a struggle which only bore fruit at the very end of the Nixon administration, years after the President had recommended the agency's elimination. Basically, President Nixon attempted to deal with the bureaucracy through infiltration of regular departments and agencies by Nixon politicos; but this only served to cause a great deal of distrust and paranoia among bureaucrats rather than accomplish the President's goal of making significant reductions in federal programs.

The assumption of office by Gerald Ford in August, 1974, caused no significant changes in the relationships between the President and the bureaucracy in spite of the fact that President Ford was as conservative, if not more conservative, than President Nixon. He dealt with the bureaucracy much more loosely, granting leeway to department heads and agencies to develop programs and giving them freer access to the White House without the usual strict requirement of channeling all requests through the Office of Management and Budget and other presidential staff agencies. President Ford recommended cutbacks in numerous federal programs, including defense, and a broad revamping of the regulatory agencies. In fact, during his administration there was no significant reduction in federal programs or personnel. In attempting to reduce program expenditures, President Ford's main weapon was the instrument of denial, the veto. In reality, however, most federal programs (for example, defense, social security, veterans' benefits, farm price supports) are supported by both parties, and are based on past statutory commitments that cannot easily be altered. Tradition, political support, and practical necessities buttress the bureaucracy against change.

As the anti-bureaucratic cry that has been traditional of the Republicans was taken up in the mid-1970s by prominent Democrats such as Jimmy Carter and Senator Edward Kennedy, it remained to be seen whether or not a Democratic President could either reduce the personnel of the executive branch or significantly alter administrative organization. Jimmy Carter significantly stated that if he became President he would not even attempt to cope with the problems of reduction of federal personnel except through attrition. This was an extraordinarily adept and realistic political move, for any promises to the contrary would border on demagoguery.

Senatorial Confirmation · The merit system is not the only legal obstacle faced by the President with respect to the appointive and removal powers. When Congress provides that administrative positions shall be filled by presidential appointments the confirmation of the Senate is usually required. And, of course, the Constitution requires senatorial confirmation of presidential appointments of ambassadors, "other public ministers and consuls," and judges of the Supreme Court. The President's Cabinet must be confirmed by the Senate, and although it is generally a formality, from time to time the Senate refuses to accept the President's choice; for example, at the end of Eisenhower's second term the Senate turned down the appointment of Lewis Strauss, an experienced but controversial public servant, to become Secretary of Commerce. He had formerly been Chairman of the Atomic Energy Commission during the Eisenhower administration. Presidents Nixon and Ford withdrew appointments to regulatory agencies rather than face almost certain Senate opposition. Although such incidents are relatively rare, the President is well aware of the need to satisfy the Senate in the appointive process. In addition to Cabinet appointments, the President has the initial power to make many thousands of appointments of subordinate officials: postmasters, judges, and so forth. Because Congress is jealous of its prerogatives it has required senatorial confirmation in virtually all these cases. The net result is that most high-level administrators engaged in policy making and adjudication must be confirmed by the Senate, and in controversial cases the President's wishes may be frustrated.[10]

The legal necessity of senatorial approval of appointments is not, however, as formidable a barrier to presidential control of the bureaucracy as the merit system. Appointments are never turned down unless there is strong political opposition capable of overcoming the political strength that always emanates from the Presidency. Moreover, Congress cannot legislate detailed provisions regarding a prospective presidential appointee. The initiative to make an appointment is considered to be an "executive" function under the Constitution. The only thing Congress can do is state general qualifications for administrative jobs, and leave the initiative in the hands of the President or another component of the administrative branch, such as the Civil Service Commission. Needless to say, in the appointive process the groups having the initiative control most of the decisions that are made.

Legal Barriers · The President also may face legal problems when he attempts to remove officials who occupy appointive positions outside the protection of the merit system. On assuming office, an incoming President must deal with previous presidential appointments of a different political persuasion. The Cabinet, of course, resigns upon the election of a new President even if he is of the same party as the incumbent. But key personnel in the regulatory agencies may choose to continue in office until their tenure, usually guaranteed by statute for a period of five to seven years, expires. If the President wishes to remove a member of one of these regulatory agencies he faces several legal barriers. First, the statute setting up the agency may specify that the administrator may not be removed during his term except for "inefficiency, neglect of duty, or malfeasance in office." This kind of provision implies that removal cannot be made for political reasons, which are usually the very factors behind presidential attempts to remove

10. A classic example of senatorial refusal to accept a presidential appointment may be found in Joseph P. Harris, "The Senatorial Rejection of Leland Olds," 35 *American Political Science Review* 674–693 (1951).

policy-making officials. If there is no statement of congressional policy regarding limitations upon the President's removal power over agency officials the courts may, upon a presidential attempt at removal, step in to protect an official, provided he has been given *judicial* responsibilities by Congress. In such a case the courts may hold that regardless of the absence of a clear congressional mandate protecting a particular agency in which administrators are engaged in adjudication, there is a congressional presumption that adjudicative functions should be exercised in an independent atmosphere. This presumption may prevent presidential removal of adjudicative officials for political reasons.

These general considerations become clear upon examination of several key court cases. In 1926 the Supreme Court decided, in the historic case of *Myers v. United States,* that an 1876 law limiting the President's removal power over postmasters was unconstitutional.[11] This decision was soon to be modified. The law in question stated:

Postmasters of the first, second and third classes shall be appointed and may be removed by the President by and with the advice and consent of the Senate and shall hold their offices for four years unless sooner removed or suspended according to law.

President Wilson appointed Myers to be a first class postmaster in Portland, Oregon, in 1917 and subsequently removed him from this position in 1920 without consulting the Senate. Myers sued for his salary in the Court of Claims, and when he received an adverse judgment an appeal was taken to the Supreme Court. Chief Justice Taft, a former President, strongly asserted in the *Myers* case the constitutional right of the President to appoint and remove subordinate officials for political and other reasons, regardless of the functions they perform. He felt such power to be implied in the constitutional provision giving the President the responsibility to see that the laws are faithfully executed, as well as in the other general executive powers stated in Article II. The main point of his argument was that the President simply cannot carry out his constitutional responsibilities if Congress interferes with his ability to control the executive branch of the government. The *Myers* opinion, which was almost belligerent in tone, as if

11. 272 U.S. 52 (1926).

Taft were still speaking from the White House, clearly overlooked the fact that parts of the bureaucracy, particularly the independent regulatory commissions, were purposely placed outside of presidential control to avoid partisan influence. Indeed, if Taft's views had been the accepted constitutional doctrine, the recent development of the bureaucracy might have been quite different, characterized by a much greater degree of administrative unity and presidential control.

The issue of the President's removal power over members of the independent regulatory commissions was raised during the New Deal and decided in 1935 by the Supreme Court in *Humphrey's Executor* (*Rathbun*) *v. United States.*[12] Humphrey was nominated to become a member of the Federal Trade Commission by President Hoover in 1931, and he was confirmed by the Senate. Federal Trade Commissioners are appointed for a term of seven years, established by Congress in the Federal Trade Commission Act of 1914. The Act states that Commissioners may be removed by the President "for inefficiency, neglect of duty, or malfeasance in office." In July, 1933, President Roosevelt requested Humphrey's resignation in a letter, giving as his reason "that the aims and purposes of the Administration with respect to the work of the commission can be carried out most effectively with personnel of my own selection." Humphrey was undecided, and another letter followed from the President in which he stated: "You will, I know, realize that I do not feel that your mind and my mind go along together on either the policies or the administering of the Federal Trade Commission, and, frankly, I think it is best for the people of this country that I should have a full confidence." Humphrey continued his refusal to resign, and in October of 1933 Roosevelt finally notified him that he had been removed. But Humphrey never agreed to his removal, and after his death in 1934 his executor, Rathbun, sued for salary he felt had been due Humphrey but never paid. The suit was brought in the Court of Claims, which certified two questions, one of a statutory and the other of a constitutional nature, to the Supreme Court to be answered before judgment could be rendered.

The questions posed for the Court in the *Humphrey* case were, first, whether or not the Federal Trade Commission Act limited

12. 295 U.S. 602 (1935).

the President's power to remove Commissioners except for the causes stated; second, if such a limitation existed was it in accordance with the Constitution? President Roosevelt had clearly indicated that the removal was for political reasons; that is, he and Humphrey did not agree on the policies the Commission should adopt. Justice Sutherland wrote the opinion of the Court, which stated that it was clearly the intent of Congress to limit the removal power of the President, and that, in answer to the second question, such a limitation was entirely constitutional. With reference to the first point the Court noted:

The [Federal Trade] Commission is to be non-partisan; and it must, from the very nature of its duties, act with entire impartiality. It is charged with the enforcement of no policy except the policy of the law. Its duties are neither political nor executive, but predominantly quasi-judicial and quasi-legislative. Like the Interstate Commerce Commission, its members are called upon to exercise the trained judgment of a body of experts "appointed by law and informed by experience." . . .[13]

The term "impartiality" coupled with the term "non-partisan" meant policies would not be administered, that is, formulated and implemented, in terms of the interests of only one of the major parties. For this reason the President's power of removal of members of the regulatory commissions was limited, and other restraints were placed upon his ability to control the activities of these agencies. Thus the Court's conclusion correctly mirrored congressional intent to limit the President; the argument was based upon very narrow definitions which did not imply the fact that the agencies are supposed to be "political" even though not completely under the control of the President. The agencies were created as arms of Congress; they always have been as deeply involved in politics as any group in government.

After determining the intent of Congress to limit the President's removal power, the Court faced the more important question of the constitutionality of such a statutory restraint. By upholding the constitutionality of this limitation in the Federal Trade Commission Act the *Humphrey* case modified the *Myers* opinion in a substantial way. The Court noted in the *Humphrey* decision that

13. *Ibid.*, p. 624.

a distinction should be made between "executive" and "administrative" functions within the bureaucracy. "Executive" functions include no responsibilities of a judicial or legislative nature; those responsibilities are considered "administrative." Under the Constitution the President controls the executive branch, which means those agencies that perform essentially executive functions. The President may control "administrative" functions only if Congress chooses to give him the power. The Court concluded that with regard to administrators engaged in legislative and judicial functions "we think it plain under the Constitution that illimitable power of removal is not possessed by the President. . . ."[14] Moreover:

> . . . The authority of Congress, in creating quasi-legislative or quasi-judicial agencies, to require them to act in discharge of their duties independently of executive control cannot well be doubted; and that authority includes, as an appropriate incident, power to fix the period during which they shall continue in office, and to forbid their removal except for cause in the meantime. For it is evident that one who holds his office only during the pleasure of another cannot be depended upon to maintain an attitude of independence against the latter's will.[15]

Where executive functions can be identified Congress cannot limit presidential control, for the President's authority stems from the Constitution. Thus the vigorous opinion of Chief Justice Taft in the *Myers* case, which so clearly was designed to give the President virtually unlimited authority to control the entire bureaucracy, was restricted in the *Humphrey* decision to include only purely executive officials.

Although the *Humphrey* case clearly limited the removal power of the President it did not answer the question of the extent of this power when there is no statutory limitation. Causes for removal are specified for Federal Trade Commissioners, but many regulatory statutes say nothing. In such instances is the President's removal power unlimited? In 1958, in *Wiener v. United States,* the Supreme Court held that if officials are engaged in adjudicative functions the President may not remove them for political reasons.[16] Wiener had been appointed to the War Claims Com-

14. *Ibid.*, p. 629.
15. *Ibid.*
16. 357 U.S. 349 (1958).

mission, an adjudicative body, by President Truman in 1950, and Senate confirmation followed. The Commission was composed of three members and was to continue in existence not later than three years after the statutory limit for the filing of war claims. When President Eisenhower assumed office he requested Wiener's resignation and, when he did not receive it, removed him with the statement that: "I regard it as in the national interest to complete the administration of the War Claims Act of 1948, as amended, with personnel of my own selection." That was similar to what President Roosevelt told Humphrey upon removing him from the Federal Trade Commission. In both instances the removals were for political purposes. Noting that the War Claims Commission is clearly an adjudicative body Justice Frankfurter concluded for a unanimous Court in the *Wiener* case:

. . . Judging the matter in all the nakedness in which it is presented, namely, the claim that the President could remove a member of an adjudicatory body like the War Claims Commission merely because he wanted his own appointees on such a Commission, we are compelled to conclude that no such power is given to the President directly by the Constitution, and none is impliedly conferred upon him by statute simply because Congress said nothing about it. The philosophy of *Humphrey's Executor*, in its explicit language as well as its implications, precludes such a claim.[17]

Thus in this type of case the judiciary may limit the legal and constitutional authority of the President over the bureaucracy in the absence of statutory restraints.

The next President after President Eisenhower to get himself into trouble over the removal of an official of the executive branch was President Nixon, who summarily fired Watergate Special Prosecutor Archibald Cox on October 20, 1973. Cox was exercising prosecutorial functions, which placed him in a different category from Humphrey and Wiener, who were exercising quasi-judicial functions. Prosecutorial functions are clearly executive, and it seems reasonable to assume that as such they would be under the control of the chief executive officer, in this case the President. Certainly, the President, in the absence of statutory limitations, can remove the Attorney General and other prosecutors within the Justice Department for political reasons.

17. *Ibid.*, p. 356.

There would be no judicial presumption of congressional intent to protect such officials in the absence of clear statutory provisions to the contrary. At the same time that Archibald Cox as Special Prosecutor was performing prosecutorial functions, he was not directly appointed by the President, but by the Attorney General under congressional statutes authorizing the establishment of an Office of Special Prosecutor. When Attorney General Eliot Richardson hired Mr. Cox, he specifically promulgated a regulation that limited his own authority to fire him. The formal Department of Justice regulation provided that "The Special Prosecutor will not be removed from his duties except for extraordinary impropriety on his part."

After the "Saturday Night Massacre," which included the firing of Archibald Cox by Acting Attorney General Robert Bork upon specific instructions by President Nixon, Ralph Nader and three members of Congress sued for a declaration that the dismissal was illegal and for an injunction against Bork. Judge Gesell, of the District Court of the District of Columbia, dismissed Nader as a plaintiff, claiming that he had no standing to pursue the suit. However, Judge Gesell granted standing to the three members of Congress, claiming that as representatives of Congress and of special committees dealing with matters concerning the role of the Special Prosecutor, their interests were substantial enough to justify a judicial determination regarding the legality of firing Cox. On the merits, the District Court held that the President had no authority to fire the Special Prosecutor because Cox was an agent of Congress, appointed by the Attorney General, who had issued a special regulation limiting the conditions of his removal. These conditions—"extraordinary impropriety"—were not demonstrated by the President nor by the Acting Attorney General, who carried out the President's orders to fire Cox.[18] Had the Attorney General, upon hiring Cox, stated no conditions limiting Cox's removal, the Special Prosecutor

18. *Nader v. Bork*, 366 F. Supp. 104 (1973). Although Ralph Nader was not granted standing, his disqualification came from the bench and the case remained in the books in his name. Archibald Cox was not a party to the suit because he had no interest in returning to his job, and when the Court finally ruled in his favor he did not resume his duties. The case, then, established a principle governing presidential removal, although it had no practical effect.

could have been summarily dismissed. Once the administrative regulations were promulgated, however, they had the full force of law and had to be obeyed.

POLITICAL SUPPORT AND ORGANIZATIONAL PATTERNS

The fact that the bureaucracy is not necessarily under the control of the President, by the terms of the Constitution, nor within his jurisdiction by statute, means that the President must deal with administrative agencies in the same way he deals with other interest groups and with Congress. He must persuade the bureaucracy to go along with him, for he cannot command it to obey him. The bureaucracy, however, is not itself unitary but is composed of a multitude of agencies that very often find themselves in sharp conflict with each other. If the President were dealing with a monolithic entity in the bureaucracy he as well as other governmental and private groups might easily be dominated. But each agency differs in terms of its authority, political support, organizational cohesiveness, and area of jurisdiction. Some agencies are of course very powerful and may be able to have their own way much of the time in their dealings with Congress, the President, and even the judiciary. But other agencies are weak in terms of the above factors relative to the strength of the President, and therefore presidential domination over their activities may follow without impediment. In such cases the agencies may turn to the President as the primary source of their own political support.

The President gains political support from a number of governmental and private groups, and from the public as a whole. If an administrative agency wishes to challenge a presidential decision ordering it to implement a particular program, it may have great difficulty unless it has strong support in Congress and from its clientele groups. The Presidency by its very nature is automatically a political force of considerable magnitude. The attention of the nation is perpetually focused upon the White House, and the President's every utterance is repeated in the various news media. He can mold public opinion, which in turn can gain him important political backing in Congress. He can also marshal the support of private pressure groups which may or may not fall outside the sphere of clientele interests of particular agencies. The fact that the President is the only nationally elected official is something no agency will overlook as it undertakes its own difficult mission of acquiring a favorable balance of political support.

Unlike Congress, and unlike many administrative agencies, the President can act with unity and with speed. Although the Presidency is now institutional, composed of a variety of staff agencies, one man still has the final power to make decisions. The political support that is gained by the Presidency can be funneled and pinpointed by one man. This kind of organizational unity is a striking contrast to the fragmented nature of Congress. An agency may divide and conquer Congress by playing off one committee against another, and by utilizing generally those congressional interests in favor of its point of view in combination with outside support to defeat those groups and individuals in Congress that may oppose it. But an agency cannot divide the Presidency if the President has firmly decided upon a particular course of action. If he has not made up his mind, the agency may be able to pressure subordinate presidential staff groups to support it and thus indirectly influence the President's final decision. But this assumes presidential indecision, which is an entirely different situation.

Although the Presidency itself may be unified to a greater extent than any other branch of the government, the President is frequently a victim of the fragmentation of the American political system. Because the Constitution requires the agreement of two houses of Congress and the President before anything can be done, the President who wishes to exercise *positive* control over the bureaucracy must have a very broad base of political support. The bureaucracy, on the other hand, will usually wish to stand pat, and hence it will primarily desire to exercise *negative* power in relation to presidential proposals. To fail to act is always easier than to act positively; that is, it is less difficult to maintain the *status quo* than to change it. The agency, then, that wishes to defy the President will actually need less political support to achieve this goal than the President will need to bring the agency into his sphere of influence. Presidential power usually requires a chain of political support which always has some vulnerable links, and a defiant agency may be particularly adept at finding these weak points.

The principal political problem the President has with respect to the agencies stems for the most part from the difficulties he faces in securing political support in Congress. Constitutional as well as political factors place the President and Congress into positions antagonistic to each other, making it impossible for the President to achieve consistent majority support in Congress. The President may be the head of his political party, but he is far from controlling it. In fact, some of the sharpest opposition to his proposals more frequently than not will come from members of his own party in Congress. Democratic Presidents from Harry Truman to Lyndon B. Johnson have attempted to reorganize various parts of the bureaucracy only to find the agencies strongly protected in Congress by its Democratic committee chairmen. Any Democratic President would find the same congressional obstacles to administrative reform. Without the cooperation of Congress it is extremely difficult if not impossible for the President to dominate the bureaucracy, since Congress has the constitutional authority to control some of the most important aspects of administrative operation. Thus, although the President may act with dispatch and firmness in reaching decisions, his endeavors to control the agencies will fail unless Congress accedes to his wishes. But if the bureaucracy is able to dominate Congress in a particular area, it is very likely that for this very reason it will also be able to defy the President within that area.

The importance of the relationship of the President and Congress to presidential ability to control the bureaucracy may be seen in the field of administrative reorganization. The determination of legal lines of accountability generally involves the relative political support that the President, congressional groups, and the agencies are able to achieve and maintain. Moreover, reorganization is one of the few areas in which the President is likely to have a program he wishes to see implemented in relation to the bureaucracy.

Since 1949 Congress has authorized the President to reorganize the bureaucracy at his own initiative provided that within sixty days after he submits a reorganization plan to Congress neither the House of Representatives nor the Senate vetoes it by a constitutional (1949 Act) or by a simple majority (1961 Act). The first Reorganization Act, in 1939, required a veto by simple majority in both houses of Congress before a presidential plan could be rejected. Congress dropped the requirement that both houses must veto a presidential reorganization plan because in effect it gives the White House almost total discretion to reorganize the administrative branch. Although the single-house veto gives Congress more flexibility in dealing with the President, it, too, has not been used frequently to turn down presidential reorganization plans. The single-house veto by a simple majority has been included in all Reorganization Acts since 1961. Only five presidential reorganization plans, however, out of a total of thirty-four that were submitted to Congress by Presidents Kennedy, Johnson, Nixon, and Ford were vetoed by Congress. When reorganization plans are in effect, the initiative clearly lies with the President.

Since reorganization authority increases presidential power over the bureaucracy, executive-legislative tension may cause Congress to allow the President's reorganization authority to lapse. Congress has always been careful to place time limits on the reorganization authority it grants to the President— usually one or two years. Reorganization Acts must be renewed in order to continue that authority. Presidents always request such a continuance, but Congress does not automatically approve. For example, in 1973, as the Watergate revelations were beginning to build, President Nixon requested a renewal of the 1971 Reorganization Act that expired on April 1, 1973. Congress, however, took no action and the President's authority lapsed. It was not renewed during the first term of the Ford administration. The first order of priority for a President wishing to reform the bureaucracy is to go to Congress to request reorganization authority subject to congressional veto.

The continuing struggle between Congress and the President over reorganization authority is illustrated by the history of Reorganization Acts since 1961. The 1961 Act itself had to be passed because Congress had allowed reorganization authority to lapse under President Eisenhower, reflecting not only the tension between a Democratic Congress and a Republican President, but also the lack of strong initiative on Eisenhower's part to reorganize the bureaucracy and to see to it that Congress maintained his reorganization authority. After the reorganization authority that had been given to President Kennedy expired in 1963, the House approved an extension, but the Senate balked in response to Kennedy's attempt to set up a Department of Urban Affairs in 1962 through use of his reorganization power rather than by submitting legislation to Congress. The House had vetoed the proposed Department of Urban Affairs in 1962. Congress did not take action to renew the President's reorganization authority until 1964, to expire on June 1, 1965. In response to the congressional disapproval of the President's attempts to establish the Department of Urban Affairs, the 1964 Reorganization Act contained an explicit provision prohibiting the President from creating a new executive department by a reorganization plan. This provision was continued in all subsequent Reorganization Acts.

In 1965, President Lyndon B. Johnson requested permanent reorganization authority, but was turned down by the Senate. The Democratic Congress again allowed the President's reorganization authority to lapse on December 31, 1968, but, at the request of President Nixon, renewed it on March 18, 1969, to expire April 1, 1971. In 1971, however, Congress did not immediately continue the President's reorganization powers, but finally, on December 1, extended his authority through April 1, 1973. It was under these Reorganization Acts that President Nixon abolished the Bureau of the Budget and created in its place the Office of Management and Budget, established the Domestic Council within the Executive Office of the President, created the Environmental Protection Agency, and eliminated within the Executive Office of the President the Office of Emergency Preparedness and the Office of Science and Technology. He also undertook to co-ordinate administrative activities in other areas.

Although the President, despite certain time lapses, has long possessed the initiative to reorganize the administrative agencies and regulatory commissions, it has not been a particularly successful presidential device in the control of the bureaucracy. This is true even though Congress must take positive action in order to reject a reorganization plan. Since 1964, departments cannot be created by reorganization, but only through legislation, which gives Congress the initiative. Although some significant reorganizations have occurred, particularly the creation of OMB and the Environmental Protection Agency, the seeming failure of Congress to veto many presidential plans is a reflection of the relative insignificance of those plans in the first place. With a few notable exceptions, such as the creation of the Department of Health, Education, and Welfare in 1953 through a reorganization plan, major shake-ups of the bureaucracy have not occurred as a result of the President's reorganization powers.

Congressional opposition has prevented the President from reorganizing the bureaucracy to bring about better control and co-ordination from the White House. Presidential reorganization attempts that have failed have, in addition, set precedents that tend to lessen presidential enthusiasm for administrative changes. Several examples will serve to illustrate this point. There have been proposals to reorganize the independent regulatory commissions since the 1930s, beginning with the proposals of the President's Committee on Administrative Management in 1937 to merge the agencies into executive departments, leaving their quasi-judicial functions to be performed by administrative courts. This suggestion was repeated in modified form by the Hoover Commissions of 1949 and 1955. The philosophy of these reports strongly supported the idea of presidential supremacy over the bureaucracy. President Truman, acting on the basis of the 1949 Hoover Commission report, recommended various changes in the regulatory agencies that would give the President greater supervisory powers. With very few exceptions, these recommendations were rejected by Congress, particularly with respect to those agencies, such as the Interstate Commerce Commission, that have powerful political support. President Kennedy again proposed changes to increase presidential power over the regulatory agencies, although he did not propose drastic reorganizations. He managed to increase the power of the chairmen of some agencies such as the Civil Aeronautics Board, the Federal Trade Commission, and the Home Loan Bank Board. This was a step in the direction of increased presidential control because it is the President who selects the chairmen of these agencies. Where Congress feels particularly protective of an agency, it may allow the President to appoint the chairman, but will not permit him to increase the chairman's authority. This was the case in 1967, when the Senate vetoed a presidential reorganization plan to increase the authority of the chairman of the Tariff Commission. President Ford's approach to regulatory reform differed from his predecessors', for it was not aimed at the organizations of the agencies but at their statutory authority to regulate in certain areas.

Presidential problems with Congress regarding administrative reorganization involve not only the independent commissions, but all agencies that have managed to develop significant political support within and without Congress. In the past, Reorganization Acts giving the President initiative have even gone so far as to exempt the more powerful agencies. After World War II, the Reorganization Act of 1945 exempted not only a number of regulatory agencies (ICC, SEC, FTC) but also the Army Corps of Engineers, an agency with the power to defy the President even though it is one of those most directly within his constitutional and statutory chain of command. Other Reorganization Acts have similarly exempted a variety of agencies from presidential control, although this has not been the case since 1949. The only limitation written into Reorganization Acts since 1949 has been a 1964 prohibition against the creation of executive departments under reorganization authority.

Agencies are not generally powerful in Congress simply because they have outside support, but because they have cultivated good congressional relationships for many years. Particular congressional committees, charged with the responsibility of "administrative oversight"—that is, supervision—often jealously guard what they consider to be their prerogative to determine when, how, and if the agencies they oversee are to be changed in terms of organization or function. If the President makes suggestions, or strongly indicates that the location and function of agencies is essentially his responsibility and not that of Congress, these committees feel that their territory has been invaded and respond accordingly. In other respects also they may seek to protect *their* agencies from presidential interference, regardless of whether they are independent by statute or within an executive department. The standing committees shield the agencies not only from excessive presidential control, but also from control by other parts of Congress itself. Presidential-congressional antagonism, then, is not the only explanation of the limits that Congress puts upon presidential authority over the administrative branch. Such limitations are also a reflection of the internal politics of Congress, in which committee chairmen and ranking committee members strive to demonstrate their power and status by their ability to determine the fate of agencies within their jurisdiction.

Congress, the judiciary, and the bureaucracy are the governmental groups that restrain the President. In addition, the existence of powerful private groups, particularly those with economic power, place restrictions upon the President. It should be added that to a considerable extent the ability of governmental (congressional committees, courts) and private groups (corporations, labor unions, farm groups, and so forth) outside the bureaucracy to resist and restrain the President is eventually manifested in the administrative branch. Particular agencies draw their strength from these groups, which in turn focus their attention upon the bureaucracy because outside of the President that is where the kind of legislative and judicial power that most directly affects their interests resides. This is true with regard to Congress as well as private groups. Thus the bureaucracy becomes a funnel into which political support is channeled from numerous sources, and for this reason it becomes in many instances the most powerful single limitation upon the President. As a whole the administrative branch represents a combination of extraordinary power. Administrative agencies never exist in a vacuum. Thus by themselves they could not challenge the President; but when Congress, private groups, and even the courts back them up there may be virtually no limit the President can place upon them. It was the courts that turned down most of President Nixon's impoundments of funds that Congress had appropriated for administrative programs, on the basis that congressional intent had been violated. When President Ford attempted a massive cutback in the food-stamp program in 1976, directing the Agriculture Department to revise its regulations for this purpose, a federal district judge held that the cutback was unauthorized by Congress and therefore illegal. In such matters as these, it is Congress and the courts that control the administrative branch, not the President. Of course the President may use the agencies as a lever against

Congress, but the opposite is more often the case. When the President turns to the agencies for political support this is not indicative of his power over them, but rather of their power over him. Thus agencies may use the President as a source of support to challenge Congress, or they may use Congress in a similar way to defy the President. In either case they are often likely to dominate the political process.

INFORMATION AND EXPERT KNOWLEDGE

A final factor that remains to be discussed in the relationship that exists between the President and the bureaucracy is information and expert knowledge. Here, perhaps, is the most important clue to an understanding of the difficulties involved in presidential control, and the resulting administrative independence.

There is little doubt that one of the greatest limitations faced by the President with respect to the bureaucracy is that neither he nor his staff agencies are able to cope with the scope and complexity of the information that administrative agencies develop and use on a day-to-day basis in program planning and implementation. Moreover, a question should be raised as to whether it is really the responsibility of the President to acquire detailed knowledge of the myriad activities engaged in by administrative agencies.

For many years students of the Presidency and public administration have insisted upon the necessity of an expansion of the Executive Office of the President—that is, his staff agencies—to funnel information to him about the numerous areas in which he bears responsibilities. There are serious limitations in the expansion of this Office on a permanent basis, for it might result in the President becoming a captive of his own staff agencies, if he is not already a captive of the permanent operating agencies. There is nothing magical about "staff," and the concept cannot provide a cure for all the ills that befall a frequently beleaguered President. President Nixon's attempts to centralize control in the White House resulted in a vast expansion of his White House staff. But he soon found that it was controlling him rather than vice versa.

The Executive Office of the President · The Executive Office of the President was first created in 1939 by executive order, and it was then composed of six agencies including the Bureau of the Budget (changed to the Office of Management and Budget in 1970) and the White House Office, the former being transferred from the Treasury Department under the authority of the 1939 Reorganization Act. The recommendations of the President's Committee on Administrative Management and their acceptance by Franklin D. Roosevelt provided the impetus for the establishment of the Office, and it was heralded as one of the greatest achievements of the century by many both within and outside the field of public administration. Since its establishment in 1939, a number of agencies have passed in and out of the Executive Office. The stable core of the Executive Office consists of a White House staff of approximately 522 people; the Office of Management and Budget, with 664 employees; the Council of Economic Advisers, created in 1946 by the Employment Act, with 51 staff members; the Council on Environmental Quality, created by the National Environmental Policy Act of 1969, with a staff of 59; the Council on International Economic Policy, composed of ex officio members, created by President Nixon in 1971, with a staff of 36; the Council on Wage and Price Stability, established by Congress in 1974, with a staff of 48; the Domestic Council, primarily an ex officio body, created by President Nixon in 1970, with a staff of 44; the National Security Council, an ex officio body, established by the National Security Act of 1947, which has 85 staff members; the Office of Special Representative for Trade Negotiations, created by executive order in 1963, which employs 56 staff members; the Office of Telecommunications Policy, created by the President in 1970, with 55 employees; and 26 persons who are special assistants to the President. The total number of Executive Office staff members is approximately 1,750, including service people in the executive residence (80 persons), the groundsmen, cooks, maids, and the keeper of the White House kennels.

The agencies within the Executive Office represent both the *institutional* and personal part of the Presidency. Most administrators in OMB have tenure under the merit system, and, to a lesser extent, the staff of other Executive Office agencies continues from one President to another. The most personal part of the Executive Office is the White House staff, appointed by the President and deputized to carry out his direct wishes. Because Executive Office agencies are not operating groups, but staff groups, they do not have private constituencies and must depend for the most part on the President for political support. The Office of Management and Budget differs from the regular staff groups in that it supplies Congress as well as the President with information, particularly since the passage of the Budget and Impoundment Control Act of 1974. Under that statute, OMB reports decisions to rescind or defer expenditures appropriated by Congress to the House and Senate Appropriations and Budget Committees and, on occasion, to the standing committees that have authorized the expenditures in the first place. OMB is required to co-operate with Congress and with all of its committees as well as with legislative staff agencies such as the Congressional Budget Office.

Although OMB is doing more work for Congress under the 1974 Budget Act than it did before, it still operates principally as a budgetary and legislative clearance agency for the executive branch. In this capacity it conducts elaborate reviews of agency budgets and develops an overall executive budget within the boundaries drawn by the President. Approximately 200 professionals within OMB are involved in the process of budgetary review. Agency budgetary requests cannot be *formally* transmitted to Congress before clearing OMB. Similarly, OMB's Legislative Reference Division, with a staff of approximately 50, must approve of agency legislative proposals before they are formally transmitted to Capitol Hill. In both its budgetary and legislative clearance functions, OMB is to represent the President and, theoretically, to bring agency proposals into line with the President's program. In reality, OMB acts as much in place of the President as under his supervision.

The Executive Office—or, as it is often called, the "President's bureaucracy"—has its own internal tensions like any other bureaucracy. Although the main source of political support for most Executive Office components is the President, they must also heed other forces. OMB, for example, must juggle agency demands with presidential directives, and in this process it does not wish to antagonize severely major departments and agencies that have powerful political support on the Hill and elsewhere. Such political support has a way of showing up in the White House sooner or later, and if OMB were continually at odds with the agencies it supposedly supervises, its job would be made impossible both politically and practically.

The regular departments and agencies constantly seek to use the presidential bureaucracy to channel their points of view to the White House. Since the Executive Office deals with an extraordinary range of matters, the President cannot have an explicit program on each and every one. His staff agencies will inevitably strike out on their own and become advocates of particular viewpoints, which, quite naturally, produces conflict within the President's "family." The White House staff and the permanent staff of OMB, for example, were in sharp conflict over many issues of policy during the Nixon years. If such conflict surfaces, it may help the President to make up his own mind. But a President who is often withdrawn, distracted, or who concentrates on only a very few areas of policy enables his bureaucracy to become a powerful force on its own. The pluralistic character of the presidential bureaucracy may afford some protection against arbitrary staff actions. Moreover, the regular bureaucracy acts as a powerful check upon the Executive Office, which it can and will circumvent by going directly to Congress or the President.

The Executive Office of the President is quite small, yet the agencies comprising it are supposed to collect information, plan programs, and generally assist the President, in a manner similar to congressional staff aids. Although there is greater unity within the Executive Office compared to its congressional counterpart, both face similar problems in their attempts to cope with the bureaucracy. Their primary source of information continues to be the operating agencies, and insofar as they depend upon the agencies, they must base their decisions upon the facts, and probably the opinions, supplied by the agencies. Although the permanent staff of the Executive Office remains around 1,750 persons, this number is augmented by people on detail from outside agencies who are assigned temporarily to the Executive Office. The same situation is true on the Hill, where hundreds of administrative staff people are on detail to congressional staff arms and committees. In this way, agency viewpoints are directly represented in the presidential and congressional bureaucracies. Increasing the size of the Executive Office, which on occasion has been done, does not solve the problem of presidential control over the bureaucracy. The additional staff members would have to be drawn from a limited pool, a significant portion of which would include agency people. Creating more Executive Office agencies would mean more staff from the regular bureaucracy on detail to it. Certainly, Congress has not solved its problem of gaining independent information by increasing its staff, which now numbers approximately 20,000 in all with many thousands of professionals.[19]

The problem of size of the Executive Office is not nearly as important as the issue of its proper role in relation to the agencies and to the political system as a whole. It is not size that makes a body expert, and capable of developing relevant information for use in policy formulation. The Executive Office by its very nature cannot possibly provide the President personally with enough information to enable him to supervise the legislative and other activities of the agencies. The scope and technical complexity of administrative legislation and adjudication alone precludes this, even if there were no legal and political obstacles to presidential control. What is of greater importance is the fact that the President cannot personally comprehend these areas. But why should he become personally involved? Because when the Presidency begins to function institutionally its constitutional and political responsibilities change, and what may be entirely proper for the President himself to do, or what is done with his knowledge and understanding, may pose problems when his staff does the same thing independently. When the President speaks for himself, entirely different implications arise than when a staff agency speaks for him. Thus there are not only many reasons why the Executive Office of the President *cannot* often control the bureaucracy, but questions must be raised as to whether or not it *should* do so. Before turning to the more important considerations involved in the determination of the proper relationship between

19. For a discussion of congressional staff, see Chapter 4, pp. 185–193.

the President and the administrative branch, a few additional points will be discussed to indicate the problems both the President and his staff face in attempting to gain information about the activities of the bureaucracy.

Information-Gathering · The most obvious problem in the gathering of information, but one that is often overlooked, is determining the questions to be asked of the agencies by the President and his staff. Are questions to be put in general terms, or are they to request specific information? Generally, in order to know what questions to ask administrative agencies the President and his staff must be able to develop independent knowledge in the fields in which the agencies function. This does not mean that the Executive Office and the President have to equal the expert knowledge of the agencies, but they must possess a certain degree of detailed understanding, which can be achieved in only relatively very few fields. Most of the President's White House staff is temporary and relatively amateurish in relation to the complex policy fields administered by the agencies. The professional staff of OMB, particularly its budget examiners, are far more expert, and, in some instances, the adversary position they may take with agencies can result in raising significant questions for the President to resolve. OMB, however, has an approximately 20-per-cent annual turnover in staff, which has been accelerating with the jump in its work load as a result of the Budget and Impoundment Control Act of 1974. For the most part, OMB's budget examiners are generalists, not specialists, which puts them at a disadvantage in dealing with the agencies. There is also a problem of co-optation of the examiners by the agencies, a natural process if examiners work with a particular agency for many years.

An important limitation on presidential information is in the sphere where the independent regulatory agencies operate. Since the agencies themselves often have no consistent policies, but develop policy on an ad hoc, case-by-case basis, the President cannot know in advance in what direction they are going. Any interference by the President in the quasi-legislative or quasi-judicial activities of the agencies brings immediate outcries from Congress and private parties involved before the agencies that the President is attempting to politicize these tribunals, which are supposed to act impartially. The rule-making and adjudicative procedures of the agencies, outlined by statutory law, determine the kinds of information they get on which they are required to act. In effect, they are not supposed to be subject to presidential control. President Ford tried to grapple directly with the agencies, and attempted to bring about de-regulation in certain areas. But, ultimately, he had to go to Congress to request legislation for this purpose. In the meantime, the agencies largely ignored him and continued to operate cozily with the industry groups they regulated and with their protective congressional committees.

Even where agencies are directly under the legal authority of the President, such as HEW, it is difficult for the President to gain information from them that will be contrary to their interests. And, in the final analysis, no effective presidential policy can be developed and implemented without the aid of the agencies. This makes the President a captive of the bureaucracy to a far greater extent than any President is willing to admit. Incoming Presidents always have grandiose ideas about changes they will implement only to find that they are almost immediately stymied by the overwhelming power and stubbornness of the agencies, which are quietly fortified by the standing committees of Congress.

These considerations lead to the conclusion that the activities of the bureaucracy in relation to the President may be placed roughly into two categories: (1) those that relate to a presidential program that has been defined with some degree of precision; (2) those that fall outside the boundaries of a presidential program. In the first category, the President at least makes an attempt to control the agencies and enlist their support in implementing his program. The second category arises because the Presidency cannot be knowledgeable enough to formulate a "policy" to guide most of the activities of the administrative branch, nor will the President's general programs involve all of the agencies.

What degree of presidential control of the bureaucracy exists if by necessity and by choice the President is not concerned directly about a great deal of what the agencies are doing? In some instances OMB may step in to *coordinate* agency policies that it feels are in conflict. But this does not work well, particularly if the agencies concerned have powerful political backing and choose to ignore OMB by failing to clear legislative and other proposals through it. If the operating agencies lack the power to defy OMB, they may watch with frustration while OMB tries to formulate policies, more or less on an *ad hoc* basis, with little if any consultation with the President.

There is little doubt that the Office of Management and Budget scans the operations of the administrative branch rather closely, but it is equally clear that it does not control substantive policy or judicial decisions made by the agencies. This is not its purpose. Nor is it the purpose of the Executive Office as a whole. The agencies are given freedom within their spheres of activity by the President and his staff unless the interests of the White House are directly affected.

The opinions of the agencies, of course, always play an important part in the formulation of any presidential policy and in many instances this influence will be decisive. But although the agencies may have extraordinary power to shape presidential programs, both the President and his staff will become personally involved and, presumably, develop an independent understanding of the issues. Once a program has been decided upon, agency action can be judged on the basis of whether or not it has been in accordance with presidential wishes. At this point and probably only at this point does it become meaningful to talk about presidential control of the bureaucracy, for if the President has a definite program it is clearly in his interest to make certain the agencies do not attack it generally or nullify it through their actions.

Examples of areas of administrative activity which do and do not relate to presidential programs may aid in clarifying the previous discussion. First, consider a few fields in which the President usually does not have a defined policy. Although deregulation became the presidential cry of the mid-1970s, vigorously pushed by President Ford, the fact remains that many regulatory areas are not of particular interest to most Presidents. There are, after all, eighty agencies with regulatory functions. President Ford's de-regulation proposals related almost solely to rail, trucking, and airline transportation. In spite of his rhetoric, he was not against regulation per se. He recommended, for example, increasing the Federal Trade Commission's independence from the White House and expansion of its regulatory powers.[20] In most regulatory areas within and without departments, the President does not have a specific program. Attacks by conservative Presidents such as Ford and Nixon on regulation are more general than specific in content. For example, when it comes to administrative regulation in such fields as air safety, food and drugs, commodities, securities and the stock exchanges, consumer products, unfair labor practices, banking practices, nuclear power plants, television and radio stations and networks (President Ford did propose de-regulating FCC control over cable television), there are more often than not no defined presidential policies. In addition to these and other regulatory fields, there are numerous areas of administrative activity with which the President is necessarily unconcerned. For example, most of the day-to-day work of the major departments, such as Health, Education, and Welfare, Agriculture, Interior, Commerce, and so forth, is not related to an overall presidential policy. In the implementation of programs, these executive departments engage in extensive rule-making and adjudication, which is generally excluded from presidential purview, as in the case of similar activities by the independent regulatory commissions.

On the other hand, definite presidential policies exist in such crucial areas as defense and foreign affairs. The strength of our ground forces, the kinds of weapons we will use, where they will be located, the circumstances under which they will be employed, and so forth, are matters on which all modern Presidents have policies. In cases of national emergency the National Security Council—or, more likely, an ad-hoc group assembled by the President—will be called into session, chaired by the President, and although possible decisions will be discussed in such meetings, a strong President will always make the final choice. In areas such as these the President is solely responsible for what is done; thus, it is desirable that he be able to gain adequate information from the bureaucracy to formulate policies which will in turn be implemented.

20. See S. 2935, 94th Cong., 2nd Sess., 1976.

Conclusion: Should the President
Control the Bureaucracy?

The realities of the relationship between the President and the bureaucracy must be recognized. In terms of our Constitution and the nature of our political system today it is not possible, necessary, or desirable that every aspect of administrative activity be controlled by the White House. If the President were to concentrate on this task it would mean a virtual abdication of his more important responsibilities. Delegation of authority and power is an integral part of our government, and it must be recognized that within broad areas administrative agencies are the primary groups responsible for legislation and adjudication.

Critics of this position contend that if the President cannot control administrative activity it is up to his staff to step in and fill the gap. Here it should be noted that it is the President who is elected by the people, not his staff. Moreover, because his staff is detached from operating activities it can in some instances function secretly and without accountability except to the President himself. The bureaucracy is a highly representative branch of our government, in many respects more representative than Congress; it should be added that the bureaucracy may be more representative in some ways than the President, and certainly more than the presidential staff. Private groups will very likely get more knowledgeable and more direct representation in those agencies to which they have access, than in the Presidency. The democratic process must reflect group demands as well as the more nebulous demands of the public at large. The President is the best representative of the latter, but the agencies are often the more effective representatives of the former.

Finally, it should be noted that in our political system the President is not always motivated to control the bureaucracy—a key consideration raised before with respect to Congress. The President's political survival depends upon a nationwide electoral process in which his personality and a few key issues determine the outcome. He need not always know what policies the agencies are following, or what decisions they are making in their judicial spheres: they are the primary concerns of the agencies themselves, and their political survival may depend upon the policies and decisions they carry out.

The American Presidency is a great institution, but the President is not in fact "Chief Administrator." He cannot, nor does he really wish to, control all the complex activities engaged in by the administrative branch. In many key areas of presidential responsibility he demands, and generally receives, loyalty from administrative agencies. But in other fields the agencies function with partial autonomy in the policy spheres that have been assigned to them by Congress.

CHAPTER 6   Conclusion

A MAJOR QUESTION remains: How does American bureaucracy fit into our system of constitutional democracy? Does it conform to our pattern of limited government? Is it responsive to popular demands that arise from time to time for changes in government policies? Are presidential candidates and members of Congress justified in their inevitable ritual attacks on the "bureaucrats" at election time? The answer is that American bureaucracy may not harmonize perfectly with the forms of our Constitution, but it is compatible with its spirit. It occupies a responsible position within our political system.

American bureaucracy is an independent force, and from its independence it draws much of its strength and prestige. It is a powerful and viable branch of government, not properly subject to complete control by Congress, the President, or the judiciary. But its independence does not mean that it possesses total discretion. It functions within a checks-and-balances system in much the same way as the original three branches of government. Its boundaries of action are set by Congress, and these must not exceed constitutional limits as determined by the courts. The President plays a varied role in relation to the agencies, but is unable and unwilling to supervise all of their myriad activities.

It is difficult to grasp the concept that the bureaucracy is not subordinate to one or more of the three initial branches of American government. But the fact is the three primary branches have necessarily supported the creation of a semiautonomous bureaucracy as an instrument to enable our government to meet the challenges it has faced. Given the needs of modern government for economic regulation, specialization, continuity, and speed in the dispatch of business, to mention only a few, it is the bureaucracy that has stepped in to fill the gap created by the inability of the other branches to fulfill all of these requirements. The other branches, particularly the Presidency and the Supreme Court, have also greatly expanded their ability and willingness to meet the challenges of the twentieth century, but they could not possibly solve by themselves the extraordinary problems that have confronted our government.

The fact that American government has been able to change to meet demands placed upon it while at the same time preserving constitutional democracy is not always fully appreciated. There has been much wringing of hands among some political scientists about "the deadlock of democracy," the inability of the President and Congress to work together through a disciplined party system.[1] This deadlock presumably prevents meaningful participation by the electorate. But neither parties, Congress, nor even the electoral system should be thought of as the only critical elements in our governmental system. The President can act without relying upon them in many instances, and for this very reason our country has survived where otherwise it might have foundered. And the bureaucracy, which is actually a more representative body than Congress, combines essential democratic ingredients at the same time that it formulates important policy. Administrative agencies, removed from the electoral process, can take action without consulting Congress, and such action is as responsive to the demands and needs of the community as any that Congress could take even if there were no "deadlock." In this respect American bureaucracy provides in part an answer to the stalemate that often exists between the President and Congress. But it should be remembered that the factors leading to the supremacy of the administrative branch in the formulation of governmental policy and in many areas of adjudication would produce exactly the same result if the parties were unified and if there were no executive-legislative conflict.

The one difference that would result from greater cohesion between the President and Congress would be a more unified bureaucracy under the legal authority of the President, as Congress would no longer be so motivated to make administrative agencies independent. But this would not diminish the overall role of the bureaucracy, which would maintain much of its independence

1. See, for example, James M. Burns, *The Deadlock of Democracy* (Englewood Cliffs: Prentice-Hall, Inc., 1963).

through political support, control over information, continuity in office, and so forth. In this respect it would be a change more in legal forms than in substance. But on the other hand it would destroy the balance of powers among the branches of government that has always been considered essential to the preservation of freedom in America. It would permit the government as a whole to overwhelm the community if it were bent upon a particular course of action, particularly because all of the vast powers of administrative agencies would be combined under presidential and party direction. One should never forget the attempt by President Nixon to seize the bureaucracy for political ends. The bureaucracy can be an important check on irresponsible actions of the President or Congress. It takes its place within the checks-and-balances system, and if it were under the exclusive authority of any one branch, the balance would be irrevocably tipped. The intrinsic power of the bureaucracy will always prevent complete control over it, regardless of the degree of unity prevailing between the President and Congress. Even in a disciplined party system, there would be large areas where no clear party policy existed, and in these spheres, the bureaucracy would go its own way, with less interference and less committee surveillance by members of Congress used to independent thought and investigation than is presently the case.

There are no political developments in the foreseeable future that will alter the nature of administrative independence and the domination of the bureaucracy in many important areas of public policy. Congressional incentives will continue to buttress the agencies against the President. The agencies themselves will continue to garner political support wherever they can find it in order to increase their power and independence. It is this political sensitivity of the bureaucracy that helps to insure its responsiveness to the other branches of government and to private interests.

With the exception of the initial executive departments, administrative agencies were created long after the Constitution was written. The precepts of constitutional democracy thus had a chance to become firmly embedded as part of the American political tradition before the administrative branch began to take shape as a significant force threatening the governmental balance of powers. This tradition has been a permanent influence shaping old and new political institutions into its own distinctive pattern, and the bureaucracy has not been an exception.

The administrative branch did not escape the effects of the separation-of-powers system, which caused a fragmentation of bureaucratic power. It did not escape the democratic forces that led to the merit system, which lessened the possibility of an elite bureaucratic class developing. Moreover, it did not escape the remnants of the spoils system, which guaranteed a circulation of the elite at the top levels. American bureaucracy is not run by a privileged group, but by men and women of diverse backgrounds. It is not separate from the community at large, but an integral part of it. Finally, the bureaucracy has always been responsive to interest groups, which now include public-interest pressure groups, an important democratic characteristic of all branches of American government.

As long as the activities of administrative agencies are viewed as being political, there will be little chance of a movement developing either within or without the bureaucracy to detach it from the political system as a whole. It is because the bureaucracy possesses such important political functions that Congress, the President, the judiciary, and private-interest groups make certain that some control is exercised over it. If "administration" were thought of as something apart from the political process, this might lead to the feeling that it should be detached from the demands of the political system. But American bureaucracy is responsive to the standards of constitutional democracy because it is an integral part of the "politics" that go to make up our governmental system. It is not neutral. Its procedures and its decisions are not subject to scientific formulation by administrative experts acting alone. Administrative agencies are forced to pay attention to political demands from many points in order to survive. This fact makes an important contribution to our system of administrative responsibility.

As American government continues to grow in response to the heavy demands that will inevitably be placed upon it, it is certain that the bureaucracy will continue to occupy a position of central importance. Administrative agencies will have more discretion in the future than they now have as public-policy needs increase and become more complex. But this growth of bureaucracy is not a cause for alarm. It adds an important new dimension to our government. American bureaucracy takes its place as an equal partner with the President, Congress, and the judiciary. Its existence not only increases the ability of our government to meet the challenges of the twentieth century, but also enhances the meaning of constitutional democracy.

Index